NEHRU'S VISION TO EMPOWER INDIAN ECONOMY

NEHRU'S VISION TO EMPOWER INDIAN ECONOMY

Edited by

APRANA BHARDWAJ

and

DR. ANIL KUMAR THAKUR

Published on behalf of
THE INDIAN ECONOMIC ASSOCIATION

DEEP & DEEP PUBLICATIONS PVT. LTD.
F-159, Rajouri Garden, New Delhi-110027

NEHRU'S VISION TO EMPOWER INDIAN ECONOMY

ISBN 978-81-8450-279-4

Typeset by S.S. COMPOSERS
3190, Mohindra Park, Shakur Basti, Delhi-110034.

Printed in India at MAYUR ENTERPRISES
WZ Plot No. 3, Gujjar Market, Tihar Village, New Delhi-110018.

Published by DEEP & DEEP PUBLICATIONS PVT. LTD.
F-159, Rajouri Garden, New Delhi-110027.
Phones: 25435369, 25440916
E-mail: ddpbooks@yahoo.co.in • ddpubs@gmail.com
Showroom:
2/13, Ansari Road, Daryaganj, New Delhi-110002 • Telefax: 23245122

Contents

Part II

NEHRU AS AN ARCHITECT OF INDIAN PLANNING

Part III

NEHRU AND HIS SOCIALIST PHILOSOPHY

PART IV

NEHRU'S ACHIEVEMENTS AND FAILURES: AN ESTIMATE

Preface

This edited volume on Nehru's Vision to Empower Indian Economy is an attempt to present the versatile faculties of Nehru's personality in its entirety. Nehru was not only a forerunner of India's freedom struggle, but a socialist philosopher of higher order. He was not a Marxist in strict sense of the term but at best an exponent of the down-trodden and their problems. He was against their political mobilization and use of force to redress their problems. He wanted their consciousness to be expanded with scientific knowledge and good human temper. He was, thus interested in creating a creative climate for social and economic development of India.

He was an economic policy-maker with a philosophical base. He was interested in development of India with a strong industrial base putting paramount place to heavy industries and supplementary to auxiliary industrial units. He was, thus an advocate of cooperation between big, large scale industries and small scale industries.

He was great planner interested in making planning a long drawn process where long-term goal of man-making matters more. The minimum asset building and infrastructure base is essential but more important than this is knowledge-base. It is this strength of Indian economy which got its important place today. This edited volume analysis all these threads of Nehru's vision with in-depth analyses spread over in four sections. This work will help academic practitioners to grasp the full perspective of Nehru's personality in a useful and constructive manner. The volume is the resultant outcome of the technical session on Nehru's Economic Philosophy at its 91st Annual Conference at Udaipur. I owe my gratitude to Anil Kumar Thakur, Secretary and Treasurer, INDIAN ECONOMIC ASSOCIATION, who gave me the opportunity to bring this issue in the present form.

APRANA BHARDWAJ

List of Contributors

Aprana Bhardwaj, M.A. Final, Dept. of Economics, A.N. College, Patna.

A. Arangasami, Lecturer (S.S) in Economics, Sir Theagaraya College, Chennai, Tamil Nadu.

A. Ranga Reddy, Professor, Department of Economics, Sri Venkateswara University, Tirupati-517 502.

A. Sangamithra, Lecturer in Economics, Bharathiar University, Coimbatore-641 046.

A.P. Tiwari, Reader, Department of Economics, Vidyant Hindu College, University of Lucknow, Lucknow.

A.S. Mohammad, Village: Mohammadpur, Mahnar, Vaishali.

Ajay Kumar Dubey, C/o P.K. Dubey, Road No. 2, Azad Nagar, Kankarbagh, Patna-800020.

Anath Bandhu Mukherjee, 2, R.N.T.P. Bye Lane, P.O.-Shyamnagar, Dist. North 24-Parganas, Pin-743127.

Anil Thakur, Deptt. of Economics, Koshi College, Khagaria (Bihar).

Bharti Shah, Professor, Economics Department Municipal Arts and U.B. Science College Mehsana-384002 (Gujarat).

Binod Choudhary, H.O.D, Rural Economics, D.N. College, Masourhi, Patna.

Birendra Kumar Jha, Reader and Head, Deptt. of Economics, D.B.K.N. College, Narhan (Samastipur, Bihar).

Biswajit Guha, Reader and Head, Department of Economics (Retired), Netaji Nagar Day College, Kolkata.

C.B. Sharma, Head Deptt. of Economics, S.S. College Jehanabad (Bihar).

C.S. Jagtap, Late Rajabhau Deshmukh Art's College, Nandgaon KH, Distt. Amravati.

Chandra Kant Singh, Nitishwar Singh College, Sarmastpur, Muzaffarpur (Bihar).

D. Rajasekhar, Reader in Economics, P.G and Research Department of Economics, Sir Theagaraya College, Chennai-21.

Gautum Bhong, Director, Post Graduate Research Centre in Economics, Abasaheb Garware College, Pune, (Maharashtra).

Hari Narayan Prasad Singh, Lecturer in Economics, Kisan College, Sohsarai, (Nalanda) M.U.

I.D. Singh, Reader in Economics, Sakaldiha P.G. College, Sakaldiha, Chandauli.

Jayaselvi, Ph.D. Research Scholar, Department of Economics, Bharathiar University, Coimbatore-46

Kishore Kumar Roy Choudhury, Reader in Economics, D.N College, P.O.: Aurangabad Dist.: Murshidabad, Pin-742201 (W.B).

M. Ramanjaneyulu, Professor and Chairman, Department of Economics, Jnanabharathi, Bangalore University, Bangalore-560 056.

Mahendra Ranawat, Principal, Head Dept. of Economic, B.N. P.G. Girls College, M.L.S. University, Udaipur.

Manisha Pathak (Dixit), Assistant Professor of Economics (Selection Grade), Govt. Hamidia Arts and Commerce College, Bhopal (M.P).

Manju Singh, Senior Fellow (Professor), Council for Social Development, Southern Regional Centre, Hyderbad-500 030.

Mukesh, Village: Purani Kherahi, Post: Shahkund, Distt.: Bhagalpur (Bihar).

R.B. Bhandwalkar, P.G. Dept. of Economics, Amolakchand Mahavidyalaya, Yavatmal.

R.P.L. Jain, Reader, Department of Economics, Faculty of Social Sciences, Banaras Hindu University, Varanasi-5

R.R. Gawhale, Professor and Head P.G. Dept. of Economics, G.S. Science, Arts and Commerce College, Khamgaon.

R.S. Nandal, Deptt. of Agril. Economics CCS, HAU, Hisar.

S. Suresh, Reader in Economics, Presidency College, Chennai-600 005.

S.K. Karimulla, Professor, Department of Economics, Sri Venkateswara University, Tirupati-517 502.

S.K. Mishra, PGT (Economics), Kendriya Vidyalaya, Uttarkashi (UA)-249193.

S.R. Jagtap, Eco. Deptt. Smt. K.L. College, Amravati, (Hist. Deptt.).

Shambhu Kumar, L.F-3, Sector-3, Room No. 189, B.H. Colony, Bhootnath Road, Patna-800026.

Srinivasan Ramachandran, Research Officer, Dr. Ambedkar Centre for Economic Studies, University of Madras.

T.M. Saravana Kumar, Ph.D. Research Scholar, Department of Economics, Bharathiar University, Coimbatore-641 046.

Umesh Prasad, Deptt. of Economics, J.N.L. College, Khagaul, Patna.

Ved Prakash Dubey, Research Scholar, Economics Department, Mahatma Gandhi Kashi Vidyapith, Varanasi.

Introduction

1.1. Pandit Jawahar Lal Nehru: The Beginning Phase of His Life Sketch

Born on Nov. 14, 1889 Pandit Jawahar Lal Nehru was the only son of Allahabad-based barrister Pandit Motilal Nehru. Being schooled at Harrow he completed his law degree from Trinity College, Cambridge. His seven years stay in England during the course of his higher learning widened his mental horizon and helped him to acquire a national skeptical outlook. He was a sampled Fabian Socialist with Indian nationalism which added to his own patriotic dedication.

Jawahar Lal Nehru returned to India in 1912 and started legal practice. After being married to Kamla Nehru in 1916 he first joined Home Rule Movement in 1917. He left his expensive possessions of past times and wore a Khadi Kurta and Gandhi Cap, after being influenced by Gandhi, with his first meeting he became an active participant in Non-co-operation Movement of 1920-22 and was arrested for the first time during this movement and was released after few months.

Jawahar Lal Nehru was elected President of Allahabad Municipal Corporation in 1924 and served for two years as City's Chief Executive. This proved to be a valuable administrative experience and stood him in good stead; later on when he became the Prime Minister of the Country. As Chief Executive of Allahabad Municipal Corporation he used this tenure to expand public education, both health care and sanitation. He resigned in 1924, due to lack of co-operation from civil servants and obstruction from British authorities.

This administrative function at the lower echelons of administration and status quest temperaments of bureaucrats and stubish attitude of British ruling class with vested parochial interest in the growing power of British Empire, sparked in Nehru, the constant and continuous will power to fight the exploitative imperial regime. He was a very active Congress leader and became its general secretary at the very early phase of the movement in 1926-28. In 1928-29, in the Congress Sessions, held under the presidentship of Motilal Nehru, J.L. Nehru and Subhas Chandra Bose backed a call for full political independence while old guards under Motilal Nehru wanted dominion status within the British Empire. Pt. Nehru led the war of independence towards a Sovereign Indian State and not Indian rule under British Suzerainty. However, the truce was maintained within the Congress fold, British Empire was given two years to grant India dominion status, if they did not the Congress would launch a national struggle for full political independence. Pt. J.N. Nehru with the help of Subhas Chandra Bose reduced the time of opportunity to one year. The British did not respond.

In 1929, in the Lahore Congress, Jawahar Lal Nehru was elected President of the Congress Party. In that session, in his leadership a resolution demanding India's independence was passed and on Jan. 26, 1930 in Lahore, Jawahar Lal Nehru unfurled free India's flag. Gandhiji, in order to achieve his goal of Independent India gave a call for civil disobedience movement in 1930. The movement was a great success and forced British Government to acknowledge the need for major political reforms.

Accordingly British promulgated the Govt. of India Act 1935 and the provincial autonomy to states were granted. Elections for states were held and the Congress Party decided to contest elections. Nehru stayed out of elections, but campaigned vigorously nation-wide for the party. The Congress formed governments in almost every province and won the largest number of seats in the Central Assembly. Nehru became so powerful within the Congress Party that he was elected to the Congress presiding in 1936, 1937 and 1946.

Thus he came to occupy a position in the national movement by dint of his organizational acumenship and administrative insight, second only to that of Gandhi. He participated in quit India movement of 1942. He was arrested and released in 1945. He took a leading part in the negotiations that culminated in the emergence of the dominions of India and Pakistan in Aug. 1947.

He became the Prime Minister of Independent India. He effectively cooped with the formidable challenges of those times; the disorders and mass exodus of minorities across the new border with Pakistan, the integration of five hundred odd princely states into the Indian Union, the framing of a new constitution and the establishment of the political and administrative infrastructure for a parliamentary democracy.

Pt. Jawahar Lal Nehru played a key role of building modern India. He set-up a Planning Commission encouraged development of science and technology and launched three successive five year plans. His policies led to sizable growth of in agricultural and industrial production. Nehru also played a major role in developing independent India's foreign policy. He called for liquidation of colonialism in Asia and Africa and along with Tito and Nasser was one of the chief architects of the non-aligned movement. He played a constructive, mediatory role in bringing the Korean war to an end and in resolving other international crisis, such as those over the Suez Canal and the Congo, offering India's session for conciliation and international policing. He contributed behind the scenes towards the solution of several other explosive issues, such as those of West Berlin, Austria and Laos.

But Jawahar Lal Nehru could not improve India's relations with Pakistan and China. The Kashmir issue proved a stumbling block in reaching an accord with Pakistan and the border dispute prevented a resolution with China inspite of its wider endeavour for brotherhood, friendship and peace with these states. The Chinese invasion in 1962, which Nehru failed to anticipate, cause as a great blow to him and probably hastened his death, which came on May 27, 1964.

I.II. Pt. J.L. Nehru: A Socialist Philosopher and an Architect of Indian National Congress

Pt. J.N. Nehru was socialist philosopher not in the sense of Marxist. He advocated democracy based on adult suffrage or adult franchise. He was thus, first a democrat and later a socialist. He was not a believer in violent class struggle. He was a believer in peaceful transition to socialism. He thus propounded a new path of non-capitalist development. He dreamed of self-sufficient economy of India that would be based on the heavy and basic industries—the temples of the modern age. He was opposed to the idea of joining either the imperialist or the capitalist bloc and the socialist bloc. He was a strong advocate of the non-aligned movement of the third world advocating a third growth path via mixed economy, where labour and capital will cooperate to produce wealth and riches in the economy. He felt that in order to harmonies the interest of the individual and the society, economic inequality between man and man should be reduced to the minimum. This could be possible only if the economic pattern attempts to achieve full employment, more production and greater social and economic justice. Nehru argues that Indian Socialism should aim at providing gainful employment to all able bodied citizens, irrespective of any kind of distinction and also reduce glaring economic and social disparities in standards of living. But this should be achieved through democratic and peaceful means and not through totalitarian and violent methods.

Thus, Nehru was the main architect of socialist patterns of society adopted at Avadi session of Indian National Congress, establishing thus seven principles which foresee the egalitarian order to come into effect. They are as follows:

(i) Right to work and full employment;
(ii) Maximum production of national wealth,
(iii) Maximum national self-sufficiency;
(iv) Social and economic justice;
(v) Use of peaceful, non-violent and democratic methods;

(vi) Decentralisation of economic and political power through the establishment of Village Panchayats and Industrial Co-operation; and

(vii) Implementation of the ideal of "Unto this last" that is the last man should be our first concern.

All these principles are in conformity with Gandhi's ideals of Sarvodaya. Thus, we see that Nehru starts with Marx's but goes much farther and adds to it new dimensions to make it relevant for the present retaining his orientation towards scientific socialism. He thus makes Marxism free from its rapidity and dogma, thereby makes socialism a progressive ideology and establishment of egalitarian economic order prime objective.

I.III. Pt. Nehru: His Economic Policies and Indian Plans

Indian Planning process as we know has been a mares nest. False publicity, sycophancy, political motivation and dishonesty are the only epithets which have clouded history of Indian planning for economic development. A man devoid of pragmatism and a sense of propriety and have a Febian ideas was put up as a man of India's destiny. It is thus a great lie and distortion of history to state that the National Planning Committee was set-up in 1944. Infact, the truth was that Jawahar Lal Nehru had nothing to do with the formation at the National Planning Committee. The truth of history being that National Planning Committee was set-up by Netaji Subhas Chandra Bose in 1938 and not in 1944 or earlier. It was with a view to placate and please Gandhiji—who was a strong opponent of industrialization and modernization of agriculture that the name of Jawahar Lal, who was in London, at that time, was proposed by one of the famous Indian scientists Dr. Meghnad Saha in place of Dr. Visvesvaraya because when the National Planning Committee was formed after a prolonged discussion in the industry ministers meeting in 1938, at Delhi, the name of the famous Engineer Dr. Visvesvaraya was proposed for chairmanship of the committee. But Dr. Saha thought that the Planning Committee's proposal for industrialization would not get the approval of Gandhijee and he would but allow it to function. So to ensure his support the name of Bapuji's most obedient man Jawahar Lal Nehru's name was proposed to chair the committee. This decision of the committee was conveyed to Nehru—who was then in London and as a gullible person, he did not hesitate to accept the proposal. So Nehru had never been the initiator of planning process in India. But a man who lived in the world of ideas and dreams, was opted as a tactical scape goat by Dr. Saha in consultation with then Congress President Subhas Chandra Bose, to get the favour of Gandhi on the issue of Planning. He was neither a professional economist nor he read economics in any college or university. He was a science graduate with Botany, Chemistry and Geology as subjects. But his study of nine years imprisonment made him well acquainted with theoretical and applied economics. The chairmanship of National Planning Committee provided him the opportunity to visualise the different aspects of planned economy of India. It also facilitated him to hear the views of 350 experts on different 29 sub-committees. So Nehruvian model of planned economy was conceptualized during the freedom struggle and its movement.

Being opted to chair the Planning Committee by Netaji, as president of Congress Committee, he relied heavily upon Dr. P.C. Mahalanobis and Dr. V.K.R.V. Rao on economic and statistical issues. It helped him to create his ideas on economic issues. Once he wrote to V.K.R.V. Rao, "I should like you go through the resolutions in the three red books and keeping them in view, note down, what further general decisions, we should take which should enable as to proceed with the draft that is to say I should like you to put down such further question of policy and principles as we should decide at our next stage. In putting down these questions, please indicate what in your opinion the decisions should be I should also like you to be brief on the general picture of national planning in India which you recommend." As chairman of the National Planning Committee Pt. Nehru was already fully trained, equipped and familiar with different aspects of planning in India before he got the responsibility to implement five years plans. It is remarkable that his recommendations in the three red books symbolizing his commitment to socialist ideas, which were written long before Mao-Tse-Tung, published his five red books.

Thus, Nehru became well acquainted with important socio-economic issues of world in general and India in particular. The national movement threw up many great leaders but what marked out Pt. J.L. Nehru was his concern with the problems of poverty and planned development in their large political and economic context and the social philosophy and values which he valued to deal with them.

The years before Independence, can be seen in retrospect as a long period of preparation for practical action. When the opportunity came the transition from the role of freedom fighter to that of gifted statesmen was therefore, easy and altogether natural.

On account of paucity of time and little practical knowledge of planning, he gave the responsibility of drafting the First Five Year Plan to Dr. Anjaria and Dr. K.N. Raj who by using simple Harrod Domar Model, propounded simple thesis of open economy, where there was little distinction between consumer goods and investment goods. It also lacked social objective.

But to Nehru the First Five Year Plan also had little scientific and industrial temper in it. Being not satisfied with the First Five Year Plan documentation, he sent Dr. Mahalanobis, Dr. Pitamber Jain and Dr. S.R. Sen to U.S.S.R., Poland and Czechoslovakia in 1954, which later on resulted in Mahalanobis thesis which was later on criticized by C.N. Vakil and P.R. Brahmananda. Pt. Nehru then invited economist from India and abroad for open debate and finally Mahalanobis model was endorsed, which was later on also called Nehruvian model, because Nehru did not accept the Mahalanobis model in its totality. He has put in it the prospects of an acceleration in economic growth but more than the seeds from which it could grow as self-reliant industrial and technological structure with emphasis on machine-building industries.

The planning process introduced by Pt. J.L. Nehru helped to complete and strengthen the process of unification of India into a single fabric. In modern India, the mobilisation of resources and effective distribution of the produced goods to all levels of population and the remote corners such as economic intervention by centre would have to be necessary concomitant with a view to achieve the economic objective of the Indian constitution which have been embodied in the directive principles.

Thus, Nehru wanted planning process to introduce changes in individual and technological structure of society by emphasizing the role of science and the scientific method on a large scale by promoting a self-reliant economy which in itself would process the means of achieving rapid economic progress and solve urgent social problems.

I.IV. Pt. J.L. Nehru as an Economic Philosopher

Nehru was never fully satisfied with social and economic comprehension of the experts. His scientific outlook, his global perspective of economic governance, his belief in deepening of democracy and his urge for upliftment of mankind made him an economic philosopher of great stature. He led as an advocate of inflow of modern technology from abroad with creation of scientific manpower. He was an institution builder and established scientific research laboratories of international of repute like Bhabha Atomic Research Centre and National Science Institute to name a few. Thus, he laid the foundation of scientific society simulated with scientific manpower. In this sense he was a forerunner economist who visualized the foundation of a knowledge base for perfect and sustainable growth of economy at higher path in future.

The three plans under Nehru, contained the essence of development in infrastructure of society. The emergence of mixed economy was the direct result of planning effort. The remaking of India on the basis of democratic planning rested on the main thrust, namely, the utilization of our resources, men and material and in particular the maximum quality and quantity of labour willingly given and rightly directed so as to promote the good of the community and individual. The foundations of sound planning rests on the realities of the day in bringing about a new social order free from exploitation. For this a climate of a scientific social reasoning and enriched knowledge base is a must.

S. Jagnarayana epitomized Nehru era with two developments for the immense and incalculable dimension for humanity and its extensive welfare domain one was the tremendous advance of science and technology resulting in development of Nuclear energy and the conquest of space throwing wide open unlimited vista of progress or destruction.

The second was the growing awakening and almost irresistible move of the long suppressed masses of humanity in the continents of Asia and Africa. Both these totally different but not necessarily antagonistic expressions of elemental energy were capable of infinite good and finite evil.

Nehru concentrated in the discussion on third plan to three aspects—first emphasis on steel, coal and other basic heavy industries.

Second, the size of investment in public sector. That was the crying need set-up for the social objectives of planning in clear terms. And third, economic goals and social objectives of planning. He eloquently sets his views on economic goals and objectives of planned economy in India in the following words:

> "Planning is a continuous process and can't be isolated for the short period. It is a continuous movement towards a desired goals because these all major decisions have to be made by agencies informed of these goals and the social purpose behind them. Thus, to Nehru, planning is not only an economic instrumentality but a social framing of societal goals or objectives with a concerted move to achieve it in a time frame. Even considering five years period, forward and long-term planning has always been kept in view. In this very perspective, planning is the essence of

> planning in Nehruvian Economic Philosophy. Because ultimately it is the development of human being and human personality that counts. Although planning in values, in material investment is essential and even more important, it is investment in man."

Thus, Nehru evolved the concept of human capital much earlier and visualized that this can be better shaped through setting long-term goals under the mechanisms of perspective planning. It helps us to estimate that he was a great economic philosopher. A rational approach devoid of emotional aberrations which led to concentration and final collapse. He emphasized the importance of the social objectives alongwith material achievement for the correct path of economic development in the country. The social and economic problems be dealt with scientifically. This requires rational approach and not emotional and forms the core of inter-related economic ideas which underlines his economic thinking for a long period. In this sense Pt. J.L. Nehru comes in the category of economic thinkers having a long run social goals like Karl Marx, J.S. Mill and A.C. Pigou.

In Discovery of India Chapt. VIII and X and his last writing on overall analysis of his own views and policies contained in an article on "Changing India" published after Chinese invasion in (1965) in the *Journal of Foreign Affairs,* Nehru said the following statement:

> "The harnessing of modern technology to economic development is very important. There are two implications of this. First was an acceptance of the emphasis on heavy industries in the process of industrialization of India, while there has been considerable controversy in India over large scale *vs.* small scale industrialization. Nehru clinched the issue in his own mind even in his early economic thinking. This issue of big and small machines *vs.* Cottage industries be stated emphatically that, "It is not a mere question of adjustment of the two forms of production

> and the economy of one must be dominating and paramount and the other as complementary. So his economic system was with a support system of auxiliary industrial units involving the masses in the development process."

The latest technical achievement of the present day economy must necessarily be dominating. The wider implications of this was his emphasis on scientific education and research. He was of the view that under proper social conditioning experimentation with the machine would inculcate the scientific temper and widen the experience and outlook of men.

Thus, Pt. Jawahar Lal Nehru was a great economic philosopher. He visualized the use of science to wider the temper and outlook of men. Thus widening the scope and created the bigger canvas for the emergence of scientific, social and economic order.

Nehru was a believer in dynamising the static character of our socio-economic system for expanding the horizon of individual mind. This is necessary to change the static character of our living conditions and make it vital, active and adventurous. New situations lead to new experiences and human mind is compelled to deal with them and adapt itself to a changing environments.

He also propounded the economic view that one must not be tied to social fabric or an industrial fabric, if it goes against, the new discovery emerges. One must think in terms of future rather than the past because the past is dead or gone and future remains. We can't go back to it. Even the present is rapidly changing. Always approach economic issues in terms of future, then many of the present conflicts seen out of place or at rate, they assume a new aspect and one get out of rate of one's old mold of thinking. This exposes, his philosophical underpining in arranging tactical devices for economic enlistment of generations to come. This economic vision of Nehru helped much in setting the economic priorities in different plans. "The three fundamental requirements of India's economic development paradigm are industrial development with heavy engineering machine-making industry, scientific research institutes and electric power." These must be in the foundations of any planning for development.

Thus, we see Nehru's vision to empower Indian economy in three phases: The visionary phase 1927 to 1936, the conceptualization phase 1938 to 1946 and the implementation phase 1946 to 1960 and his own estimation of overall performance 1960-64 and at the last pointed out that the success points go further with growing capacity building in common man via minimum asset availability and growing knowledge capacity building, thus preparing the ground for a minimum material base and rich knowledge base for the economy as a whole.

In this present edited volume altogether 32 articles have been included analyzing different dimension of Nehruvian vision to empower Indian Economy. The contents explains that Nehru's vision as a socialist philosopher contains 5 articles written by scholars of repute. Where articles by A. Santhanan, Jayaselvi, Binod Chaudhary and Dr. Umesh Prasad is important.

The Part II of the content discusses Nehru as an architect of Indian planning, where article by Dr. D. Rajshekhar and Anand Bandhu Mukerjee is an important eye opener.

Part III of this volume discusses Nehru as an economic philosopher and an economic policy-maker. Where Dr. Manju Singh, Dr. M. Ramajaneyula, Dr. A. Sangamitra and T.M. Sravana Kumar, S.K. Karimulla, A. Ranga Reddy's papers desire special attention.

Finally Part IV discusses Nehruvian Policy: Failures and Success stories. The estimation of Nehru's vision finally place us in the position of telling the fact that Nehru, as a visionary was a successful statesman, shaping India's future as a knowledge-based democratic socialist order. Here articles by Harinarayan Pd. Singh, C.B. Sharma, Prof. R.R. Gawhale and Dr. R.B. Bhanduralkan are praiseworthy.

References

Martyschin Orest: Jawahar Lal Nehru and his Political Views, Progress Publication, Moscow, 1989.

Mishra, Neelam, Socialist Orientation of Pt. Jawahar Lal Nehru, Gyan Publishing House, New Delhi (1889).

Pt. Jawahar Lal Nehru Letter to V.K.R.V. Rao, July 10, 1940, Published on selected works of Jawarhar Lal Nehru, VI, XI, p. 236.

Pt. J.L. Nehru, Speeches in Lok Sabha on Dec. 5, 1952.

S. Chakrawarti, Development Planning: The Indian Experience, Oxford Univ. Press (1937), pp. 3-4.

Pt. J.L. Nehru, Speeches in Lok Sabha on 15 Dec. 1952.

Pt. J.L. Nehru Speeches at Silver Jubilee Celebration of Central Broad of Irrigation and Power, No. 17, 1952.

Pt J.L. Nehru Speeches on NDC Meeting, Nov. 9, 1954.

Mukerjee, Hiren, The Gentle Colossus—A Study of Jawahar Lal Nehru, Manish Garanthalya Pvt. Ltd., Kolkata, 1964.

Narayan Sriram: Towards a Socialist Economy, Indian National Congress, 1956.

Tarlok Singh, Nehru and Planning in India, Edited, pp. 29-30, Concept Publishing Company, New Delhi.

1

Pandit Jawahar Lal Nehru—A Visionary Economic Philosopher and Prospective Planner

Aprana Bhardwaj

Pandit Jawahar Lal Nehru was not a professional economist. Neither did he read economics in any college or university. He was a science graduate with Botany, Chemistry and Geology and then studied law.[1] The growing contact with millions of masses and deep study of books on social science while he was in prison for more than nine years, made him well acquainted with both theoretical and applied economics. Moreover; his chairmanship of National Planning Committee provided an opportunity to visualize the different aspects of planned economy of India. It also facilitated him to hear the views of 350 experts on different 29 sub-committees.[2] So, Nehruvian model of planned economy was conceptualized during the freedom movement itself.

When Netajee Subhash Chandra Bose was elected president in Haripura Congress, he constituted a National Planning Committee with Pt. Nehru as its chairman. He relied heavily upon Dr. P.C. Mahalanobis and Dr. V.K.R.V. Rao on economic and statistical issues. It helped him to concrete his ideas on economic issues once he wrote to Dr. V.K.R.V. Rao, "I should like you go through the resolutions in the three books and keeping them in view, note down what further general decisions we should take which should enable us to proceed with the draft that is to say I should like you to put down such further question of policy and principles as we should decide at our next stage. In putting down these questions, please indicate what in your opinion the decisions should be.

> "I should also like you to a brief not on the general picture of national planning in India which you recommend.[3] As such he was "learned theory approach".

In this way we see that as chairman of National Planning Committee, Pt. Nehru was already fully trained, equipped and familiar with the different aspects of planning in India before he got the responsibility to implement Five Years Plans. It is remarkable that his recommendations in three red books symbolizing his commitment to socialist ideas which were written long before Mao-tse-Tung published his five red books.

On the eve of independence, Pt. Nehru was already acquainted with all the important socio-economic issues of the world in general and India in particular. "The national movement threw up many great figures, but what marked out Jawaharlal Nehru was his concern with the problems of poverty and planned development in their large political and economic context and the social philosophy and values which he valued to deal with them. The years before independence can be seen in retrospect as a long period of preparation for practical action. When the opportunity came the transition from the role of freedom fighter to that of gifted statesman was, therefore, easy and altogether natural."[4]

On account of paucity of time and little practical knowledge of planning, Dr. Anjaria and Dr. K.N. Raj who drafted the First Plan, used the simple Harrod-Domer model.

The simple thesis of an almost open economy where there was little distinction between consumer goods and investment goods. It also lacked social objectives.[5] However, Pandit Nehru was emotionally delighted to see that a plan document was ready for implementation that he carried the First Plan document balancing on his head when he entered in the cabinet meeting to present the First Plan draft.[6]

Pt. Nehru was not entirely satisfied with the social and economic comprehension of the experts who put out the First Plan. It lacked the perspective and there was little of scientific or industrial temper in it. He sent Dr. Mahalanobis, Dr. Pitamber Pan and Dr. Sen to USSR, Poland and Czechoslavakia in 1954 and here emerged Mahalanobis thesis which was criticized by several economists. Pt. Nehru invited economist from India and abroad for open debate and finally Mahalanobis model took shape which has been called also Nehruvian model. But Pt. Nehru did not accept the Mahalanobis model in its totality. He has in it the prospects of an acceleration in economic growth but more than that the seeds from which could grow as self reliant industrial and technological structure with emphasis on machine-building industries.[7]

The planning technique introduced by Mr. Nehru for ameliorating economic and social backwardness of the people had helped also to complete the process of unification of India into a single fabric. In the modern India where planning would have to be resorted to for the mobilization of resources and effective distribution of the produced goods to all levels of population and the remote corners such economic intervention by the centre would have to be necessary concomitant with a view to achieve the economic objective of the Indian constitution which have been embodied in the Directive Principles.[8]

With the help of planning technique Pt. Nehru wanted to introduce changes in the individual and technological structure of society by emphasizing the role of science and the scientific method on a large scale and by promoting a self-reliant economy which within itself would process the means of achieving rapid economic progress and solve urgent social problems. He was for inflow of modern technology from abroad. Simultaneous with the scientific Manpower Committee. This laid the basis for the remarkable advance of the scientific and technological education in later years to come.[9]

The three plans under Nehru's leadership, contained the essence of development in the infrastructure of society. The emergence of mixed economy was the direct result of planning effort. The remaking of India on the basis of democratic planning rested on the main crest, namely, the utilization of our resource, men and material and in particular the maximum quality and quantity of labour willingly given and rightly directed so as to promote the good of the community and the individual. The foundations of sound planning was laid on the realities of the day in bringing about a new social order free from exploitation. As Pt. Nehru himself pointed out it was set-up towards the establishment of a society which gave security to individuals and offered employment and encouragement to future activity and adventure.[10]

In the Nehru era of economic planning two important developments of immense and incalculable dimensions for humanity had taken place. One was the tremendous advance of science and technology resulting in the development of nuclear energy and the conquest of space throwing wide open unlimited Vista of progress or destruction. The second was the growing awakening and an almost irresistible move of the long suppressed masses of humanity in the continents particularly in Asia and Africa. Both these totally different but not necessarily antagonistic expressions of elemental energy were capable of infinite good as well as finite evil.[11]

When discussions began on the Draft outline of the Third Plan, Nehru paid special attention to three aspects. First was his emphasis upon steel, coal and other basic and heavy industries. His priority was Bokaro Steel Plant. The second aspect was the size of investment in public sector. That was the crying need to set for the social objectives of planning in clear terms,[12] Pt. Nehru went on Himalayan holiday, revised the draft and what emerged as the first chapter of Third Plan document in which he eloquently sets his views on economic goals and objectives of planned economy in India in the following words:

'Planning is a continuous process and cannot be isolated for short period. Thus the Third Five Year Plan is in continuation of the First and Second Plan and it will lead to the Fourth and subsequent plans. Planning is a continuous movement towards desired goals and because these all major decisions have to be made by agencies informed of these goals and the social purpose behind them. Even in considering a five year period, forward and long-term planning has always to be kept in view. Indeed perspective planning is the essence of planning process. Ultimately it is the development of human being and the human personality that counts. Although planning in values material investment, even more important is investment in man'.[13]

Pt. Nehru always emphasized the social objectives along with material achievement for the correct path of economic development in the country. He believed that social and economic problems to be dealt with scientifically, i.e. the approach should be rational and not emotional.[14] A core of inter-related economic ideas underlines economic thinking through a long period.[15] This came out very strikingly if one compares sections of Discovery of India (Chapters VIII and X) and one of his last overall analysis of his own policies and views contained in the article on changing India published after the Chinese invasion in Foreign Affairs (April 1965).[16]

To Nehru, the harnessing of modern technology to economic development was very important. There were two implications of this. The first was an acceptance of the emphasis on heavy industries in the process of industrialization of India. While there has been considerable controversy in India in large scale *vs.* small sale industrialization. Nehru himself had clinched the issue in his own mind even in his early economic thinking. This was perhaps one of the few economic choices he really made discussing this issue of the big machines *vs.* cottage industries, he stated emphatically that "it is not a mere question of adjustment of the two forms of production and economy of one must be dominating and paramount with the other as complementary to its fitting in where it can.[17] The economy based on the latest technical achievement is of the day must necessarily be the dominating one. The second wider implication of this approach was his emphasis on scientific education and research. He seems to have particular fascination for the idea that under proper social conditions experimentation with the machine would inoculate the scientific temper and widen the experience and outlook of men.[18]

Pt. Nehru believed in dynamising the static character of our socio-economic system. In India we have been wedded for long past forms and made of thought and action. Now expanding, horizons are necessary. Thus we will change the static character of our living and make it dynamic and vital and our minds will become active and adventurous. New situation lead to new experiences, as mind is compelled to deal with them and adapt itself to a changing environment.[19]

It also means not being tied down the social fabric or an industrial fabric, if it goes against the new discovery.[20]

Moreover, he always thought for future for whose sake he started planned economy for the country. In his own words, "One must think in terms of future rather than the past because the past is dead and gone and we cannot go back to it and even the present is rapidly changing present. It you approach it in terms of the future, then many of the present conflicts seem out of place or at any rate, they assume a new aspect and you get out of the rate of your old mode of thinking.[21]

It was his economic vision that the priorities of Indian plans were fixed. According to him, "The three fundamental requirements of India, if she is to develop industrially and otherwise, are heavy engineering and machine-making industry, scientific research institutes, electric power. These must be the foundations of all planning and the National Planning Committee laid greatest emphasis upon them.[22] Pt. Nehru held the view that "Planning does not merely mean putting up a factory here or factory there. Planning implies the interlocking of the production, consumption, employment and a large number of other such as transport, social services, education and health. The whole thing has somehow to be brought together of course, human relationship in a vast country of three hundred seventy million people cannot be dealt with in a mathematical way. There are numerous uncertain actors, the coming of the monsoon for instance. Yet the element of uncertainty and error can be greatly reduced by planning."[23] Again he observed: "Gradually we have proceeded along the path of planning. And I have no doubt that we ought to continue this and learn more and more, often make mistakes, nevertheless growing progressively a little more expert of this business of planning. We want to arrive at stage when we can assess more or less accurately, what the next stage is going to be and to provide for it and to visualize our problems in advance to take appropriate action to meet them before events force out hands.[24]

On socialism Nehru was not dogmatic. In his own words, "What do we mean when we say our objective is a "socialist pattern of life." Surely we mean a society in which there is a social cohesion, which is without classes, where is equality of opportunity and the possibility for every one to live a good life. Surely we mean a society in which there is social cohesion which is without classes, where there is equality of opportunity and the possibility for every one to live a good life. Obviously this cannot be attained unless we produce to achieve these standards to enable us to lead a good life. So, we have to lay great stress on equality, on the removal of disparities, and it has to be remembered always that socialism does not consist in the spreading out of poverty. "The essential thing is that there must be wealth and production."[25]

In this way, we see that Pt. Nehru was not dogmatic on socialism while starting the planned economic development. The only issue on which there was to be no compromise was advancement through technological progress, planning and the necessary degree of social control were to be hand maidens to this objective.[26]

Pt. Nehru had a clear vision that a socialist society can be established only in a planned economy and without the establishment of a socialist society the removal of poverty, unemployment and inequality from Indian Political Economy is not possible. Nehru's socialism which can be termed as "Nehruist" provides the whole underdeveloped world with a pattern of development which makes communism or state socialism look both old fashioned and barbarian by comparison. It is rather a special form of socialism whose emphasis is on equality and prosperity or mankind. It attached more importance to people's consent and cooperation than anything else. So, his vision of planned economy was democratic and by active participation of mass and not authoritarian and totalitarian as in USSR. Nehru himself was very concerned on the implementation and achievement of plans. He himself mentioned, "I think that on the whole we plan well. I thing also that on the whole, we do not implement well. It is not good to have a theoretical plan and not implement it.[27]

While summing up the discussion on Pt. Nehru's Philosophy and planned economy of India we may safety say that what he visualized on his visit to Soviet Union in 1927 was conceptualized by him as chairman of National planning committee and implemented by him as Chairman of Planning Commission. So far Nehru planning went with three states, Visualization (1927-37), Conceptualization (1938-47), Implementation (1948-63). Nehru was both the ideologue and pragmatic personality in regard to planning in India, The most dearest terms to his mental thinking were democracy, socialism, and planning. To him socialism was an end, democracy was means and planning was tools to achieve the ideal of socialism through democratic means. To criticize Nehru's role as chairman of Planning Commission of the failure of Indian plans is not fair. These failures were inevitable in a socio-political system under which he had to work. It is impact of his contribution that despite 17 years period of economic reforms none dare to move the resolution to drop the word 'Socialism' from the preamble of the constitution of India. Planning has come to stay in India and no supporter of economic reforms dare to suggest to stop planning in the reform era. It is on account of the deep-rooted penetrating of planning by Mr. Nehru during his tenure as chairman, In fact he visioned planning for India while leading freedom movement and dedicated India and himself to planning in free India. He lived for planning, thought for planning and died for planning. Despite many shortcomings, the planned economy of India got a definite direction with the Nehruvian model expressed in

Mahalanobis model upto the 7th Plan and after that gradually the planners of the country have silently bequeathed Nehruvian model and openly moving towards indicative planning under economic reform measures. Pt. Nehru is quoted on lip only. It is why Finance Ministry is becoming stronger than Planning Commission.

Pt. Nehru was the founder of planned economic development of India and knew no fatigue and was unparalleled man of action dedicated to the good of all suffering masses through planned economy of India, He was not only chairman of Planning Commission but friend, philosopher and guide of the planned economic development of India from First Plan to the Third Plan. In the history of India, he will be always remembered for his contributions to nation building as chairman of Planning Commission despite failure and non-achievements of the objectives set in the plans from First to the Third. Withdrawal from Nehruvian model is a mean betrayal of the masses from the commitments which our freedom fighters made to the poor people long ago under the leadership of Gandhi and Nehru.

Notes and References

1. Pt. Jawaharlal Nehru, An Autobiography, p. 25.
2. Pt. Jawaharlal Nehru, The Discovery of India, p. 400
3. Pt. Jawaharlal Nehru, Letter to Dr. V.K.R.V. Rao, on June 10, 1940, published on selected works of Jawaharlal Nehru VI, XI, p. 326.
4. Tarlok Singh, Jawaharlal Nehru and planned development of India published in Nehru and Planning in India (Edited), pp. 29-30 Concept Publishing Company, New Delhi.
5. S. Chakrawarti, "Development Planning: The Indian Experience", Oxford, pp. 3-4 (1987).
6. Pt. Nehru, Speech in Lok Sabha on December 15, 1952.
7. Pt. Nehru, Speech in National Development Council, 20 October, 1954.
8. Theodoren Gregory, India on the Eve of Third Five Year Plan.
9. S. Jagannarayan, India Under Nehru, p. 33.
10. *Ibid.*, pp. 37-38.
11. *Ibid.*, pp. 40-45.
12. Tarlok Singh, *op. cit.*
13. Jawaharlal Nehru: First Chapter in the Third Plan document, pp. 1-3.

14. Tarlok Singh, *op. cit.*
15. Pt. Nehru, Speech in Lok Sabha on Dec. 15, 1952.
16. Y.K. Alagh, Nehru, Planning Commission and planned economic development published in Nehru and planning in India (Edited).
17. Pt. Nehru, Speech in Lok Sabha on December 15, 1952.
18. Pt. Nehru, Speech at Silver Jubilee Celebration of Central Board of Irrigation and Power, Nov. 17, 1952.
19. Pt. Nehru, The Discovery of India, p. 412.
20. Pt. Nehru, Speech at the opening ceremony of the Fuel Research Institute, Digwadi, April 22, 1950.
21. Pt. Nehru, Speeches, Sept. 1946-May 1949, Vol. I, p. 99.
22. J.L. Nehru, The Discovery of India, p. 412.
23. Pt. Nehru, Speech delivered at the NDC meeting on Nov. 9, 1954.
24. Pt. Nehru, Speech delivered in the Lok Sabha initiating the debate on the Second Five Year Plan, May 23, 1956.
25. Pt. Nehru, *Ibid.*
26. Jawaharlal Nehru's Speeches, Vol. I, Sept. 1946-May 1949, pp. 113-14.
27. Pt. Nehru, First Five Year Plan, GOI.

2

Nehru's Vision to Empower Indian Economy

Mahendra Ranawat

Jawahar Lal Nehru's fascination and dream for planned economic infrastructural development is a known fact, before independence also he had a great vision for sustainable economic development. Through this planning and pragmatic approach he gave birth to 'Mixed Economy', which was felt need of that hour, but now it has become fashion in present economic circles to criticize that model. The proposed topic of paper is focusing on the historical process of ideological development of Nehruvian economic policies and its relevance in the present scenario.

The economic policies of Jawaharlal Nehru have been subjected to much controversy in the past few decades. However, it is important to place Nehru's economic policies in context for a proper appreciation of his policies. Nehru's commitment to the cause of India's development remains unquestioned, and it is no doubt that much of his plans and speculations were jeopardized by the unexpected partition that came along with the independence of India, which brought about an unprecedented fissure in the economic resources of the Indian mainland. Nehru himself confessed that the partition brought about a large share of problems, including a great rift in thee agricultural land sell in Pakistan, whereas the corresponding industries remained in Indian dominion. The problem faced by the Jute producing areas were in Pakistan, whereas the Jute processing factories remained in India, thereby affecting jute production on both sides of the border.[1]

Early Economic Reforms of Nehru: Nehru started his career as the Prime Minister of independent India in 1947, and immediately launched a number of economic reforms. Nehru was firm believer in state control over the economic sectors. His socialist ideals revealed themselves in the way he introduced laws for land redistribution, in order to curtail the economic disparity in India among the landed and the land—less classes. One was introduce to determine the mode government expenditure and grants in important development sectors like agriculture and education.

As a Fabian Socialist, Nehru had great faith in economic planning and personally chaired his government's Planning Commission. Food grain production increased from 51 million tons in 1951 to 82 million tons by the end of the Second Five Year Plan (1956-61). During that same decade,

however, India's population grew from about 360 million to 440 million, which eliminated real economic benefits for all but large landowners and the wealthiest and best educated quarter of India's urban population. The landless and unemployed lower half of India's fast growing population remained inadequately fed, ill housed, and illiterate. However, Nehru's wisdom in keeping his nation nonaligned helped accelerate the country's economic development, as India received substantial aid from both side of the Cold War, with the Soviet Union and Eastern Europe contributing almost as much in capital goods and technical assistance as did the United States, Great Britain, and West Germany. The growth of iron and steel industries soon became a truly international example of coexistence, with the United States building one plant, the Soviet Union another, Britain a third, and West Germany a fourth. For the Third Five–Year Plan (1961-66), launched during Nehru's era, an

Aid India Consortium of the major Western powers and Japan provided some $5 billion in capital and credits, and as a result, India's annual iron output rose to nearly 25 million tons by the plan's end, with about three times that amount of coal produced and almost 40 billion kilowatt—hours of electric power generated. India had become the words of output, through it remained per capital one of the productive of the world's major countries.

The First Five Year Plan emphasized on irrigation sector because of food shortage in India but the second five year was based on Mahalanobis model, which was focused on industrial development, therefore transportation and power sector received high attention in this plan.[2]

THE IDEOLOGY GUIDING NEHRU'S ECONOMIC POLICIES

Nehru's economics policies have often been considered to be Socialist in nature. It is no doubt that Socialism did play a very important role in Nehru's ideological make up. But at the same time, it is also important to consider that Nehru himself denied any kind of overt Socialist tendencies in the economic policies adopted by him. Nehru advocated a kind of mixed economy. Any kind of unquestioned ideological adherence to any form of economic tenet, or "ism", he realized, would be detrimental to India's growth. He wanted a practical approach in farming the Indian economy, which would suit best in the betterment of rural economy. On the other hand, he had a strong belief that industrial development would be the best way to serve India's economic interests.

Nehru as the grand architecture of the Indian economic identity, instead of following the western type 'Capitalism' or the Russian type 'Socialism', wanted India to follow a 'mixed economy so he perceived that the good elements of capitalism and socialism be enjoyed in the 'mixed economy' instead of socialism, he proposed the formulation of a 'Socialistic Pattern of society' with public sector achieving the 'commanding heights'.

Nehru wanted the country to accept the goal of

socialism for free India. In his numerous writing and speeches, Nehru declared himself to be a socialist. At the Lahore session of the congress (December 1929) in his presidential address, Nehru said" I must frankly confess that "I am a socialist and a republican we must realize that the philosophy of socialism has permeated the entries structure of society of the world over, and almost the only points in dispute are the pace and method of advance to its full realization. Nehru's efforts to move to socialism and to promote causality of opportunity a personal growth and moral development proved to be an even more difficult proposition than goals of lightly abolishing unsociability and resaving opportunities for those previously excluded.[3]

Nehru was essentially a democrat of the western liberal category. This was due to the impact of his early education in England. He accepted the essential of Marxism and appreciated Soviet Russia and its system of economic planning but under Gandhian impact did not accept Communist methods, and even gave secondary position to the concept of class-struggle.

Nehru was concerned with evolving a set of principles and ideas to achieve a socialist reconstruction of society with democratic means rather than trough a violent revolution.

As India was nearing freedom, there were multiple views on the 'economic identity' for the emerging Indian nation among the members of the India national congress. While leaders like Sardar Vallabh Bhai Patel and C. Rajagopalachari stood for a western type of liberal economic order for India, the Marxist list oriented members including M.N. Ray, Subhash Chandra Bose, and others advocated for socialism. Gandhian economists like J.C. Kumarappa wanted the emerging Indian economy freed from any type of foreign influence Pandit Jawaharlal Nehru assimilated all these suggestions and put forward an integrated economic identify for India.[4]

NEHRU'S INDUSTRIAL POLICIES

Nehru wanted to create a balance between the rural and the urban sectors in his economic policies. He stated that there was no contradiction between the two and that both could go hand in hand. He denied to carry forward the age old city versus village controversy and that in India, both could go hand in hand. Nehru was intent to harness and fully exploit the natural resources of India for the benefit of his countrymen. The main sector he identified was hydroelectricity, and he constructed a number of dams to achieve that end. The dams would not only harness energy, but would also support irrigation to a great degree. Nehru considered dams to be the very symbol of India's collective growth as they were the platforms. Nehru also considered the possibility of nuclear growth during his tenure as the prime minister of India.

Prior to 1947, there was virtually no "Public sector" in the Indian economy. The only instances worthy of mention were Railways, the Posts and the Telegraphs, the Port Trusts, the Ordnance and Aircraft Factories and a few state managed undertakings like the government salt factories, quinine factories, etc. The idea that economic development should be promoted by the State actually managing industrial concerns did not take root in India before 1947, even thought the concept of planning was very much discussed by Congress government in the Indian provinces. However, in the post-independence period, the expansion of public sector was undertaken as an integral part of the 1956 Industrial Policy.[5]

The Industrial Policy Resolution 1956 gave the public a strategic role in the Indian economy. For one thing, at the time of independence, the country was backward and underdeveloped—basically an agrarian economy with a weak industrial base, heavy unemployment, low level of saving and investment and near absence of infrastructural facilities, India economy needed a big push. This push could not come from the Indian private sector, which was starved of funds and of managerial ability and was incapable of undertaking risks involved in large long—gestation investment. It was assumed at that time that only the Government intervention and industrial production, expand employment opportunities, reduce poverty, etc. In other words the public sector was thought of as the engine for self reliant economic growth to develop a sound agricultural and industrial base, diversify the economy and overcome economic and social backwardness.[6]

To this basic argument for the expansion of the public sector, the Government adds additional reasons over time, e.g.:

1. to accelerate the growth of the core sectors of the economy;
2. to serve the equipment needs of strategically important sectors like Railways, Telecommunication, Nuclear Power, Defense, etc.
3. to exert countervailing power on the operation of private monopolies and multinationals in selected arrears;
4. to ensure easier availability of articles of mass consumption, to check prices of important articles, etc.-the rationale behind setting up consumer-oriented industries.
5. to protect employment, the government was forced to take over sick industrial units.

In fact, over a period of time, the government entered into many sectors for all types of good and bad reasons and in many cases for no reasons at all.[7]

NEHRU AND FOREIGN INVESTMENT

Nehru inspired the industrialists to provide a fillip to India's economy; however, he had strict reservation on the question of foreign investment. Nehru was wary of foreign investment. Nehru's nationalist ideals confirmed in him the belief that India was self- sufficient to bolster its own growth. Although he did not officially decry the possibility of foreign investment in direct terms, he did stress that the sectors of foreign investment would be regularized, and terms and conditions of investment and employment would be strictly controlled by government rules in case there were possibilities of a foreign investment. Nehru, moreover, emphasized that the key sectors will always be in government hand. This step of Nehru is much criticized now.

Yet, it cannot be denied that Nehru aptly looked forward to long-term investments for which he banked more on Indian industries. It is also often suggested that his endeavor to harness international support to develop India's infrastructural profile between 1947 and 1955 did not one of great economic growth for India. Although his economic policies are blamed for the failure of India to turn into a major more long-term basis. It is often inferred that the economic liberation of the years was possible only because of Nehru's policies in the initial stages.

The state Control in Nehru's Economic Policies: The most distinctive, and often debated feature of Nehru's economics policies, was the high level of state and central control that was exercised on the industrial and business sectors of the country. Nehru emphasized that state would control almost all key areas of country's economy, either centrally or on a state-wise basis. His Socialist emphasis on state control somehow seemed to undermine his stress on industrial policies. The rigorous state laws and License rules put a great degree of restrain on the free execution of industrial policies. Even the farmers, along with the business personnel, found themselves to be at the receiving end of rigorous state control policies and high taxation. Poverty and unemployment were widespread were widespread throughout Nehru's governance.

NEHRU'S VIEWS ON RURAL ECONOMY

Nehru's policies towards the rural economy of India were also significant. Nehru felt for the rural self-development of India very strongly. He tried to boost India's cottage industries. Much on the lines of Gandhi, Nehru believed that the rural and cottage industries of India played a major role in the economic fabric of the country. But most of his cottage industry development programs were as a part of community development. He was also of the belief that small scale industries and cottage industries were effective solutions to the massive employment problems that remained a perpetual issue of concern throughout his tenure.

The economic policies of Nehru are often blamed for

the poor economy of India in the subsequent years. However, it cannot be denied that his decision was necessitated by the needs of the times. India needed to effectively harness its domestic means as well as strengthen its governmental control to lay the future privatization. It is often speculated that Nehru would have embraced the economic reforms and economic liberalization of the late twentieth century if he was alive.

Nehru was fascinated by the Soviet Union's Piatiletka or 5 years plans. But he wrote after a visit there in the 1920's that the human costs are unpayable'. A believer in the mixed economy of Harold Laski and influenced by the Fabian Society, Nehru wished the economy of India to be partially capitalist, but with the state occupying a large, especially in the commanding heights of the economy.

In setting a path for the economic policy after Independence, he chose from a set of options considerably more limited than those available today, and followed to a large degree the conventional wisdom among Capitalist Indian academic economists of the time. India's growth rate was moderately above 4% during planning period. It is hard to say definitely how much growth there might have been with different economics policies: predominantly capitalist Western Europe grew slightly faster than India during the Nehru years (especially during the decade after World War II); but so did the command economies of communist China and the Soviet Union. The strongly capitalist USA grew somewhat more slowly, as did most of the newly independent nations that followed WWII (with the exception of oil- producing nations).

Some recent (but isolated) studies influenced by "Chicago School Economists" such as one by "Golman Sachsae" have that India, had the potential to grow faster than it did in the post Nehru 1960—1980 timeframe. According to this thinking, that opportunity was wasted out of a misplaced faith in the power of economics planning. Economist Jagdish Bhagwati has rightly remarked that India's problem has been that it has too many brilliant economists; Bhagwati believes the stalwarts of Nehru's Planning Commission began to believe in their own infallibility, to the detriment of the Indian nation. B.R. Shenoy a contemporary opponent of Nehru's Second Five Year Plan, notably, is now considered a significant theorist in the Austrian School of Economics.

The Soviet Union was the only major power during Nehru's tenure to aid India in developing independent capabilities areas of heavy industry, engineering, and technology. This political fact, combined with Nehru's preference for state-led development, promoted suspicion about the Nehruvian model failed in many of its objectives; however, many Indian economists" particularly among Nehru's contemporaries" believe Nehru emphasis on central planning was the right policy for India of that time.[8]

Some critics of Indian economics development believe that the economy of the Nehruvian and post-Nehruvian era, with inefficient public sector entities on the one hand, and crony- capitalist private sector entities that used the so- called license raj to have carve out lucrative niches for themselves on the other, was a product of economic policy foundations laid during Nehru's tenure.

Nehru's economic policies are sometimes confused by critics with those of his daughter, Indira Gandhi, which were more statistic and deregister in orientation. Nehru's economics of state intervention and investment were conceived at a time when transfer of capital and technology important to India were not easily forthcoming from the developed world (which at time also had plenty of state-sponsored capital controls)

HISTORICAL BACK GROUND OF NEHRUVIAN PLANNING MIXED ECONOMY

The Indian National Congress, under the inspiration of Jawaharlal Nehru, set-up the National Planning Committee towards the end of 1938. The Committee produced a series of studies on different subjects concerned with economic development.

The committee laid down that the state should own or control all key industries and services, mineral resources and railways, waterways, shipping and other public utilities and.

In fact, all those large- scale industries which were likely to become monopolistic in character.[9]

Beside the National Planning Committee (NPC), eight industrialists conceived" A Plan of Economic Development" which was popularly known as the Bombay Plan. There was also a Gandhian Plan which was prepared by Shrman Narayan, the world famous revolutionary M.N. Roy formulated the People's Plan. All these plans are of historical importance never implemented.

Just after the attainment of Independence the government if India set-up the Planning Commission in 1950 to assess the country's needs of material capital and human resources so as to formulate plan for their more balanced and effective utilization. The First Five Year Plan commenced in 1950-51 and it was followed by a series of Five Year Plans.

OBJECTIVES OF ECONOMIC PLANNING IN INDIA

The Directive Principles of our Constitution laid down: "The State shall in particular direct its policy towards securing—(a) that citizens, men and women equally, have the right to an adequate means of livelihood: (b) that the ownership.

B.S. Minhas states: "Securing rapid economic growth and expansion of employment, reeducation. Disparities in income and wealth, prevention of concentration of economic power, and creation of the values and attitudes of a free equal society have been among the objectives of all our plans".[10]

When India became independent the Indian people were steeped in mass poverty, unemployment and underemployment. India had an illiterate and untrained labour force, static, agriculture with semi feudal relations and a comparatively less developed industrial sector, and woefully inadequate infrastructure in the form of transportation and communication, energy and power, banking and finance, etc. thus, India's problems required a big national effort and there fore India adopted "Planning as a lever of social and economic change". "Jawaharlal Nehru, rightly said, greatly admired the achievements of Soviet planning and so borrowed the concept of socialism from the Russian but, he also regarded the democratic values of the capitalist society as indispensable for the full growth of a just society. Thus, in his endeavor to take advantage of the virtues of the two extreme societies which were themselves also undergoing a transformation, Nehru's vision of the new India was described as "democratic socialism".

EVOLUTION OF THE CONCEPT OF MIXED ECONOMY

Mixed economy is the outcome of the compromise between the two diametrically opposite schools of thought- the one which champions the cause of capitalism and the other which strongly pleads for the socialization of all the means of production and of the socialization of all the entire economy by the state. The economic development of U.K., U.S.A. and many free nations of Europe and America was due to private enterprise. This explains why in the writings of the 18th and 19th century economists, the concept of mixed economy finds no mention, since in those days, economics liberty and non-interference of the state in economic affairs were cardinal principles. According to the economic system worked smoothly and what was most profitable for the individual, was also most conducive to the economic welfare of the community at large. Perfect harmony in the economic system could be achieved through the acceptance of the invisible hand of self-interest and the use if market forces of demand and supply

While Karl Marx was laying the foundations of a socialist system, the capitalist system failed to respond to the needs of the people during the great depression of the 1930's and thus opened the eyes of the economists and statesmen to its intrinsic weakness. Lord Keynes wrote in 1926: "The world is not so governed from above that, private and social interests always coincide..... It is not a correct dedication from the principles of economics that enlightened self-interest always operates in the public interest. Nor is it true that self-interest is generally enlightened."[11] Keynes was proved correct when the Great Depression of the 1930's showed the hollowness of the classical claim of the smooth working of the economics system.

As a direct reaction to the failure of the old capitalist order, the socialist economy was advocated as an alternative system. It was maintained that complete socialization of the means of production and state direction of production and distribution would be the ideals solution to the pressing problems of the contemporary society. Even professor Pigou, the last of the classical, had to admit: "the system of socialist central planning, if it could be effectively organized, would be in many respects preferable to our existing capitalist system."

Keynes, however, thought that capitalism shorn of some of its defects, was an admirable system as it helps to promote competition and efficiency in production. At the same time, socialism of the authoritarian type would spell death to individual freedom, both economic and political. But state control and direction was inevitable in the modern complex society. A compromise was, therefore, necessary between the high degree of state intervention and participation in the socialist economy on the one side and free enterprise capitalist economy based of Keynes that the concept of mixed economy was evolved.[12]

CRITICAL ESTIMATION OF THE NEHRU'S ECONOMIC MODEL

The experiment of mixed economy in India has been carried on for nearly five decades now. Both Central and state Governments in India set-up several public sector enterprises in many lines of production, trade and finance. In some cases, successful private sector units were nationalized (insurance companies and bank by the central Governments and road transport system by the Central Governments). Often sick private units were taken over by the Government (e.g. textiles mills and engineering units). Many states set-up public sector enterprises just to accommodate party legislators as chairmen to provide them with ministerial status and perquisites. In general, most public sector enterprises in India have been running inefficiently involving huge losses to the

Government and ultimately to the tax- payers. As in the case of erstwhile Soviet Russia and East European communist countries, the public sector enterprises have wasted precious resources and, therefore, have come in for utter contempt from the general public; their staunch defenders begin the left politicians and trade unions leaders.

Further, the private sector has been constantly and incessantly trying to evade and, in many ways, distort the planning process. The private sector has corrupted the bureaucracy and the politicians-in-power. Consequently relaxations in plan priorities were permitted. For instance, as revealed by the Subimal Dutt committee the government has permitted the private sector to set-up industrial units in areas reserved for the public sector. Similarly, while imports were to be permitted in areas of sophisticated technology, they were permitted in areas of low priority under one pretext or the other. The profit motive and the acquisitive spirit of the private sector on the one side and the competition and inefficiency of the public sector on the other have resulted in serious distortions in the planning process. The main distortion is:

1. Distortion of the production structure because of the persistence of inequalities under of income and wealth—a very significant preparation of the national resources is used to satisfy the wants of the elite;
2. Growth of unemployment, despite creation of additional employment opportunities under each plan, party because of failure to control the rapid growth of population and partly because of emphasis on capital-intensive production;
3. Failure of the state to check concentration of economic power.
4. Emergence of black economy or parallel economy in India—the instrument of progressive taxation has been blunted by widespread tax evasion and the rapid growth of black money.
5. Failure to check the increase in prices, particularly the prices of essential articles of mass consumption such as sugar, edible oils, foodgrains, etc.

6. Failure to bring about a redistribution of income in favour of the working class—Real wages of the working class have not shown an increase commensurate with the rise in national productivity.
7. Failure of the planned economy to significantly reduce the proportion of population below the poverty line.[13]

The upshot of the above analysis is whether investment is made in the public sector or the private sector, the major beneficiaries of growth have been the big business houses, the big trades and the landlords. These are the inherent contradictions of the mixed economy.

Notes and References

1. S. Gopal, J.L. Nehru: A biography, selected writings of J.L. Nehru, Vols. VI to XII, Teen Murtihouse, Delhi.
2. Planning Commission reports (Ist Five Year Plan to IIIrd Five Year Plan) Centre for Monitoring Indian Economy (1951-91).
3. Zaidi and Zaidi—Encyclopedia of Congress, Vol. 1929-30, S. Gopal, Nehru—A Biography
4. Gandhi Raymohan, "Sardar—Biography of Sardar Patel, Navjeevan Press.
5. Mathai, M.O., "Reminiscences of the Nehru Age", Vikas Publishing House, New Delhi.
6. Economic Survey of various years.
7. Industrial Policy Resolution, 1956.
8. Oral History Transcripts an Interview with C.D. Deshmukh. Teen Murtihouse, Delhi.
9. Zaidi and Zaidi, Encyclopedia of Indian National Congress, Vol. 1938, Chandra, Bipan, Indian Freedom Struggle, Published by Penguin India Ltd.
10. Minhas, B.S., Planning and the Poor, p. (vii).
11. Keynes, J.M., The End of Laissez Faire.
12. *Ibid.*
13. Subimal Dutt Committee Report.

3

Nehru Vision: Strengthening Science for Benefitting People

MANJU SINGH

This was the remark of Pandit Jawaharlal Nehru while addressing the Indian Science Congress as the President, held in New Delhi in 1947, the year of Indian Independence. Nehru was clear in his mind about the relationship between science and development of the society as a whole and its relevance, in the Indian context, for meeting the basic needs of large numbers. This was a recurring theme in his thought and deliberations. It was Nehru who envisioned the role of S&T to underpin and accelerate national development, science being an important element in modernizing the country to bring about what he repeatedly referred to as scientific temper in society, an essential aspect of the culture of a new civilization. Nehru promoted the growth of science in every conceivable way. It was a fairly unique statement then for any country, leaves alone a developing country. The Nehru period was thus characterized by massive development of an infrastructure for S&T, and for the promotion of quality and excellence.

Within the parameters of free, secular and democratic values he wanted to build an India with a strong infrastructure in Science and Technology. He always felt that India had missed out on the Industrial revolution and he wanted to make sure that it did not miss out on the Electronics revolution. He got together with people like Bhabha, Bhatnagar, Sarabhai, Krishnan and Mahalanobis to build the Science and Technology infrastructure. Dr Ambedkar helped him not only to write the constitution but also helped him implement the Hindu code bill which took the large bulk of the country towards the modernization path which we are witnessing today giving women the rightful role that they deserve.

When the country talks about becoming a Science and Technology powerhouse in the 21st century, it may be nice to step back and evaluate why such a robust optimism is possible at all. It may be appropriate to recall the rich legacy that Pandit Jawaharlal Nehru left behind and his permanent footprint in terms of building a modern secular and democratic India with a firm commitment to science and technology. Long before India became independent he had a shadow planning committee under the Indian National Congress in the late 1930's charting out what India should do when it became independent. When it did in 1947, he lost no time in working towards that dream.

Undoubtedly the development of science and technology in India has been based on Jawaharlal Nehru's unswerving faith in the importance of science and scientific institutions for national progress. Many successive governments have shared Nehru's commitment to science.

Nehru's vision left its indelible imprint. His ideas on economic development, industrialization with heavy industry and development of science and technology, including space and atomic energy, set the basis of our planning. Agricultural development programmes, supported by large budget allocation was to be promoted by institutional reforms, community development programmes and land reforms, as well as irrigation programmes and new technology setting the base for the green revolution, which gathered momentum in the late 1960s. Along this, the founding fathers were also deeply aware of the need for social change, with the Hindu Code Bill and the Anti-untouchability Law of 1955 and the appointment of the Commissioner of Scheduled Castes and Scheduled Tribes. Nehru in particular was emphasizing the need for gender equity and development as well as the essentiality of education, at the primary and the secondary level and also at the level of university and high technology.

Nehru's commitment to the cause of India's development remains unquestioned. He wanted a practical approach in framing the Indian economy, which would suit best the country's needs. On the one hand, as a devoted Gandhian, he had strong belief in the betterment of rural economy. On the other hand, he had a strong belief that with strong technological base, heavy industrial development would be the best way to serve India's economic interests.

Nehru's policy towards sustainable development with focus on the rural economy of India was also significant. Nehru felt for the rural self-development of India very strongly. He tried to boost India's cottage industries. Much on the lines of Gandhi, Nehru believed that the rural and cottage industries of India played a major role in the economic fabric of the country and also for sustainable growth of India. But most of his cottage industry development programs were meant as a part of community development. He was also of the belief that small scale industries and cottage industries were effective solutions for the sustainable development through solving the massive employment problems that remained a perpetual issue of concern throughout his tenure.

Nehru was always convinced of the positive good that could result from science. Addressing the Indian Science Congress in 1938, he emphasized his faith in science as follows:

> "The application of science is inevitable and unavoidable for all countries and people today. But something more that its application is necessary. It is the scientific approach, the adventurous and yet the critical temper of science, the capacity to change previous conclusions in the face of new evidence, the

> reliance on observed fact and not on pre-conceived theory - all this is necessary not merely for the application of science, but for life itself and the solution of its many problems." [Bright, 1978]

Looking to the global threat of world population which is expected to reach nine billion by 2050 and the demand for food is expected to more than double in a similar time frame, Science-based solutions for sustaining increases in productivity while protecting ecosystems are the key to addressing these challenges. In many circumstances, the benefits of increasing agricultural production are outweighed by the drawbacks in the efforts to achieve them, including: degradation of the natural resource base; declining human health (associated with agricultural practices); and social exclusion. Some 30 per cent of irrigated lands are already degraded and water use is expected to increase by 50 per cent over the next 30 years. There is concern that the agricultural growth required to meet society's increasing demand for food will further degrade the environment and that this will, in turn, further undermine food systems and destabilise long-term food security.

Nehru was of firm belief that science must always grapple with the key challenges facing the country. These include the pressures of increasing population, greater health risks, changing demographics, degraded natural resources, and dwindling farmlands. Accordingly now we need new science and technologies, new priorities and new paradigms to address these fundamental challenges. These are of direct relevance to the Millennium Development Goals. We need to underline and emphasise our priorities in all these areas. As Jawaharlal Nehru said in 1961,

> 'It is science alone that can solve the problems of hunger and poverty, insanitation and illiteracy, of superstition and deadening custom and tradition, of vast resources running to waste, of a rich country inhabited by starving people...Who indeed could afford to ignore science today? At every turn we have to seek its aid...the future belongs to science and to those who make friends with science'.

The last decade has witnessed the emergence of an array of increasingly vibrant movements to harness science and technology (S&T) in the quest for a transition toward sustainability. These movements take as their point of departure a widely shared view that the challenge of sustainable development is the reconciliation of society's development goals with the planet's environmental limits over the long-term. In seeking to help meet this sustainability challenge, the multiple movements to harness science and technology for sustainability focus on the dynamic interactions between nature and society, with equal attention to how social change shapes the environment and how environmental change shapes society. These movements seek to address the essential complexity of those interactions, recognizing that understanding the individual components of nature–society systems provides insufficient understanding about the behavior of the systems themselves. They are problem-driven, with the goal of creating and applying knowledge in support of decision making for sustainable development.

The need for sustainable development initiatives to mobilize appropriate science and technology has long been recognized. The case for making appropriate research and development (R&D) an integral component of sustainable development strategies was broadened by a number of international scientific organizations during the mid-1980s, promoted by the Brundtland Commission's report Our Common Future in 1987, and enshrined in the Agenda 21 action plan that emerged from the United Nations Conference on Environment and Development in 1992. Over the succeeding decade, the discussion of how S&T could contribute more effectively to sustainability intensified, involving numerous researchers, practitioners, scientific academies, and development organizations from around the world. By the time of the World Summit on Sustainable Development, held in Johannesburg in 2002, a broadly based consensus had begun to take shape on the most important ways in which S&T has already contributed to sustainability, on what new R&D is most important, and on what stands in the way of getting it done. This trend itself is witness of strong approval of Nehru vision.

Many of the most valuable contributions of S&T to sustainable development predate the term itself. These range from the 'mundane technologies' that have improved delivery of basic needs for sanitation and cooking, through the yield-enhancing, land-saving accomplishments of the international agricultural research system, to the fundamental scholarship of geographers and anthropologists on nature–society interactions. The strongest message to emerge from dialogues induced by the Johannesburg Summit was that the research community needs to complement its historic role in identifying problems of sustainability with a greater willingness to join with the development and other communities to work on practical solutions to those problems. This means bringing our S&T to bear on the highest-priority goals of a sustainability transition, with those goals defined not by scientists alone but rather through a dialogue between scientists and the people engaged in the practice of 'meeting human needs while conserving the earth's life support systems and reducing hunger and poverty'. At the international level, the Johannesburg Summit, building on the United Nations Millennium Declaration, has defined these priorities in terms of the so-called "WEHAB" targets for water, energy, health, agriculture, and biodiversity. As important as this international consensus on goals and targets may be for targeting problem- driven research in support of a sustainability transition, however, it is not sufficient. The transcendent challenge is to help promote the relatively 'local' (place- or enterprise-based) dialogues from which meaningful priorities can emerge, and to put in place the local support systems that will allow those priorities to be implemented". Where such systems exist, the production of usable, place-based knowledge for promoting sustainability has been impressive indeed.

This perception reinforces Nehru's vision that had always emphasized that Science and Technology are essential for development and sustainable development hinges on them. The work of the scientific community should be harnessed for winning the war on poverty and achieving equitable growth. Reducing economic disparities among people and between nations is a real challenge. The scientific community has a social responsibility to improve the quality of life of all and a global responsibility to advance peace and to nurture a healthy planet.

He always believed that application of science and technology for development should be made an integral part of people's life. People should be made to realize the role played by science in their daily lives. Government, NGOs and individuals should help in popularizing science by conducting awareness programmes to make science understandable to the people at large. The outreach efforts should expand through diverse media like print media, electronic media and the Internet. Research and development efforts should be designed to serve the people of the country and, indeed of the world. Apart from working on cutting edge technologies, scientists should also find low cost technological solutions that are easy to implement and within the reach of the end-users. Better farming techniques, low energy intensive machines, and disease prevention are some areas which can greatly benefit from new technologies. Interaction between the scientific community and the general public will establish a two way communication, where scientists can understand the needs of people and incorporate it in their research, and people get an opportunity to explain their requirements and problems to researchers.

The population of the world has already crossed six billion and India accounts for one sixth of this population. Meeting the needs of a large population will be compounded further by poverty, hunger, malnutrition and illiteracy in a few decades, if appropriate steps are not taken immediately. To face the situation squarely, it would be important to adopt a scientific approach to these challenges.

Jawaharlal Nehru firmly believed that Science and Technology can be the twin tools that would help bring about social equity and economic development to enable India join the mainstream of the world community. This conviction was reflected in the Scientific Policy Resolution (SPR) of 1958, the aim of which was:

> "To foster, promote and sustain the cultivation of sciences and scientific research in the country and to

secure for the people all the benefits that can accrue from the acquisition and application of scientific knowledge".

References

Clark, W.C., Lebel, L., Gallopin, G., Jaeger, J., Mabogunje, A., Dowdeswell, E., Hassan, M., Juma, C., Kates, R., Corell, R., *et al.* (2002) in Science and Technology for Sustainable Development (Int. Council for Science, Paris).

Dorothy, Norman (ed.), "Nehru: The First 60 Years" (1965), The Bodley Head, London.

International Council for Science (2002), Science and Technology for Sustainable Development (Int. Council for Science, Paris), www.icsu.org_Library_WSSD-Rep_Vol. 9. pdf.

Initiative on Science and Technology for Sustainability (2003), Forum on Science and Technology for Sustainability, http:__ sustainabilityscience.org.

Jagat, S. Bright (ed.), "Collected Speeches of Jawaharlal Nehru", Vol. 1, Lahore (1938), cited in Shyam Bhatia, "India's Nuclear Bomb" (1979) Vikas Publishing House, New Delhi.

National Research Council (1999), Our Common Journey (Natl. Acad. Press, Washington, DC).

Phanikumar, G., Pursuit and Promotion of Science: The Indian Experience, INSA Publication, ppsie_insa.pdf

Science and Technology for Sustainable Development, Consensus Report and Background Document, Mexico City, Synthesis Conference,

United Nations World Summit on Sustainable Development (2002), WEHAB Framework Papers, www.johannesburgsummit.org_html_documents_ wehab_papers.html.

Senior Fellow (Professor), Council for Social Development, Southern Regional Centre, Hyderabad 500 030. manjusinghajm@gmail.com

Senior Fellow (Professor), Council for Social Development, Southern Regional Centre, Hyderbad 500 030. manjusinghajm@gmail.com

Economic Policies of Jawaharlal Nehru for Indifferent India

M. RAMANJANEYULU

INTRODUCTION

Jawaharlal Nehru was a great statesman of India, who summed up the resurgence of the Third World, and fully absorbed, after the settlement of the disorders immediately after independence. He is the instrumental for work of national reconstruction with heavy responsibility of external affairs. For building a new nation strong in the sectors of agriculture, industry, science and hard labour to expedite the development process, curtailment of unnecessary expenditure, self sufficient in food, working for the planned economy were Nehru's major domestic concerns and outcome for progress. He had close touch with common people of this country and believed in faith of people on government. He had the suspicion that "the people of India are known as the common of India". The affection of that he had shouldering the pleasant burden. He said emphatically towards the approach to the problem of India that all kinds and groups of people in this country whether it is the industrialist or labour, or workers, merchants or any body else or politicians that we have not adjusted ourselves to changing conditions sufficiently. He said that people have not brought our minds in line, in tune, with the world as it is. It is a difficult task that because swift as thought is, the mind and man's thoughts lags behind events.

He recognized the basic problem of India was food, clothing and housing, etc. He did not talk about the world, because country has its own problems and its own way of approach on basic industries, the key industries, private sector and public sector and nationalization. The formation of Planning Commission was made to look after the economic affairs of the nation. In connection with foreign investments, participation of foreign capital in industries, Indian capital needs to be supplemented by foreign capital not only because our national savings will not be enough for the rapid development of the country on the scale it requires but also because in many cases scientific, technical, industrial knowledge and capital equipments can be secured along with foreign capital.

The Policy of the government was quite clear in the context of foreign investors' participation of capital remittance of profits, and the treatment of foreign enterprise. India had to confirm to the general requirements of their industrial policy. The government of India had no desire to injure in any way British or other non-Indian interests in India and would gladly invited their contribution in a constructive and cooperative role in the development of Indian economy.

OBJECTIVES

The present paper on "Economic Policies of Jawaharlal Nehru for Independent India" aims at the following objectives; which are:

1. To study the economic policies of Jawaharlal Nehru for development of the nation of Independent India.
2. To study the development policies of great visionary Jawaharlal Nehru as a First Prime Minister of India contribution to the development of India.

Self-sufficiency in Food

The acute shortage of food grains is a challenging to our intellect, resourcefulness and to our very existence. Crores of rupees were spent every year for importing food grains to meet requirements of the nation. It was a great financial drain on our resources. The decision was taken to make India self sufficient in the matter of food grains with in a two years. The government has taken various schemes of reclamation of wastelands and developments of river valleys. This was important for increase the productivity of soil already result taken advantage of by the common cultivators. The disseminating knowledge of the latest scientific methods of agriculture was also important attempt made by him.

Expenditure on Education Schemes

Nehru said relating to education and its impact on development that "you must understand that if you stop reading and learning even for a little while you will become backward in the world". You must keep the windows of your mind; your eyes and ears constantly open. Real reading should enrich the mind train if to think and help in understanding a little the problem of the world. He also said fearlessness is the highest achievement for any human being.

He had a vision tied up with growth of big industry which should certainly grow and the nation should help to grow but any solution of the unemployment problem must take into consideration a fairly, large scale growth of small industry. The manufacture of some fancy article must grow by the smaller and the cottage industries. They must do encouraged making article of widespread use, more especially in terms of economic crisis of today. The first unit of the Hindustan Machine Tools was inaugurated by Nehru at Jalahalli, Bangalore on 5th October 1955.

River Valley Development

Nehru had a thought of wealth producing activities, of works which add more land for cultivation, provide more power for industry, and generally lead to a higher standard of the living. Increased production is essential for that means more wealth in the country. But increased production can only take place if there is increased consumption and consumption means the raising of the standards of our people. The great schemes of river valley development, and dams, reservoirs and irrigation channels and hydro electric power, which are various stages of development all over India, are the basic foundation for this future growth. Among these, one of the most important was the Bhakra Dam Scheme and the Nangal Hydal Canal. It is very necessary that a project should not look upon merely as that of building a dam and producing hydro electric power. These were the builders of the India has great importance today and tomorrow and a high responsibility attached to them and it was a spirit of service.

The development of electric power depends on production of more national wealth. The engineers should not lose sight of the vast sociological changes taking place in India and the world. The engineers should utilize their talents in developing power projects. The greatest need is of getting speedy results from the development of various power projects so that national wealth can be increased and the standard of living of the masses also be raised. The people can be a source of enormous strength if all their minds and all activities are turned towards a certain end.

Industrialisation

In the convocation address, he talked a great deal of progress, development, projects and schemes in India. Need of industrialisation and big river valley projects, more science applications, development of India some thing like United Provinces. The resources are tremendous potential, which can be easily trained including manpower. The financial resources or resources are in the shape of skilled manpower. The borrowing from abroad may get help in the shape of technical advice, planning approach for progress and advancement of India of increase standard of living, to abolish poverty and unemployment, bettering the conditional of Indian people, economic, social and industrial plans are absolutely necessary. Whatever economic plans country may have still nation must train engineers for that economic plan that is obvious. The Indian Industry developed in spite of great obstructions and opposition from the then British government in fifty, sixty, seventy and eighty years ago. India has developed in Jute and Cotton, which are necessary things but not basic things. It is depending almost entirely for every basic and important thing on other countries.

Industrialisation means having those basic and key industries on which every other industry depends. It means if you go still further back to the development of scientific research and the application of science, it means the development of power. Without power the economy cannot be achieved any real development. It means having certain basic things like the steel industry. Further real development means finally the machine making industry as nothing else counts. Suppose not developed the machine making industry means you are thoroughly depending on others. Now here we have been talking about industrialization for last sixty, seventy or eighty years and we can hardly make anything at all not even small things like spare parts. We have to rush to America or England or Japan or some other countries.

Those men who have money in this country are the ones whom people wrongly call industrialists. There are hardly any industrialists in this country. They don't think in terms of industry or real industrial progress. They are interested certainly in helping India by producing goods. But they are also interested in getting profits rather too soon. It is inevitable that at a certain stage of growth they cannot put their money to get profits 15 years later only. A well-developed industry, which has great resources, can afford to put in money and wait for 10 or 15 years for a dividend.

The outlook of India has not been considered elements of planning and thinking of the basic things on which industry is to flourish. He said that India's problems and difficulties are a challenging to our manhood and to our sense of patriotism, disciplined and cooperative effort to achieve higher path of development.

A VISION FOR THE FUTURE

Nehru said that there is a need and importance of marriage of science and industry. Because it means that we utilize science to the immediate advantage of the betterment of our people. He also said that Laboratories do not signify progress in themselves, but they are foundation of progress. There can be not real progress without its being found and based on science, on the scientific application to many things in life and on the scientific temper of the minds of the people. He also quoted the silver lines of Dr. Bhatnagar and his message that replica of the Asoka Pillar that we have to put a noble symbol of many things. India has adopted those tops, the capital of that pillar, as our crest and symbol. He said that the wheel of the capital of the pillar that is known as Asoka Charka was a symbol of peace and righteousness. It was also a symbol of scientific and industrial progress. It also served as an inspiration to those who wanted to combine the past and the future of India.

The common man progress and plans for development was one of this visionaries which is a conception of whole a developing each aspect of that whole in relation to other parts. All round development of national economy and national life is the prerequisite of the nation. The tremendous investment in Irrigation Projects was a measure of self-sufficient to achieve food.

Science in the Service of the Community

The science is not merely an individual's research for truth. It is something infinitely more than that if it worked for the community. For a hungry man or women truth has little meaning. He wants food, for a hungry man God has no meaning. He wants food to think about himself. And India is a hungry, starving country and to talk of truth and God and even of many of the fine things of life to the millions who are starving is a mockery. He said that we have to find food, clothing, housing, education and health for them, these are all absolute necessaries of life that every man should possess.

The Crisis in Production

The most important for the nation is to produce men and women, good and true. One such person is in India who, through his goodness, truth and power of spirit brightness of this ancient land and casts his radians on us, weak and erring mortal sand stops us when we go astray. Indian have strayed enough from the right path and wasted our inheritance and our good repute. We have had enough of this now. We must go ahead on the path of creation, construction, cooperation and good will to over fellowmen.

The production means wealth of individual or nation. If we do not produce, we do not have enough wealth. Distribution is equally important, so that wealth does not accumulate in the hands of a few. But nevertheless, before we think of distribution, there must be production. The economic problems relating to control of inflation, scarcity of goods, slow rate of economy, a stream of wealth powering out from our fields, factories and workshops. Nehru also accepted that the political freedom alone does not take us far unless there is economic freedom. Indeed, there is no such freedom for a man who is starving or striving for a country, which is poor. Therefore, we have to produce in order to have sufficient wealth distribute by proper economic planning, so that it may go to the millions, more specially to the common man. Never the less, a new country, a new state, which has recently achieved its independence, must take great care to guard its freedom. It has rightly been said that eternal vigilance is the price of liberty. The schemes of reforms of development need of wealth, we cannot live on borrowed money for long time. We must be strong enough to invest it along proper channels. All these require production—production is the immediate present to fulfil our immediate needs. So, that we have something to play by for those productive schemes of development. Now, production means hard work, unremitting labour, production means not stoppage of work.

It is important for Indian to have period of industrial calm and peace so that we may all join together to increase the production in the country and building up the country by pulling through the vast schemes of development. We know that these schemes for a long time remain on power. There are among them great river valley schemes, which would irrigate the land, prevent floods produce hydroelectric power prevent malaria and other diseases, but generally prod conditions for the rapid development of indus modernization of industries and modernization of agriculture. The full employment can easily attained by increasing wealth of the country; thereby it can also remove unemployment and poverty. The work with real hard work will produce for the nation to raise the standards of the people of the nation depends on resources, manpower, peace, international peace, national peace, economic peace in the labour world and industrial world.

Increasing Production in the Battle against Poverty

The freedom and independence cannot be completed unless the difficulties of the people are removed and there is a proper arrangement for food, clothing, housing and education. Another battle is to remove the poverty of the masses and inflation. In this battle we have fight to work in a way, which would increase production. The number of farmers constitutes in the largest strength and agriculture is the main industry. It is also necessary to increase the fertility of the land, to bring prosperity to the peasants and the country.

THE WEALTH OF INDIA

India must try to produce what ever people need in our own country. It will benefit the people and the country. It is crucial for us to produce as quickly as possible, new wealth in the country. India must increase production of essential goods, which is the wealth of the nation. Unless the wealth of the nation grows, what can we distribute the wealth. The gold and silver are not wealth. The real wealth of a nation is that which we produce in the country. So it is very essential that we should produce enormous quantities of goods by every available means, from land, from factories and in other ways like building ships. The steel is essential to build ships and unless we produce steel in vast quantities, there will be delay in building ships in the country. The faster growth in production, the greater will be the wealth of the nation. It will mean more employment and people will become better off and India will become strong and stable. Now let us to work hard in harmony so that the common people will be benefited. Suppose, people do not hard work, any thing, which will slow down our work.

A Flexible Economic Policy

The policy of nationalization has been the first and far most priority of the Pandit Jawaharlal Nehru. The long-term policies through Planning Commission, which would, precisely lay down priorities to plan and coordinate various sectors of economic life. Nationalization of new and existing industries is an absolute necessary to meet the requirements of production. Nationalization of Reserve Bank of India and the imperial Bank of India were the best examples of his new economic policy.

The Progress of science and technology is so enormous and so rapid changes in short span of life. The industrial revolution did 200 years ago in England and in the rest of Europe. All these enormous changes are going to take place and Nehru found that many of us unaware of the big chances that are taking place. We are so unaware of this that we think merely in terms, not of the greater wealth coming into existence by fresh methods, but rather only of changing the ownership of industry from the point of view of advancing towards equality. Distribution is very important but what the most important is the dynamic future. In the changed situation all over the world, new sources of power might completely revolutionize our agriculture as well as our industry. The construction of big resources, hydroelectric work, irrigation canals, prevention of erosion, prevention of malaria, etc., are going to require a vast deal of money and by the most important of all future growth. A scientific manpower for future progress, he linked to have collective and cooperative farming in this country at on a small scale. A particular statement of policy in regard to our industrial programme is to increase production obviously which depends on a very great deal of cooperation among those people who are most concerned with production. The country want the goodwill of the industrialists of the country to the nationalize industries from private enterprises.

CONCLUSIONS

Jawaharlal Nehru was the First Prime Minister of Independent India who brought a tremendous change through his economic policies and though the vision of planned development. He has great vision for the development of agriculture and industry, science and technology to increase the production of the nation. His achievements were enormous in all sub sectors of the economy in his tenure. He had given first priority for agriculture sector in the First Five Year Plan and Industry in Second Five Year Plan. His activities for struggle for freedom made him an intense nationalist and one of the leaders of humanism. He himself was a socialist and a democrat, faith in civil liberty with the necessary of political, social and economic freedom. He is an endeavour of one who was not only a leader of man and a lover of mankind but also a completely integrated human being.

References

Jawaharlal Nehru, (1962), An Autobiography, Allied Publishers, New Delhi.

Selected works of Jawaharlal Nehru, Second Series 1-14, Jawaharlal Nehru Memorial-Fund, Teen Murthi house, New Delhi, 1990.

Speech in the Constituent Assembly (Legislative) on a resolution moved by Kzi Syed Karimuddin urging the government to accept and implement a socialist economy, 17 February, 1948.

Constituent Assembly of India (Legislative) Debates Official report, Vol. II, 1948., pp. 825-34.

The report was endorsed by the AICC on 22 February, 1948.

The reference is to the Economic Programme Committee, which had submitted its report to the Congress Working Committee on 25 January, 1948.

5

Nehru's Model for Economic Development

MUKESH, AJAY KUMAR DUBEY AND SHAMBHU KUMAR

INTRODUCTION

Nehru was a socialist. He made that clear from early times. He even indicated that Congress as it was constituted then may not quite accept socialism as the basis of a society that should emerge after independence. His other ideas regarding the society were essentially a by-product of his commitment to socialism, viz., social justice, planning as a basis for development. Another aspect that is relevant in Nehru approach is the commitment to scientific outlook.

It would be obvious that for Nehru, socialism was not only an approach to solve India's problems but also a philosophy of life. One other point that may be keep in mind is that while he was committed to socialism, he also realized that given the social and economic realities there had to be some adaptations, some flexibilities in introducing socialism in India. The phrase 'socialistic pattern of society' indicates flexible approach, needless to say that mixed economy is another aspect of the adaptability. The vision of the Indian society that should evolve that Nehru had was based in his understanding of socialism. This understanding was a striving force in operationalising his ideas to the realities of the Indian situation and the way of achieving the desired goals.

Nehru said: " I am certainly a socialist in the sense that I believe in the socialist theory and method of approach. I am not a communist chiefly because I resist the communist tendency to treat communism as a holy doctrine and I do not like being told what to think and what to do. I suppose, I am too much of an individualist. But my general approach is largely Marxist, though not in a technical sense."

I have progressively accepted the ideology of a scientific socialism and I may now claim to be a socialist in the full sense of the term... I have mentioned two ways that they moved me and I take it that they move also in varying degrees, many of the countrymen.

These are the nationalism and political freedom as represented by the Congress and social freedom as represented by socialism. It is obvious it includes political freedom for without it there can be no social and economic freedom. But, India is unhappily still politically a subject country, nationalism is a governing urge of most politically-minded classes, that is a factor of primary importance and any socialist who ignores it does so at his peril. But no socialist need be reminded that nationalism by itself offers no solution to the vast problems that confront our country and our world. To continue these two outlooks and make their organic whole is the problem of the Indian socialist. Scientific socialism itself teaches us not to follow slavishly any dogma of any other country's example which may have resulted from entirely different set of circumstances. Armed with a philosophy which reveals that inner work of history and human relations and scientific outlook to guide, the socialist tries to solve the problem of our country in relation to its varied background and stage of economic development and also in relation to the world. It is hard task but there is no easy way...... Further he said: "I am convinced that the only key solution of the world's problem and of India's problems lies in socialism, and when I use this word I do so not in a vague humanitarian way but in the scientific, economic sense.

Socialism is, however, something even more than an economic doctrine, it is a philosophy of life and as such also it appeals to me, I see no way of ending the poverty, the vast unemployment, the degradation and the subjection of the Indian people except through socialism, That involves vast and revolutionary changes in our political and social structure, the ending of vested interests in land and industry, as well as the feudal and autocratic Indian states systems. That means the ending of private property, except in a restricted sense, and the replacement of the present profit system by a higher ideal of co-operative service. It means ultimately a change in our instincts and habits and desires. In short, it means a new civilization, radically different from the present capitalist order."

NEHRU'S IDEAS OF SOCIAL JUSTICE

Let us now look at Nehru's idea of social justice. One can do no better than to quote Shri Krishna Menon, "For Panditji, the content of liberty was equality and from that there has been no deviation, so far as he is concerned, or this country is concerned, except for last few years when vested interest have questioned the proposition that the content of liberty is equality... that has been his contribution which has been projected in the Indian struggle for independence and if there is anything that Panditji can be spoken of as an embodiment, it is this there is no liberty without equality.

His ideas on socialism or as a matter of fact his entire philosophy can be understood only in the light of his mental and spiritual make up. His ideal of socialism " was not by sharp stage, but was rather a steady development over a long period of time. Nehru's belief socialism traversed a long road, right from his student carrier where in Cambridge he was vaguely attracted to the Fabian and socialistic ideas, to the Congress Session of Bhuvaneshwar where he committed the Congress as well as the nation to the socialistic goal. It is not our purpose here to trace the growth of Nehru's socialism but to discuss what did Nehru mean by socialism? How did he implement these ideas in his own characteristic way? And what Nehru's importance and contribution in enriching socialism in India?

Origin of Nehru's socialism was in this sense of pride and dignity as a man. It was this pride which enabled him to plunge in the national struggle and it was this dignity which provided him the fervour to fight against those ideas and institutions which tended to separate man from man. To Nehru, "it was unmanly to reconcile one's self with injustice that endangered human dignity; ideas and institutions which supported such injustice had to be changed and it did not behave the dignity of man to submit to such wrongs." Accordingly, he declared in 1929 in Lahore Session of the Indian National Congress: " I must frankly confess that I am a socialist and am no believer in kings and princes, or in the order which produces the modern kings of industry, who have greater power over the lives and fortunes of men than even the kings of old." In Indian context recognition of individual dignity was a major step towards socialism. Though it may not conform to the conventional sense of socialism, yet it was by and large a necessity. He not only wanted equality in economic terms but also saw its importance in the socio-cultural fields. For this reason he fought with forces of ignorance and tried to demolish communal and caste walls.

Nehru's socialism also has a distinct impress of Indian thinking and particularly that of Mahatma Gandhi. Nehru was aware of the vast exploitation of Indian economy by the Britishers as well as the predominance of peasant class. When he visited certain villages. Here his idealism was confronted with practical problems and he looked for a solution to eradicate poverty and emancipate society from many social evils. He could see the way only through socialism. Gandhi too was moved by the poverty and termed the poor as Daridranarayan and asked the rich to act as trustees. Nehru was never satisfied with this glorification of poverty and critically reacted. " I confess that I have always been wholly unable to understand how any person can reasonably expect this to happen, or imagine that therein lies the solution of the social problem." However Nehru's approach to socialism was influenced immensely by Gandhian non-violence. He was convinced about the desirability of non-violence and was confident about its application to any problem.

NEHRU'S SOCIAL JUSTICE AND EQUAL OPPORTUNITY

He emphasized equal opportunity and minimum standard of life to make it a reality. From this point of view, it might be suggested for Nehru that social justice was not an end in itself—but an essential aspect for national development. There has been reference by many of his biographers of 'harmonization of goals', social justice and economic development. Mrs. Alva Myrdel in analyzing Nehru's ideas on this says: "The low levels consumption, prevalent for the great masses in underdeveloped countries where social and economic inequality persists, hamper economic development because of their detrimental effect on productivity..."a rise in consumption in the lowest economic strata and in regard to items of intake, health care and educational level should have beneficial effects on productivity.....our present knowledge about the interdependence of development factors will then support Nehru's intuitive conviction that to raise the level of living of the poor is productive and that work for social justice might well be harmonized with work for economic development."

Social inequality too comes in the way of economic development as it acts as an obstacle to mobility and to fair competition—both of which are necessary for the process of economic development. It is in this context that Nehru's statement in introducing the First Five Year Plan needs to be understood. He wanted class differences to be ended and economic equality to be achieved. Towards this end, he propagated rapid industrialization, strong agricultural economy, controlled and mixed economy, community development and land reforms aimed at revolutionizing the basis of basis of India's rural economy.

NEHRU SOCIAL CHANGE AND ECONOMIC DEVELOPMENT

Nehru advocated controlled economy. To understand his contribution to social change and economic development, one has to look at his views on planning. From early times he was committed to the idea of planning. In 1929 Session of

Congress he had pleaded for it. The national problems would be solved only by conscious, constructive and planned efforts. Without planning, he said, there would be anarchy in our economic development. In 1938, he was a Chairman of the Congress National Planning Committee. From the beginning of the settlement up of the Planning Commission (1950) he was a Chairman till his end (1964). We are concerned as to why he was for planning. He said: " If left to normal forces, under the capitalist system, there is no doubt at all that the poor will get poorer and handful of the rich richer. Planning is essentially a process whereby we stop these cumulative forces at work which make the poor poorer and start a new series of cumulative forces which make them get over that difficulty. We have to plan at both ends. We have to stop the cumulative forces which make the rich richer and we have to start the cumulative forces which enable the poor to get over the barrier of poverty. In Russia this was done, but at a terrific cost in human suffering. The problem which we have to face is how to cross the barrier of poverty without paying the terrible task and without impinging individual freedom. "To him, planning was the process through which production would be increased and greater distributive justice achieved. It was only through planning that the goal of integration development could be reached." This approach is an attempt to look at our great country with its manifold activities as a whole and to find out what our resources are, what our activities are and how best to use them without waste. V.K.R.V. Rao says: "Planning for Nehru was essentially linked up with an industrialization and eventual self-reliance for the country economy on a self-accelerating basis." What is being suggested is that one should not look at Nehru only as a planner but what he considered would be the end-result of planning. The objectives as declared in the second plan give ideas of how he tried to operationalise the ideas into a programme.

1. A sizable increase in national economy so as to raise the level of living in the country.
2. Repaid industrialization with particular emphasis on the development of basic and heavy industries.

3. A large expansion of employment opportunities.
4. Reduction of inequalities in income and even distribution of economic power.

CONCLUDING REMARKS

Nehru believed the way to transform the society was through a scientific approach. He once said: " Politics led me to economics and this inevitably to science and scientific approach to all of our problems and life itself." He felt that the methods an approach of science had revolutionized the human life. He believed that the large number of applications of science and technology would help the rapid economic development of the country. He was concerned at the ambivalence of even the intellectuals to science and rationality. The science policy resolution was formulated mostly due to his interest. The setting up of science laboratories, expansion in engineering and technology and emphasis of science in education were all his efforts to forge a society which was dominated by 'scientific culture' V.K.R.V. Rao say: "Modernisation of Indian society and induction into it of scientific climate and temper both go together and constitute an important part of Nehru legacy."

The planning for economic development and social reform is one of his major legacies. He was not happy with violent revolution. He was upset at the human sufferings that the Russian revolution had caused. He accepted that the non-violent approach would be more positive in bringing about change which would be more lasting and less turbulent. One associates impatience, quicker temper a desire to get on with things quickly with Nehru. These may be over manifestations. However, he believed there would be no short-cut to changing the socio-economic structure. He believed in what might be termed 'gradualism'. He said: "We realise that the process of bringing socialism to India especially in the way we are doing it, that is, the democratic way will inevitable take time."

References

C.G. Shah, Marxism, Gandhism and Stalinism, Popular Prakashan, Bombay, p. 19.

Savya Sachi, Nehru's Conception of Socialism, Economic Weekly, Special Number, July 1964, p. 1227.

Michael Brecher, Nehru: A Political biography, p. 1.

Savya Sachi, op. cit., p. 1227.

M.N. Das, The political Philosophy of Nehru; George Allen and Unwin Ltd;, London, 1961, p. 132.

Jawaharlal Nehru, An Autobiography, pp. 362-63.

On March 28, 1939, Subhash Bose wrote to Nehru in which he had written: " How a socialist can be an individualist as you regard yourself beats me. The one is the anti-thesis of the other. How socialism can ever come into existence through individualism of your type is also an enigma to me".

Bunch of old Letters, London, 1936, p. 328.

Congress and Socialism Essays, pp. 39-40

Jawaharlal Nehru, Discovery of India, 196, p. 16.

He writes in his autobiography, "I was filled with shame and sorrow, theme at my own easy going and comfortable life and our petty politics of the city which ignored this vast multitude of semi-naked sons and daughters of India. Sorrow at degeneration and overwhelming poverty of India, p. 52.

Autobiography, op cit, p. 197

Sampurnanad, Memories and Reflections, Asia Publishing House, 1962, p. 84.

Norman Dorothy, Nehru: The First Sixth Year, Vol. II Asia Publishing House, p. 783.

Nehru: His Economic Ideas and Influences

A. Sangamithra and T.M. Saravana Kumar

INTRODUCTION

As India's first prime minister. Jawaharlal Nehru played a major role in shaping modern India's government and political culture. He is praised for creating a system providing universal primary education, reaching children in the farthest corners of rural India. Nehru's education policy is also credited for the development of world class educational institutions such as the Indian Institute of Technology, the National Institute of Technology and the Indian Institute of Management.

Nehru is credited for establishing a widespread system of affirmative action to provide equal opportunities and rights for Indian's ethnic groups. Minorities, women, scheduled castes and schedule tribes. Nehru's passion for egalitarianism helped end widespread practices of discrimination against women and depressed classes. Nehru is widely lauded for pioneering non alignment and encouraging a global environment of peace and security amidst escalating cold war tensions. Nehru was one of the transitional figures of modern times. He was perhaps the only leader in history to turn down absolute power. He simply felt that his people deserved better than that.

ECONOMIC THOUGHT OF JAWHARLAL NEHRU

Nehru mind was awakened to the problems confronting the masses and he started imaging about the panacea for those ills. His European tour between March 1926 and December 1927, in the course of which he paid his first visit to Russia, had a profound effect on his economic thinking. "Soviet Russia" he wrote, "despite certain unpleasant aspects attracted him greatly and "seemed to hold forth a message of hope". He wrote later in Discovery of India that the passion for progress filled him with a wish to emulate other countries which had gone so far ahead in many ways." (Dr.Purnima P. Kapoor, 1985)

He became convicted that "without social freedom and a socialistic structure of society and state, neither the country nor the individual could develop much". The writings of Karl Marx impressed him and "lightened up many a dark corner of his mind; "history had new interpretation for him and "Communist philosophy" gave him comfort and hope" From the lessons of the NINETEENTH CENTURY ECONOMIC THOUGHT Nehru's logical, sensitive and scientific mind DISCOVERED "some of the wider and deeper social and psychological forces" that "moved the masses", to which therefore, "economic and political arrangements had to adapt themselves". His quest for Socialism started and his first attempt was to understand Gandhian Economic Philosophy. To him it was 'secondary' whether people accepted everything that Gandhi preached but "fearlessness, truth and welfare of the masses" formed the basis of his teachings, which appealed to him the most.

Gandhi's approach was not easily understood and many times it was estimated wrong by him, and he felt it was unreal" but he derived the main stream of inspirations from his economic philosophy only and he felt that his "Socialism" was definitely an alternative to the "Laissez Faire Competitive Industrialism" in its end" although the "means" were to provide a congenial background for the "GROWTH OF SOCIALISM". He developed interest in "UTOPIAN SOCIALISM" and not in "SCIENTIFIC SOCIALISM" at this stage and "even this was all very academic". Probably his interest was due to a vague feeling that in such socialist ideologies there was IMPLIED IDEA OF "ANTI COLONIALISM". Thus the initial inspiration towards socialist ideology appeared to have been inculcated in him, because of his feeling that socialism was a theory and practice which helped in denouncing "colonialism" a burning urge of the Indian youth them. India embarked upon a mission of re-discovering herself. This was the struggle into which Jawaharlal plunged to "RE-DISCOVER" India amidst "doldrums" and "Communalism". He sought refuge in "municipal work" though mind was" befogged" and he had no clear vision.

Gandhi evolved a peculiar and unique approach to this struggle though "Ahimsa" and Nehru committed himself to the cause of rebuilding. He very soon established himself as the "Idol of his people and the quintessence of the spirit of the independence". "He was young, vibrant and visionary." He influenced his people by his speeches and sharing and created "AWARENESS" among the masses by his intellectual and economical approach to the problem. The problem before him was more economic and humane than political. But nothing socio-economic could spur the momentum unless political freedom was obtained.

The balance between "emotion and intellect" in Jawaharlal's individuality "projected itself on the individuality of India" and through his visions the "Indian National Congress sought to bear an Economic Creed", which was closer to him than Gandhi. The nucleus and the essence of all his mental rebellion, struggle for freedom and sacrifice aimed to remove degrading poverty of India. The years of 'CIVIL DISOBEDIENCE' deepened his urges and saw him as a national leader.

Jawaharlal Nehru perceived that the economic history of pre-war years seemed to divided in three parts. The forces which first came to the forefront during the decade 1860-70 were prominent throughout those years. "The results of the contact with the economic structure of the West were shaping events in India". 1860 to 1875 was a period of PROSPERITY which was arrested by terrible famine. 1880 to 1895 was fairly prosperous. Then occurred tow famines even more terrible than the previous one. By 1900 country started recovering and gradually prospering. This was "a rhythm" which could be compared to the analogous movements of trade cycles, which clearly revealed "prosperity and adversity", which enlightened his economic perception.

The first period witnessed the beginning of the factories and plantations. The second period marked a decline in the handicrafts and after that a slow progress began all over the country in the late nineties; a considerable growth of small miscellaneous industries started as a stream. The agriculture industry had always been overwhelmingly important as to decide the fate of economic prosperity or calamity in the country.

The economic ups and downs taught him the true nature of the economy and he felt that political freedom was an absolute necessity to curb such cycles to utilize "surplus man power and unexploited natural resources". He pondered that the state of affairs were probably due to the "STAGNANCY" of techniques, which inhibited socio-economic factors, and prevents growth and development.

So he felt that RATIONAL ECONOMIC PLAN could galvanize all the socio-economic forces and the vast resources, if India could develop economically. He was thinking of a device that would suit India's economic conditions, and would be acceptable to the people. This was the most for aid able task he had undertaken himself as an ardent patriot.

Socialist planning in Soviet Russia offered one solution to his awakening of the economic situation and problem in the country. Number of tours to Russia, the influence of its accomplishments through "Socialist planning" and his bubbling enthusiasm, were subject to "MOCKERY" and "criticism", i.e. that he acted as a "liaison agent between Moscow and India", but he did not leave hope and experienced and educated himself on he basis of the world history, politics and "European Socialists" he found that "equality and freedom were the basic arguments against 'imperialism' or 'capitalism' and "they remained the basic arguments against poverty, ignorance and disease" and 'Socialism' could be a means to achieve a classless society where equalization of wealth, opportunity and social justice could be attained forcibly." Jawaharlal became an ardent admirer of Socialism, but he disliked "force" and was "not prepared to brook dictatorship of any kind—either of capital or of proletariat."

IDEALS AND INFLUENCES

With Gandhi's fundamental approach to economic problems, he had strong differences. He could not agree with him that higher standard of life would lead to self-indulgence and sin. He felt that Gandhi wanted to improve "individual" internally, morally and spiritually, and thereby change the external environment, society and economics. Such a society would be a "Utopian" one, which seemed impractical to him, who wrote in the early that "I realize now that there are basic differences between Gandhi's ideals and the Socialist objective." But Gandhi did not believe in ideological conflicts. He had "an extraordinary capacity to sense a situation" and early he recognized his youthful colleague's natural political talent, and continued to favour Jawaharlal for his zeal, dedication and deep concern for the nation, and realize that he was a "dead-weight" on the CONGRESS AND NEHRU was the "RIGHTFUL HELSMAN OF THE ORGANISATION." Gandhi had the rare gift of probing deep into persons' mind and he opined that Jawaharlal was what his name signified 'a Jawahar, i.e. a jewel' Gandhi held him in high esteem and could depend on his capability, and fundamental 'elements' of his ideology. Gandhi wished to instill his economic ideas clearly into his mind and indirectly he wished that they should be understood to follow. The "essence" of his economic philosophy as understood by Jawaharlal was "that man should rest content with what his real needs are, and become self-sufficient. If he does not have this control, he cannot save himself. After all the world is made up of individuals just as it is (of) drops that constitute the ocean... "I have said nothing new; this is well known truth." Further he added that... "my ideal village will contain intelligent human beings. They will not live in dirt and darkness as animals", but for many Gandhi "was greater that what he wrote" and appeared "as an extraordinary paradox", and occasionally Gandhi mentioned his "socialistic ideas" in a sense peculiar to himself, which had little or nothing to do with the "economic framework of society." Either Jawaharlal was confused, due to complex situation and immense burden on the young mind, or he just disliked the very idea of 'poverty' and expressed that he almost had "a horror of it and instead of submitting to it" he would want to drag out" even the peasantry from in not to urbanization, but to the spread of urban cultural facilities to rural areas" Gandhi wrote that he clearly saw that Jawaharlal "must carry on open warfare against him and his views", as ideological differences were vast, but he never wished the least his "comradeship to dissolute" or "personal intimacy" to be affected in any way". "Despite the tone of Gandhi's letters "an open break was never entertained by Jawaharlal either and "invariable he would remain loyal to his master", but Jawaharlal's hostility to orthodoxy "crystallized" and he felt that " people who are slaves to dogmas" can never progress happily. "These were learning years for Jawaharlal when he wished to enlarge the scope of SOCIAL SERVICES and infuse "a moribund organization with efficiency" and wanted to take a challenge of Reform.

He had "established his Independence league which swept away the more prudent counsels of advocates, 88 although he never shirked even a bit in recognizing the great economic service done to India" by Gandhi, "through an emphasis" on village-industry programme, as the pure "Satyagrahi of East", while he was the "realistic statesman" of the West, who stood for "a life of harmony in vastness and variety." Jawaharlal reared, as he was in a modern environment imbued with progressive contemporary thinking was able to adapt himself to the experiments, but "found it less easy to instill the same dedication in his followers and colleagues though he believed that his leadership could alone deliver the goods in the first formative years of independence and lift the country out of old ruts" he was fully aware of the need for DEMOCRATIC BEHAVIOUR. He thought democratic setup prepares its own representatives in initiating a process of development and progress with the means of DEMOCRACY and SOCIALISM. (Dr. Purnima P. Kapoor, 1985)

The agrarian question in United Provinces revealed Jawaharlal's firm trials and experiments for a CONSTRUCTIVE AGRARIAN PROGRAMME. The "Zamindars were crushing kisans", and he was firm for some PERMANENT SOLUTION for the peasants and Emerson was impressed by his conviction more than Gandhi. Jawaharlal looked eagerly for Gandhi's counseling in many of his tensed hours when vital problems confronted and haunted him. He was deeply concerned about the lot of the peasants who were "oppressed" and "terrified", and with his impressive and robust personality. He was able to motivate the British Overloads not to torture the innocent masses unnecessarily and cruelly. His strong point was the vision a notch higher "every time". The new technique he viewed was a MIDDLE-WAY between CAPITALISTIC SOCIO-ECONOMIC DEVELOPMENT and what he called TOTALITARIAN-SOCIALISM." It was evident that Gandhi "could take in his stride the issues of Socialism planned industrialization on modern lines an building on economy of abundance". His "new content and revolutionary-orientation" pushed him beyond "the bounds of traditional economic thinking." "To Gandhi it was dialectical process which to some extent produced a SYNTHESIS out of a conflict of ideologies". But this brought a clash between ideas of Jawaharlal and Gandhi. Though he lived in "Gandhi's world in a vital manner, he nevertheless tried to make his own world (which he wished to share with his countrymen) under the influence of great ideas shaping the contemporary "Western world."

"Gandhi was strongly conscious of the specificity of his own plan of socio-economic transformation as an alternative to socialism: as his ideas resembled on the plane of the socialism in "Soviet Union" and on the point of "abolition of private property" Gandhi felt that this objective could be achieved by the 'ethical doctrine of non possession' and force was not needed. He believed in the "Swaraj" of the poor and this 'Swaraj' for Jawaharlal, in which the 'individuality' of the poor was maintained and "Socialization' was achieved through their free will, which needed "self" and "Social awareness" and was difficult to be attained immediately after freedom, unless their minds reached that vigilance and awakening. Illiteracy was one of the greatest handicaps to such "Swaraj". 'He made a concession' out of respect for a modern visionary like Nehru, who could not think of free India's national defence without its strong base in important key industries which he thought, were needed even otherwise", and stated that he "could not be a party to state capitalism in the name of Socialism:, and did not reconcile in this matter. Jawaharlal thought in "a lop-sided way many times and "ignored the human-aspect" of the problems, as he felt that: village can no longer be a self-contained economic unit." Besides, while the central principle of Gandhian "non-violent society is individual freedom, that of Nehru's socialistic state is equality."

The objective aimed at by both, were the same, i.e. "maximum production, equitable distribution and no unemployment" but their devices differed to a great extent and Jawaharlal's ideas started percolating to the masses almost as "acutely and instinctively" as Gandhi's. As to the "MEANS" and the Programmes for achieving their ideals, Gandhi insisted on "Non-Violence" but Jawaharlal preferred "freedom with violence to subjection with non—violence" 107 Gandhi hoped to bring about" non-violent socialism through "Bread Labour" Trusteeship, Varna-Vyasvastha and decentralized village industries. Jawaharlal was silent about "Bread Labour" and felt that theory of trusteeship was impractical and "barren" and disapproved of the "Varna-Vyavastha" in the framework of the "democratic ideal" He advocated an ideal of all round development of the merit and ability. He consented the "dispossession of vested interests", e.g. capitalist. Zamindars, princes, through legislations and even force. He put forward an alternative for 'Trusteeship' and pleaded for 'state control' of capital and natural resources and clearly asked all hands to engage in "production" or "creation" of wealth, which meant "Labour" for "Bread" and thus "ends and means" formed together "one organic whole". Gandhi felt that big industries could certainly result in much greater production of some commodities, but employment problem would remain unsolved, and so would remain the problem of distribution, and it was essential that both big ad small industries were to develop simultaneously to prepare a sound base for India's economy and Jawaharlal's ideas were in perfect coherence with this ideal.

Nehru set down his thoughts more systematically in "Wither India" which presented a "provocative" series of articles on "what do we want and why?" In western terms, he emerged as a "left-socialist" of the Australian School. Marxist in theory democratic in practice." Such a "democratic-socialism", according to him. Could only be achieved by SYSTEMATIZED AND CONSCIOUS EFFORTS IN THE FORM OF A "NATIONAL PLANNING". This was to be effective only independence was won. Besides, planning could be significant only "with great deal of STATE-CONTROL" and for this purpose. He proposed that "if India was to rise above the brutal level of "wars and strife" then "a co-operative Commonwealth " was indispensable to wipe off the DISEQUILBRIUM OF THE ECONOMY. On this JUNCTURE GANDHI AND NEHRU INFLUENCES WERE RECIPROCAL and on many occasions Gandhi" committed himself to the ideas of Jawaharlal". From the letters and talks of Jawaharlal, Gandhi gathered this "impression that there was not much difference" in their outlooks and he was sure that in due course Jawaharlal "will speak his language" The gist of ideas are summed up as follows:

(1) "The real question is how to bring about man's highest intellectual, economic, political and moral development", to which Gandhi agreed entirely.

(2) "There should be an equal right and opportunity for all"

(3) "There should be equality between the town dwellers and the villagers in standard of food and drink, clothing and other living conditions. In order to achieve this equality, people should be able to produce for themselves the necessities of life, i.e. clothing, food stuff, dwellings, lighting and water"

These ideas were similar to those of Jawaharlal's "they were one in spirit" "on the need of Swaraj" though not on economic substance".

IDEOLOGY SUMMARIZED

Jawaharlal stood for "Mixed Economy" which was "Socialistic" to a great extent but he was not a Marxist, his Socialistic ideal implied "planned production and its equitable distribution", which was to be included "legitimately and peacefully". His action programme included reforms, equitable distribution of income, development of cottage industries and friendly relations between capital and labour.

The masses depended on agriculture for their living and 'emphasis' was shifting to "proletariat". The programme was as Socialistic an progressive as it could be under the circumstances which aimed to ameliorate the lot of downtrodden masses. Jawaharlal's economic policy became progressive and it "Concert Socialism" in wide sense of term by arousing an "Asian Sentiment" and conscience of PLANNING for shaping India's destiny.

A PRECIS OF THE THOUGHT AND ACTION

Jawaharlal's economic ideal took a definite pattern in the wake of independence. In a true democratic fashion he designed his policy. He was clear about his basic objectives and means to achieve them. He made his position clear about the pattern of ownership and succeeded in unifying the conflicting communities. In achieving his objective he accorded primary position to Planning. Indeed to him the role of Planning in ushering in a Socialist pattern was crucial. While emphasizing the need to develop heavy industries, he was fully conscious of the need for all round development-especially in the sphere of agriculture and rural industries and added special emphasis upon land-reforms. Production, according to them was essential both in agriculture and industry to fight poverty and raise standard of living. He aimed to modernize the tradition-bound society with the help of science and technology and he pinned much hope on the technique of Planning to entail happiness to his people. The process of policy information, the choice of middle way and the creation of social institution, revealed his true democratic character and deep love for his people. His foreign policy was a counterpart of his economic policy and aimed to achieve a trusteeship of nations in the process of country's development. He became the true Trustee of the Nation.

References

Jawaharlal Nehru—A Study in Ideology and Social Change, 1988, R.P. Dube, Mittal Publications.

Life and Works of India's First Prime Minister—Jawaharlal Nehru, S. Balasubramaniam, 2007, Vijay Goel Publishers.

Jawaharlal Nehru—A Biography, Vol. 2, 1947-56.

Economic Thought of Jawaharlal Nehru, Dr. Purnima P. Kapoor, 1985, Deep & Deep Publications, New Delhi.

Jawaharlal Nehru, The Discovery of India Economic Doctrine—G.B. Seshadri.

A.R Desai, Recent Trends in Indian Nationalism, Bombay, Popular Book Depot, 1960.

Nehru quoted by H.K. Manmohan Singh, "Jawaharlal Nehru and Economic Change," *Economic and Political Weekly*, (Special Number, August, 1975).

Nehru: A Visionary for Democracy and Development

S.K. Karimulla and A. Ranga Reddy

I. ORIGIN OF PARLIAMENTARY SYSTEM

The Institutions of parliament is the greatest political inventions of man, Parliament should reflect the will of the people of the country as a whole. Parliament democracy will fail, unless we learn to work together in national interest. Democracy without discipline leads to *mobocracy* and chaos, and discipline without 'democracy leads to slavery'. In the 14th century parliament began to present petitions (bills) to the king, which with his assent would become law. Legislative Assembly of Britain and of other governments modeled after it. The British Parliament consists of the Monarch, the House of Lords and the House of Commons, and its roots to the Union (C.1300) of the Great Council of the Kings Court, two bodies that treated with and advised the King. In the 14th century, Parliament was split into two houses—with the lords spiritual and temporal debating in one and the Knights and burgesses in the other. Robert's Walpole was the first party leader to Head the Government as Prime

Minister (1721-42). Rules of parliamentary procedure originated in Britain in the 16th and 17th centuries and were subsequently adopted by legislatures around the world., Roberts Rules of order, codified in 1876 by U.S. General Henry M. Robert (1837-1923) and regularly refined and enlarged, is the standard set of rules used by legislatures in the U.S. Generally accepted rules, procedures and practices used in the governance of deliberative assemblies. They are intended to maintain decorum, ascertain the will of the majority, preserve the rights of the minority, and facilitate the orderly transaction of business. Nehru, the Prime Minister of India laid solid foundation for democracy and development in India.[1]

2. A BRIEF BIO-DATA OF JAWAHARLAL NEHRU

(born Nov 14, 1889, Allahabad died May 27, 1964, New Delhi). He was the first Prime Minister of India (1947-64), Son of Independence, advocate Motilal Nehru (1861-1931). Nehru was educated at home and in Britain and became a lawyer in 1912. More interested in Politics than law, he was impressed by Mohandas K. Gandhi's approach to Indian independence. His close association with the Indian National Congress began in 1919; in 1929 he became its president, presiding over the historic Lahore session that proclaimed complete independence as India's Political goal.. He was imprisoned nine times between 1921 and 1945 for his political activity. When India was granted limited self government in 1935 the Congress Party under Nehru refused to form coalition governments with the Muslim league in some provinces; the hardening of relations between Hindus and Muslims that followed ultimately led to the partition of India and the creation of Pakistan. Shortly before Gandhi's assassination in 1948, Nehru became the first Prime Minister of Independent India. He attempted a foreign policy of non-alignment during the cold war, drawing harsh criticism if he appeared to favour either camp. During his tenure India clashed with Pakistan over the Kashmir region and with China over the Brahmaputra River valley. He wrested Goa from Portuguese. Domestically he promoted democracy, socialism, Secularism and Unity, adapting modern values to India conditions. His daughter Indira Gandhi became Prime Minister two years after his death.[2]

3 VITAL ECONOMIC ISSUES

In Agriculture, large scale State intervention in the shape of extinguishing or modifying rights in property, controlling farm practice and regimenting the peoples' way of life from a prior considerations may be ever disastrous. Talk of a socialist pattern of society has been very much in the air. Nehru couples it with the welfare state as a twin objectives which congress party has accepted. Of course *Sarvodaya* group was against Socialism as a goal. Nehru has discounted the importance of the communist, Communal and Praja Socialist parties. He realizes that there can be no socialism on the basis of a pauper economy, which production is the key to progress. For elimination of inequality social ownership or control of the principal means of production is not an inescapable necessity. On the contrary from the point of view of rapidly increasing production without adapting totalitarian coercion, there is everything to be said for an enlightened policy to encouraging private industry. Maulana Azad gave cogent reasons why nationalsation is no panacea, and British experience seemly fully to bear this out. But a far more potent reason which was weighted with countries bred in -the democratic tradition against going in for socialism or for a socialistic pattern is their rooted faith in liberty as the very life breath of democracy. We in India who have accepted the democratic way of life cannot afford to jeopardize that supreme value.

1. Move to Socialistic Pattern Society

Britain had welfare state without socialism and doing very well on it. Nehru had painstakingly sought to explain that they are not thinking of that kind of socialism at all that they contemplate something which will be as distinct from the Marxist- Leninist conception of socialism as from capitalism. Nehru's instincts are essentially democratic. He realizes that socialism of his dream can not be realized in a day. He knows that means are no less important than ends. If confronted with the choice between socialism and democracy, we have no doubt he would prefer the latter any day.

The Hindu in November 1958 wrote that our failure to reach the plans food targets shows that not enough was invested in agriculture. Industrialization is not an end in itself what should be aimed at is the reconstruction of the whole country from the village up. Today we have roads and railways which link the big towns, we have business and industry and education mainly sited in the towns. But the purchasing power of the villager does not rise. The villagers want schools, bridges, markets, improved tools and machines, fertilizers as well as irrigation and electricity.

2. Mixed Economic System

Mixed economy is an inescapable consequence of the political and economic character of the country. The role of the state should be that of a catalyst. It should not become an octopus that seeks to control every thing.

Our plans have failed so far mainly in this latter aspect. There has been too much dependence and Central Government direction and too little of local initiative and inspiration. Neither the progress of agriculture, which is so vital for the solution of the food problem nor the diversification of industry which is essential for providing employment, will be possible unless the impulse for improvement and organization comes from the bottom, from the village and district level.[3]

3. Rainbow of Secularism

Nehru felt that secularism did not mean something opposed to religion or "a state where religion as such is discouraged. It means freedom of religion and conscience, including freedom for those who may have no religion". And it means a "State which honours all faiths equally and gives them equal opportunities and does not allow itself to be attached to one faith or religion.[4]

Delhi is the eternal city, as the ruins of its forerunners- Indraprastha and Hastinapur— testify. It is the heart of India only a nit-wit can regard it as belonging to the Hindus or Sikhs alone. From Kanyakumari to Kashmir and from Gujarat to Assam, all Hindus, Muslims, Sikhs, Parsis, Christians and Jews who people this vast sub-continent and have adopted it as their dear motherland have an equal right to it. No one had the right to say it belongs to the majority only and that the minority can remain only as the underdog. Whoever serves it with the purest devotion must have the first claim.5

4. KASHMIR AND INDIA

On the eve of Independence, All India Congress Committees (AICC) stand as declared in its resolution of June 15, 1947 was that "the people of the States must have a dominating voice in any decisions regarding them". In contrast Mohammad Ali Jinnah asserted on July 30, that the ruler would decide which of the two States to accede to" or to remain independent. When a dispute arose with Pakistan over Kashmir's accession to India on Oct 26, 1947 following a tribal raid from Pakistan, Nehru said repeatedly the people would nonetheless, decide the issue in plebiscite. The international agreement that was used by V.K. Krishna Menon's words on the modalities of a plebiscite in the form of two resolutions of the UN Commission for India and Pakistan (UNCIP) dated August 13, 1948 and Jan, 5, 1949. Sheikh M. Abdullah, Prime Minister (from 1947 till 1952) had a strong disapproval of plebiscite. On August 8, 1953 Sheikh Abdullah was sacked from the office of Prime Minister of Jammu and Kashmir and put him behind the bars. Nehru felt that why would they live in a country where the Jan Sangh (presently Bharatiya Janata Party) and the Rastriya Swayamsevak Sangh are constantly beleaguering them. Nehru was always preaching the Mission of Secular democracy

At present, Kashmir is an integral part of Indian Union on the basis of 'Accession' and as a symbol of Indian Secularism. Bharatiya Janata Party demanded that Kashmir is an integral part of India by removing article 370[6]. Even today, Kashmir became a burning problem. Which has swallowed lot of wealth, men and energy, we are looking for amicable solution in this decade.

5. THE KAMARAJ PLAN

In August 1963, an attempt was indeed undertaken to enhance the party influence over the government through, what came to be known as "the Kamaraj Plan". The idea was to revert back government Ministers to party positions after certain tenure and *vice versa*. Jawaharlal Nehru sympathized this theory, but hardly put his weight behind its implementation. Instead, his colleagues like Morarji Desai alleged that he used the Kamaraj plan to remove all possible contenders" from the path of his daughter, Indira Gandhi". Besides, the Kamaraj plan created a new dispossessed group within the congress who had been deprived of their Ministerial positions. This increased intra-party factional squabbles. The spirit of the Kamaraj plan was thus greatly lost.7

6. DEMOCRACY AND DEVELOPMENT

Development involves investment. It naturally involves savings, private and public. Both are necessary. He would not like to spend a large part of resources in making more and more weapons. The industrial background has to grow, which means that we should provide for this process of development all the more. In planning, you must have clear social imperatives. In a democratic country like India, we cannot think of any social objective which does not touch the vast masses of the people. We want to produce more and more wealth and also have it properly distributed. We should continue with democracy, functioning in as wide a measure as is possible, even though the shadow of war and other troubles have hovered over us. Democracy is a complicated way of functioning and sometimes it involves delays. I think we should get rid of these delays. India is not merely a land of mountains, rivers, forests, cities, towns; it is a mass of human beings, many of them struggling for a bare pittance. We have to have perspective planning, that is, we must plan for the next 15 years or 20 years.

Ever since we become free, we have been absorbed in this major war against poverty, ignorance, illiteracy and all that. The democracy we profess and practice has not substantially grown in most countries. We established the democracy largely taken from the British and partly from the American practice.[8]

7. CONCLUSION

Nehru-multifaceted personality, had introduced Parliamentary Democracy and Five Year Plans for development. Which became solid and strong roots for fast development. Villages were founded as 'engine of growth' for all round development. Mixed economy was considered as a competitive boon system!" Secularism was treated in Constitution and in practice, as a backbone. Even under globalization era, Kashmir is even today become a bone of contention for both countries. Democracy and development were interdependent for curing all ills, and pushing economy for welfare of all.

References

Britannica (2005): Britannica Ready Reference Encyclopedia, New Delhi, Vol. 7, p. 218.

Britannica (2005): Britannica Ready Reference Encyclopedia, Vol. 7, New Delhi, p. 84.

Rangaswamy Parthasarathy (1978): A Hundred Years of The Hindu, the Epic Story of Indian Nationalism, Kasturi and Sons Ltd., Madras, pp. 703-14.

S. Gopal (1980): Jawaharlal Nehru: An Anthology (Ed. Vol.), OUP, Delhi, pp. 327-30.

The Hindustan Times (1948): Delhi Belonged to Everyone, January 18.

A.G. Noorani (1999): How and why Nehru and Abdullah Fell Out, *Economic and Political Weekly*, pp. 268-72.

Suranjan Das, (2001): The Nehru years of Indian Politics, Edinburgh Papers, *Centre for South Asian Studies*, No. 16.

Publication Division (1983): Jawaharlal Nehru's Speeches, 1963-64, Vol. V, 49.

8

Nehruvian Economic Ideas: The Framework of Mahalanobis Model

S.K. MISHRA

Pt. Jawahar Lal Nehru was not only a Political thinker and freedom fighter. He was an Educationist and economic thinker whose thought was to establish the perception of 'self reliance' in the sphere of economic proficiency specially in policy making so that India may realise the dream of a developed, vibrant, strong and stable India.

It is well known that India was famous all over the world for her wealth. All the countries of the world thought and rightly regarded India as the land of Milk and Honey. Leading economists Dada Bhai Naoroji, Lord Curzon, Prof. Kala, Dr. Balkrishna have conducted investigations into the average income of the people of India. The findings vary. There was a time when people came here to make money; today Indians are the poorest of the poor.

Pt. Nehru was the man who wanted to transform India a developed, vibrant, strong and stable Countries of the world. So he thought that without the base of heavy and basic Industries India can never conquer the world and with this strategic Industries India will become the self- reliance economy. Soon Nehru had a great discussion about the importance and need for planning and the role of statistics in planning (because Russia was the example of development with planning) with the great architect of Country, Prof. P.C. Mahalanobis. Nehru became impressed with the work done at Indian Statistical Institute and indispensability of statistics in planning in the future programme of development in the country.

The work of planning could not make much headway till India attained independence in August, 1947 with Pt. Nehru as Prime Minister. The All India Congress Committee appointed an Economic Programme Committee in November, 1947 with Nehru as Chairman. The Committee recommended, inter-alia, the appointment of a permanent Planning Commission, which was subsequently set-up in 1950 with Prime Minister as Chairman. The First Five Year Plan (1951-1956) was formulated soon after, though this plan was a grand success because emphasis was on Agriculture in this Plan. The shortage of Steel became so acute that the Prime Minister was convinced about the immediate need for increasing its production.

In the meantime, Mahalanobis was appointed the Statistical Adviser of the Cabinet, Govt. of India. On the desire of then Prime Minister Pt. Nehru, the National Sample Survey was established in 1950 for collecting information on social, economic and demographic conditions for the entire Country.

With the valuable suggestions of Pt. Nehru, Mahalanobis prepared 'Operational Research Model to Planning in India', which is a mile stone in the field of economic planning. Programmes for rapid development have been the central theme of four sector Operational Research Model of Mahalanobis. It is an allocation model because the object of the model is to get a consistent solution to obtain a desired rise in National income as result of given amount of investment and at the same time creating a desired volume of employment.

Prof. Mahalanobis had tried to set-up a conceptual framework in his Operational Research Model which would be of help for practical purposes to solve the basic problems of Indian economy within a definite period. The Model stands as the centre of India's planning frame. It has not remained simply a matter of analytical appreciations as a Model of Second Five Year Plan. It has turned out to be a guiding force in the Model building activity in our planning system.

At the instance of Jawahar Lal Nehru, Prof. Mahalanobis took upon the task of working out a Draft Plan Frame for Second Five Year Plan. In order to benefit from the best economic expertise available in the world. Mahalanobis gathered in the Indian Statistical Institute, of which he was the Secretary, a large team of economists drawn from different parts of the world. A part from the whole delegation of experts from the GOSPLAN, the U.S.S.R. State Committee of Planning, among the visiting the economists were such stalwarts as Oscar Lange (Poland), Ragnar Frisch (Norway) Charles Bettelheim (France), Jan Tinbergen, Nicholas Kaldor, Kennett Galbrath, Paul Baren and Richard Goodwin (University of Cambridge). Goodwin played a leading part in the work that was started by a team of Researchers for the construction of an inter-Industry table. Frisch began the construction of a multi-Sector programming model which was among the first attempts at the application of linear programming to country wide economic planning. Other lines of work that was get started were in the fields of commodity balancing and demand projection for consumer goods with the help of Engel Curves fitted to National Sample Survey data.

With the help of the broad suggestions by eminent persons, suitable to the Indian conditions, Prof. Mahalanobis developed his Operational Research Model for the Second Five Year Plan. Mahalanobis was of the view that it would be necessary to use much scientific and technical knowledge and also to organise continuing research at various levels for this purpose. But Research would not be the primary objectives, the aim would be to solve our particular problem. When a Practicing Physician gives medical treatment to a patient he uses much scientific knowledge and may even do some research but his chief aim would be to cure the patient. T observations or experiments on the patient may ad medical knowledge but the treatment given is not primarily for purpose of research. The distinction is important. In Mahalanobis view their studies also have the primary aim of solving a particular problem (and not of doing any theoretical research for its own sake). This is why he named his model Operational Research Model which is a Decision Model based on the Indian conditions in various sectors of the economy.

Nehru-Mahalanobis considered the question of economic development over a long period of time. The rate of development over a long period, however, intimately connected with the pattern of investment. India has plenty of Iron-ore, Coal and other natural resources. The long-term aim should, therefore, be to manufacture Capital Goods within the country rather than to import them. The proper strategy would be to bring about a rapid development of the Industries producing investment goods in the beginning by increasing appreciably the proportion of investment in the basic Industries. As the capacity to manufacture both heavy and light machinery and other capital goods increase, the capacity invest would also increase steadily and India would become more and more independent of the import of foreign machinery and capital goods.

What should be proportion of total investment to be allocated to the industries producing capital goods in the most crucial decision in perspective or long run planning. Once the choice is made of the share of investment in capital goods industries, the availability of capital goods in future years would become more or less determined. Having settled the share of investment for the capital goods industries, broadly from considerations of long period development, the next step would be to decide the detailed allocation of investment to individual industries and services. Mahalanobis used three sets of contingent parameters in considering different possibilities. He was interested firstly, in the ratio of the increase in output of new investment, i.e. the output per unit of new investment or the output co-efficient of capital, secondly, in the ratio of the increase in net value added to new investment, i.e. increase in income per unit of new investment or the income co-efficient of capital 'â' and thirdly, the ratio of investment to the number of persons employed, i.e. the amount of capital required per worker or the capital co-efficient of labour 'è'.

According to the technical methods used in the plan frame the total amount of investment available having been provisionally settled, it may proceed to distribute the investment to groups of industries or to individual industries and services. In each industry (or groups of industries) the amount of investment having been (provisionally) settled, it would be possible to estimate the expected output in physical term and in money value, the expected contribution to national income and the expected volume of employment generated.

The physical target of production, investment, income and employment are thus completely interlocked in Nehru-Mahalanobis Model.

Prof. Mahalanobis divided the total net investment into two parts, one part (a fraction, say lK) is used to increase the production of basic capital goods (which may be called K-sector) and the other part (a fraction, say, lC) is used to increase the production of consumer goods (to be called the C-sector). It should be noted that lK and lC are fraction of total investment, so that:

$$lK + lC = 1$$

Prof. Mahalanobis extended his two sector model to a four sectoral formulation by breaking down consumption goods sector 'C' into three components, namely:

C_1 = Factories producing consumer goods
C_2 = Agriculture and household industries
C_3 = Services (i.e. education, health, etc.) sectors

So, Mahalanobis's four sector was = $K + C_1 + C_2 + C_3$

While the earlier models were growth models, this model should properly be called an allocation model or decision model. The object of the model is to get a consistent solution to obtain a desired rise in national income as a result of given amount of investment, and at the same time a desired volume of employment. It was necessary to use such a model to get the broad sector allocations of investment in the Draft Plan Frame for the Second Plan prepared by Mahalanobis. Mahalanobis allocated the investment in different sectors, which may be written as:

$$lK + l_1 + l_2 + l_3$$

The incremental net output–investment (or called capital–output ratio as:

$$\hat{a}k + \hat{a}_1 + \hat{a}_2 + \hat{a}_3$$

As employment is to be specially considered in the model a set of parameter is introduced giving the investment required per engaged person (i.e. capital-labour ratio è) in the four sectors respectively as:

$$\grave{e}\,k + \grave{e}_1 + \grave{e}_2 + \grave{e}_3$$

The variables, income (E) and investment (A), are depicted by a new notation because these give the respective increments over the plan period of five years; and a new variable 'N' is also introduced giving the increment in employment over the plan period of five years. The basic set-up is ultimately given by:

$$N = nk + n_1 + n_2 + n_3$$
$$A = l_kA + l_1A + l_2A + l_3A$$
$$E = Ek + E_1 + E_2 + E_3$$

Increment in income in each sector can be shown as:

$$Ek = lkA/\hat{a}k$$
$$E_1 = l_1A/\hat{a}_1$$
$$E_2 = l_2A/\hat{a}_2$$
$$E_3 = l_3A/\hat{a}_3$$

And increment in employment in each sector will be as:

$$Nk = lkA/\grave{e}k$$

$N = l_1A/è_1$
$N = l_2A/è_2$
$N = l_3A/è_3$

The actual situation before the preparation of the plan frame was some what like this:

Yè = initial national income= Rs. 10,800 crores
A = total investment fund =Rs. 5,600 crores 10 to 11% of national income
n = rate of increase of national income 5% per year
N = total new employment to be created 110 lakhs (= 11 million)
lk = proportion of investment in industries producing investment goods = 33% (settled from considerations of growth over a long period)

The capital and labour requirements per unit of increase in national income differ among these four sectors. The basic problem of economic planning is then how to distribute a given amount of available investment funds among these sectors so as to achieve both the target for the rate of increase in national income and full employment of the labour force.

In distributing investment funds, however, sector K was given special priority of total funds for new investment 1/3 was allocated to sector K. This allocation was arrived at from considerations of longer run economic growth over 20 or 30 years.

Tables 1 and 2 shows the parameters of capital-output ratio and capital-labour ratio prepared by Mahalanobis for the Second Five Year Plan Period.

On the basis of parameters Mahalanobis calculated the income and employment position for the whole second plan period. (Table 3)

After split up the estimates relating the C_2 sector in between agriculture and small and household industries the following expresses (Table 4)

The table indicates that 33% of total investment in the capital goods sectors contributes only 12.76% of total income

TABLE 1

Parameters of Capital and Labour Requirements

(per one million rupees of income)

Sector Description	*Capital (Rs. Million)*	*Labour (Man Years)*
K Basic investment goods	$\beta k = 5.00$	$\theta k = 250$
C_1 Factory consumers goods	$\beta_1 = 2.86$	$\theta_1 = 327$
C_2 Agriculture and household Industries	$\beta_2 = 0.80$	$\theta_2 = 320$
C_3 Service sector	$\beta_3 = 2.22$	$\theta_3 = 593$

TABLE 2

Parameters for C sectors

Sector Description	*Capital (Rs. Million)*	*Labour (Man Years)*
C_2 Agriculture	$\beta_2 = 0.91$	$\theta_2 = 146$
Household industries	$\beta_2 = 0.50$	$\theta_3 = 801$

Source: Mishra, S.K. 'Mahalanobis Approach to Planning in India' Deep & Deep publication, New Delhi, 1994, p. 31.

TABLE 3

Income and Employment Estimation for Second Five Year Plan

Sectors	*Investment (A)*	Increase in *Income (E)*	*Employment (N)*
		(Rs. Crores)	*(Million)*
K	1850 = 33%	370 = 12.76%	0.9 = 8.18%
C_1	980 = 17%	340 = 11.72%	1.1 = 10.00%
C_2	1180 = 21%	1470 = 50.69%	4.7 =42.73%
C_3	1600 = 29%	720 = 24.89%	4.3 = 39.09%
	5610 = 100%	2900 = 100%	11 =100%

Source: Mishra, S.K. 'Mahalanobis Approach to Planning in India' Deep & Deep publication, New Delhi 1994 p. 32.

TABLE 4

Income and Employment Estimation for Second Five Year Plan from C_2 Sector

Sector Description	*Investment (Rs. Crores)*	*Increase in Income (Rs. Crores)*	*Increase in Employment (Million)*
a: Agriculture	986	1083	1.58
h: Household enterprises	194	387	3.12
	1180	1470	4.70

Source: Mishra, S.K., 'Mahalanobis Approach to Planning in India', Deep & Deep Publications, New Delhi, 1994, p. 32.

and 8.18% of total employment meaning that the productivity of capital in 'K' sector is less than that in other sectors, while the capital-labour ratio in this sector is very high. The target values of income and employment were fixed in such a way as to satisfy the requirements of perspective planning and also conform to the needs of a capital poor and welfare conscious economy. The instruments were the proportions of distribution of total investment between sectors. Though C_2 sector has quick yielding, but Mahalanobis was of the view that 'K' sector is essential for the sound development of the country in the long run. 17% total investment in C_1 contributes 11.72% of total income and 10.00% of total employment. C_2 sector, i.e. household and agriculture needs only 21% of total investment to contribute 50.69% of total income and 42.73% of total employment. Inspite of low capital-labour and capital-output ratio, Mahalanobis allocated 50% of the investment outlay for 'K' and 'C_1' sector in view of long-term interests. Mahalanobis's approach was nearer to the approach of Lewis, who was also confident about the ultimate transfer of manpower from subsistence sector to capitalist sector, i.e. large industries sectors in the development process.

Mahalanobis's strategy essentially aimed at removing long-term structural constraints by creating a high skill base through human capital formation, industrialization in depth by creating the base of heavy industry and by stepping up the rates of domestic savings and capital accumulation. Mahalanobis had proposed his model on the economic idea of Jawahar Lal Nehru. Due to full support of Nehru, the model was accepted for the Second Five Year Plan of India by the Planning Commission. Not only this the model has dominated the over all scenario till Seventh Five Year Plan of India.

References

P.R. Brahmanand: Planning for a Futureless Economy, Himalaya Publishing House, Bombay, 1978, p. 61.

Ashok Rudra: Indian Plan Models, Allied Publishers Pvt. Ltd., New Delhi, 1976, p. 8.

J.N. Bhagwati and S. Chakravarty, Contribution to Indian Economic Analysis; A Survey, Lalvani Publishing House, Bombay, 1971, pp. 4-8.

P.K. Bose and M. Mukherjee, (eds); P.C. Mahalanobis; papers on Planning, Statistical Publishing Society, Calcutta, 1985, pp. 83-86.

P.C. Mahalanobis, The Approach of Operational Research to Planning in India, Asia Publishing House, Calcutta, 1963, pp. 32-33.

Ajit Kumar Sinha; Some Emerging Issues of Indian Economy, A Theme Paper presented on the occasion of the Seminar on 4th August, 1991.

S.K. Mishra, 'Mahalanobis Approach to Planning in India' Deep and Deep publications, New Delhi, 1994.

Nehru: Selected Works, Vol. 3, Savgan Books Division of Orient Longman Ltd., New Delhi.

Socio-economic Ideas of Nehru and Globalisation

S. Suresh

INTRODUCTION

Just after Independence of India on 15 the August 1947, Indian economy, under the premiership of Jawaharlal Nehru, was built through planning in the lines of Soviet Russia. Due to global significance of the socio-economic ideas of Jawaharlal Nehru economic development was adopted as national motto.

NEHRU'S IDEAS AND GLOBALIZATION

His ideas are still very useful in terms of globalization; liberalization and economic reform. Globalization makes an attempt to examine the role of the socio-economic ideas of Nehru. Globalization means increasing integration of developing countries into Global Economy. It is achieved through liberalization of trade and capital market, increasing internationalization of corporate production and technological change that is rapidly dismantling barriers to the international trade ability of goods and services and the mobility of capital.

Laissez Fair Idea and Economic Reforms

His idea of laissez fair policy is directly related at present economic reform and globalization policy.

His ISI Strategy and Liberalization

The ISI strategy was adopted in India by Jawaharlal Nehru which was explicitly incorporated in India's Second Five Year Plan (1956-61) and was expected to pave the way for export promotion efforts over a sufficient broad based. Due to Nehru in the planned gradual transformation of the economy, the state was supposed to play the key role. In a mixed capitalist economic structure which we proposed the establish the role of the state was supposed to be led by public sector enterprises where these public sector enterprises were assigned the task of producing capital goods and thereby commanding the economy.

Table 1 shows reduced import availability ratio in 1965-66 relative to those in 1959-60 which is a state of generally high and accelerating industrial growth. Only the basic goods under the use based classification and chemicals based goods under input based classification show deceleration.

Table 2 shows that show that it was relatively easy to reduce imports of customer goods as percentage of total imports, relative to that of reducing imports of capital goods and maintenance imports. The inability to reduce the share of capital goods and maintenance goods is to be judged in the context of an initial weak supply of capital goods relative to requirement of capital goods needed for industrialization as prescribed by Mahalanobis.

Table 3 shows the import availability ratio for food grains, fertilizers and tractors, on each from consumer goods, capital goods and maintenance imports.

Table 4 shows our trade balance its ratio with GDP and the position of foreign exchange reserves.

In sum, while growth performance on the industrial front was not bad, we did not perform well in terms of trade

TABLE 1

Growth Rate of Industrial Production and Import Availability Ratio (Percent 1951-56)

(Base year 1956)

Industries	*Growth*		*Rates*	*Imports*	
	1951-55	*1965-66*	*1960-65*	*1959-60*	*1965-66*
Total	5.7	7.2	9.6	18.1	14.1
A. Use Based Classification					
a. Basic Goods	4.7	12.0	10.4	34.1	22.5
b. Intermediate	7.8	6.4	6.9	21.3	10.9
c. Capital	9.8	13.1	19.6	44.0	36.4
d. Consumer	4.8	4.4	4.9	5.7	4.9
B. Input Based Classification					
a. Agro-based	4.0	3.8	4.0	4.7	2.7
b. Metal-based	7.5	14.1	18.2	39.3	31.6
c. Clinical-based	8.5	12.2	9.0	35.3	21.9

Source: S.L. Shetty, Structural Retrogression in the Indian Economy since Mid-Sixties. (*Economic Political Weekly*), Vol. XIII, (Annual No.) Feb. 1998, p. 186, and I.J. Ahluwalia, Industrial Growth in India Stagnation since Mid-Sixties, OPU, 1985, pp. 9, 21, 120 (For import availability radio).

TABLE 2

Import by Exhaustive Components as Percentage of Total Imports (1951-64)

Plan	*Period*	*Capital Goods*	*Consumer Goods*	*Maintenance Goods*
First	1951-56	21.38	24.95	48.83
Second	1956-61	29.24	17.74	47.39
Third	1961-64	34.87	16.51	43.79

Source: NCAER (1967), Maintenance Import, New Delhi, p. 2.

TABLE 3

Import Availability Ratio (%) 1955-56

Year	*Food grain*	*Fertilizers*	*Tractors*
1955-56	2.2	40.64	-
1960-61	4.6	73.64	-
1961-62	4.8	61.14	77.30
1962-63	6.1	53.34	64.91
1963-64	8.0	46.85	54.19
1964-65	8.8	44.87	34.95
1965-66	14.1	54.56	25.82
Third Plan (1961-66)	8.31	51.89	46.16

Source: Govt. of India, Economic Survey, 1983-84, pp. 94-95 (for food and fertilizers), NCAER, 1980. Implication of Tractionasation for Farm Employment, Productivity and Income, Vol. I, p. 53 (for tractors).

TABLE 4

Trade Balance and Foreign Exchange Reserve (Rs. Crore) 1951-66

Year	*Trade Balance*	*Trade Balance GDP Ratio*	*Foreign Exchange Changes Reserve*
1951-52	174	1.75	864
1955-56	165	1.61	902
1960-61	480	2.96	304
1961-62	430	2.50	297
1962-63	446	2.41	295
1963-64	430-	2.02	306
1964-65	533	2.15	250
1965-66	599-	2.29	298

Source: Ibid.

balance and were faced external liquidity crises at the period of Jawaharlal Nehru.

We find that the economy took a U-turn during post-1966 period which incidentally coincided with number of external shocks, including the significant devaluation in June 1966. The pre-1966 quantitative controls led to the protection domestic industries irrespective of cost structure leading to inefficient import substitution. The post-1966 emergence of excess capacity in capital goods sector was supposed to be tackled by vent for surplus. Thus the shift from ISI to EOI may be interpreted as a shift from dependence on home market to Independence on world market. This was a period particularly seventies and eighties, when the potential exporters got high export assistance from government of India particularly industries produces engineering and chemicals goods. It led to a slight size in export of engineering good

As a percentage of India's total exports, but could not ensure increasing command on global front. By the mid-sixties India came to assure less than one per cent of world exports and stagnated at half of one per cent from mid-seventies. All these had their effects on trade balance and forging exchange reserves.

NEP 1991 AND NEHRU

The New Economic Policy introduced since 1991 made it clear that India can grow faster as part of the world economy and not in isolation. Our trade policy must therefore, create an environment that will provide story impetus to exports and render export activity profitable. The package of trade policy reforms announced in July, 1991 aimed at access to high technology and world markets.

The economic reform, thus, aimed at strengthening export incentives eliminating a substantial volume of import licensing and optimal import compression in view of the balance of payment situation. The New Policy aims at reducing the interference of government if not totally abolishes it, in matters related to import of technology by Indian firms particularly in high technology and high investment priority industries.

The New Industries-*cum*-trade policies thus, reveal an "input liberalizing-*cum*-export promoting" or what we call an ODI strategy.

PROFIT MOTIVE IN PRESENT CONTEXT

In an acquisitive society based on profit-motive, appeared Jawaharlal Nehru out of date in the new world that is growing up, it does not mean that there should no incentive. Though, incentives may not be confirmed to financial benefits, may always be necessary. Jawaharlal Nehru was against profit-motive. He revealed that in the context of world today, such a motive is becoming increasing not only wrong from the economic point of view, but a vulgar thing from any sensitive point of view changes are bound to repeat.

Nehru was against free economy. To him, laissez faire variety of economic policy brought the law of jungle, which was called by Carlyle as 'Pig-philosophy'. The theory of individual freedom failed at the period of Nehru but it has again become effective and useful at the present stage. He observed that liberty of the individual in the laissez faire economy was a mere myth in itself.

His democracy under laissez-faire is very significant even today as he maintained that democracy under laissez-faire was only a political democracy not economic democracy. With out equality, democracy and liberty have no meaning at all.

But, now all centralization is a sight encroachment in the freedom of the individual. To him, the real problem of India economy was maintaining balance between the two. He argued that the political right of individual be safeguarded by the constitution of the state. He believed in a policy of flexibility in term of economic function of the state.

NEHRU'S IDEAS OF POVERTY IN ECONOMIC REFORM

India is a poor country, our development efforts during the last fifty five years always aimed at reduction in the incidence and severity of poverty across masses scattered over different regions and states. It is well known result that the decline in the incidence of rural poverty is very closely associated with the growth in the agricultural sector particularly in the agricultural productivity over the years. The record of poverty alleviation varied significantly across states of India and across rural and urban areas. Education and health care are two important elements in the process of elevation of one's well-being and capability in the long run.

Unless the programmes for rural infrastructure development like extension of irrigation facilities and land distribution are accompanied by carefully thought out schemes for taxing the beneficiaries of rural investment and development and investigating the surplus so acquired for the betterment of the true have nots in the rural economy, the macro programmes like Jawahar Rojgar Yojana (JRY) and/or land distribution, even if meticulously implemented will not be able to eradicate poverty among the bottom layers of income distribution.

LAND REFORM

There has been another policy flow of approaching village poverty as a wage problem because the surplus labour can be easily dispensed with by transfer to other wage sectors. Such employments are supposed to be springing up under the trickle down effects of urban growth. Infect the so called redundant zero productive labour would hamper agriculture if transferred, besides the fact that such transfers would be costly and casual. What was needed in a massive poverty eradication scheme was the growth of land substitute factors like irrigation and growth of complementary capital within the villages accompanied with the policy input of land reforms.

OBJECTIVES OF SOCIO-ECONOMIC IDEAS OF NEHRU

The main socio-economic ideas of Jawaharlal Nehru was to make India economically strong, stable and self-sufficient so that economic and political freedom might be meaningful. His all these ideas and thinking should be viewed in the context of the Indian social and economic setting. His ideas of mixed economy, planning, socialism, industrialization, agriculture and co-operation, etc. Were all directed towards a strong foundation of the shattered economy of India.

India suffered from inefficiency of production, inequality of distribution and instability of economic life at the time of economic planning. The result of his socio-economic ideas during the period ranging from 1950-51 to 1965-66 was an overall strengthening of the Indian economy and its heading towards desired goals. The national income at constant (19648-49) prices went up from Rs. 8850 crores in 1950-51 to Rs. 14930 crores in 1964-65 and the per capital income from Rs. 14930 to Rs. 14930 (both at constant prices). During 15 years index number of agricultural production of all commodities (1949-50=100) rose from 95.6 to 157.6 and index of industrial production (1956=100) increased from 73.5 in 1951 to 174.8 in 1964-65)

PRESENT ECONOMIC PLANNING AND NEHRU

His ideas on economic planning included in its orbit adoption of democratic socialism, development of basic and heavy industries, beginning of land reform and co-operatives for agricultural re-organization. In most of these directions a satisfactory rate of progress was achieved in spite of several shortfalls, pitfalls and unfavorable climate for development. It went a long way in building up the modern India and prevented her from stepped towards military rule like other developing nations of Asia and Africa. To quote Mr. S. Kesava Iyenger. "The democratic planning in India with about 450 million population is undoubtedly the most significant experiment without any per cent of parallel any where in the world."

The deviction for the ideas and thinking from Nehru in present global perspective has also resulted inefficiency of production, inequality of distribution and instability of economic and political instability.

An elaborate study of Nehru's economic policies lead us to the conclusion that Nehru believed that for full realization of political and social freedom it was essential to have economic freedom for 'there could be no real freedom without economic freedom. To call a starving man free is but to mock him" Full fledge political freedom means progressively what might broadly be called economic freedom. According to him:

"To give an opportunity to large number of people to profit by democratic method and to have more or less equal chances to progress". A political vote has its own value but it is useless" if it is decompanied by hunger and starvation". Nehru defined economic freedom thus. Firm of all that means working for a certain measure of well being for all, call it welfare state. Secondly, at means working for a certain measure of equality of opportunity in the economic sphere.

ECONOMIC FREEDOM

His concept of economic freedom include an economic structure based on:

(a) Economic equality
(b) On the well being of the masses, and
(c) On co-operative sprite.

His ideal of an egalitarian society was " a co-operative ideal based on social justice and economic equality. " 20 In 1955, while speaking at Trichur Nehru announced, "I also want a classless society in India and the world. I do not want any privileged class. I do not want a great deal of inequality among people.

The issues of both the approach Nehruvian and present are to some extent similar:

I. Expansion of per capita income
II. Achievement of food security
III. Elimination of poverty
IV. Reduction of inequalities (both internal and external)
V. Removal of infrastructure constraints
VI. Realizing growth with stability
VII. Strengthening the knowledge and technology base

VIII. Achieving production efficiency at the maximum possible limited
IX. Achieving strong financial sector
X. Restoring values in the society
XI. Ensuring sustainable development
XII. Realizing full employment
XIII. Human resource development
XIV. Providing education and health to one and all
XV. Strengthening social security and safety net programme
XVI. Realizing optimum water management in the rural and urban economics.

We should not pursue the policy instruments of development namely globalization, liberation and privatisation as an ends in themselves without critically examining their implications for the cherished goals and aspirations of the common man in the Indian economic society. India is an economy with a very large potential of demand of its population belong to the middle class which has significant demand potential for durable and non-durable goods.

REFERENCES

Govt. of India, Eighth Five Year Plan, 1992-97, Vol. II, Planning Commission, New Delhi (1992), p. 104.

Majumdar, Bhaskar, "Capitalist Globalisation of the Third World, Compulsions and Choice", 79th Conference Volume, The Indian Economic Association (1996), Gwalior, (Quoted from Marx and Engles, 1997, p. 46s).

Chaubey, P.K., Majumdar, B., "Open Door Industrial: A Panacea for the Poor Economy of India", The Indian Economic Association, 1st April, (Jubilee), 80th Conference Volume, Hydrabad, 1997, p. 455.

Singh, Manmohan, Planning Commission, 1956, pp. 43-49.

Gupta, S.P. (1995), "Important of Economic Reform on Poor", *Economic and Political Weekly*, Vol. XXX, 20 June, 1995.

Nehru Speeches, Vol. IV, Speeches in Bangalore, February 6, 1962, p. 150.

10

Economic Philosophy of Jawaharlal Nehru

GAUTAM BHONG

I. INTRODUCTION

This paper highlights on "Nehru on Mixed Economy" Pandit Jawaharlal Nehru's love for socialism was perhaps next only to his love for India. His passion for building up a socialistic pattern of society in India had become so deep in recent years that some have even suggested that his political creed partook more of a totalitarian philosophy akin to communism.

Socialism appealed to him as a "philosophy of life", as the inevitable solution to banish from India the poverty unemployment and degradation of its teeming millions.

A classless society with no privileged sections in it and with the minimum of inequality among the people was the ideal he aimed at not only for India but for the whole world. The largest good of the largest number was the prime objective.

The socialistic pattern of society can be built in India only by raising the standard of life of the masses providing them with the means of decent existence and enabling them to progress in life materially, culturally, spiritually.

Jawaharlal Nehru had before him the example of soviet Russia's Five Year Plans after revolution in October 1917. His deep interest in the idea of planning was appreciated and recognized when he was appointed as chairman of National Planning Commission in the Year 1938. According to him the socialistic pattern of society was the means to be adopted in evolving a welfare state in India.

Nehru was not a doctrinaire socialist. He was a realist and pragmatist. He deliberately chooses the concept of mixed economy.

2. CONCEPT OF MIXED ECONOMY

Mixed economy is a system of economy in which both the public and private sectors of economy are allowed to exist side by side. The state fixes certain targets to be achieved annually as well as during particular period. After these targets have been fixed the state decides to the extent to which it can manage the resources for financing the industries for achieving the goals. Then it is left to the private sector to fill the gap. Private sector is given all encouragement and facilities to step in. Once it has decided what is to be left to the care of private sector and what is to be taken over by the state the private sector is allowed to flourish. It is allowed to earn profit and retain that not only this but his successors are allowed to inherit the property created by the industrialist.

The industrialists are also provided facilities to exploit unexpected resources. They are permitted to research, locate and fill the gap of economy.

In the area left to the state, the state employees suitable personnel and gives them the work. The state is empowered to locate natural resources, technical know now and proper machinery, along with foreign exchange. The state is responsible to declare prices, regulate distribution.

The role of the state in mixed economy system is usually more important than that of the private sector. It is because where the later fails, former steps in and the gap is not allowed to remain unfilled.

3. NEED OF MIXED ECONOMY

The nations which have mixed system of economy have there own arguments to advance. According to them both these system go to the care of the private sector, resulting the naked exploitation and concentration of wealth in the hand of only few families under capitalism.

On the other hand communist system of economy makes man a machine and takes away all its initiative. Therefore, they feel that there should be a system of economy in which both the systems blended together and brought nearer to each other, so that the society is benefited by both the systems. India is a country which public and private sectors have been allowed to exist and to develop side by side and it closes cooperation with each sector.

4. EVOLUTIONARY/REVOLUTIONARY WAY FOR MIXED ECONOMY

Today the society is leaning towards socialistic system with the result that the concept of mixed economy is receiving more and more encouragement. This has led to a discussion namely evolutionary or revolutionary. Those who favor evolutionary system are of the view that gradually system of mixed economy should be introduced and extreme system should be replaced. On the other hand those who hare revolutionary orientation are of the view that this system should be introduced all of a sudden and every thing else will take it own care.

Therefore, they do not favor other process. But usually evolutionary system is favored over revolutionary because that avoids sudden fluctuations and dislocations. In the word of Sivayya and Dass, "the evolutionist admitting that a peaceful transition to full socialism has never taken place in modern society, still favor the gradual socialism so as to minimize the opposition from the private owners and to avoid the unnecessary physics destruction that may take place as a result of revolution".

5. JAWAHARLAL NEHRU'S PERCEPTION OF MIXED ECONOMY

Community projects and the national extension services were expected to form the base for the national edifice of a socialistic pattern of society the odd half hearted phrase adopted by the congress at the session in January 1955. The Nehru era is for the 16 years from 1947 to 1963.

Nehru himself preferred straight forwardly to use the word ' socialist and socialistic' soon dropped out of use. But the word had its advantage at the start, even If it was not coined by Nehru. What he had in mind is that the country was expecting not a rigid or doctrinaire framework of ideology but certain methods of economy and social change. The socialism to which Nehru committed India was to adopt the definition of modern philosopher, not so much a certain desirable set of social relations as a way of solving social problems.

The ways in which the socialism was made possible in India were very similar to those which Anthony Crosland formulated for British. India was striving to move ahead from a low stage of economic backwardness.

The approach which Nehru favored was on the lines of British left wing thinking. The ownership of industry was in itself unimportant and nothing was gained by nationalizing existing industries solely in order to gain control. But it was important for the state to control the strategic points of production. There was no doubt that the public sector would grow and gradually dominate the scene. The arguments that private enterprise is sacrosanct dose not hold good in India today. But both the sectors had their roles in increasing production within the broad limits of general control by the state and could even help by healthy rivalry in keeping each other up to the mark. Indeed, the kind of socialism which Nehru had in mind would be more easily achieved in a mixed than in a wholly state owned economy.

Socialism appeared to him in his younger days as a philosophy of life. With the passing of the years his faith in the efficacy of socialism as a sort of miracle worker to end al l human ills had grown stronger. He swore by it as the principal tenet of his political creed and philosophy not only for India but for all under developed countries.

6. MIXED ECONOMY IN INDIA

Whatever the motive force, Nehru's speeches in the autumn of 1954 ushered in a new phase in Indian economy policy. First came the Avadi resolution on "socialist pattern of society". Then came the budget for 1955-56 termed by some (incorrectly) the first socialist budget because of social taxes on salaried business executives, preferential rates for cottage industries and the promise of substantial deficit financing to meet envelopment costs. Soon after the taxation Inquiry Commission recommended a statutory ceiling on incomes. Ironically this socialist proposal came from a group headed by Dr. Mathai, a prominent industrialist and was rejected by a government pledged to a socialist pattern. The constitutional amendment in 1954 empowered the government to determine the amount of compensation for expropriated property.

Immediately in 1955, Imperial Bank of India was converted to the State Bank of India.

Pandit Nehru did not favor state socialism. He wanted decentralization of economic power. But Mahalanobis was forceful exponent of enlarging the public sector at the expense of the private enterprise, particularly with respect to basic industry.

Gandhians welcomed the stress on cottage industries. Nehru was impressed with the fusion of western and Gandhian economic ideas for development and the emphasis on the public sector. The business community however was alarmed.

The initial Industrial Policy Resolution in 1948, Nehru's retreat from socialism had confined exclusive state activity to six fields. The second plan proposed marked expansion in publicly controlled industry.

7. PRESENT STATUS OF MIXED ECONOMY

The main objectives of economic planning as they have

been spelt out in various plans can not be realized simultaneously. In India's mixed economy the objectives of rapid economic growth and reduction in income inequalities seem to be in conflict and the planners clearly betray awareness of trade-off between them. The objective of Fourth Five Year Plan was to reduce in equalities in income and wealth. However, the indifference of the Planning Commission towards this objective was unconcealed. This objective could be achieved by reducing income inequality through fiscal measures. The Fifth Plan also referred to the necessity of eliminating poverty. But Suresh Tendulkar was criticized it saying that the programs for the removal of poverty are vague in terms of their qualitative effects on the attainment of the social objectives.

During the First and Second Plans, of the total investment, 54 percent was in the public sector and 46 percent in the private sector. The share of the public sector rose to 60 percent in the Third Plan. It was 59 percent in Fourth Plan, followed by 57.6 percent in Fifth Plan and 53 percent in Sixth Plan. But for the first time, the Seventh Plan reduced the share of public sector investment to 47.8 percent. In Eighth Plan the public sector investment reduced further to 45.2 percent.

There has been a precipitous fall in the share of public sector. It was 16.2 percent in 1980-81, 7.3 percent in 1992-93 and 6.9 percent in 1994-95.

8. ISSUE OF PRIVATISATION

The new Industrial policy announced by the Government in July 1991 emphasized on the following four major measures:

(a) Reduction in number of industries reserved for public sector from 17 percent to 8 percent (reduced still further to 6 later on) and the introduction of selective competition in the reserved area.

(b) The disinvestment of shares of select set of public sector enterprises in order to raise resources and encourage wider participation of general public and workers in the ownership of public sector enterprises.

(c) The policy towards sick public sector enterprises to be the same. As that for the private sector.

(d) The improvement of the performance through an Memorandum of Understanding in (MOU) system by which managements are to be Granted greater autonomy but held accountable for specified results.

In addition, there was a drastic reduction in the budgetary Support it sick or potentially sick public sector undertakings.

9. CONCLUSION

Kaushik Basu points out that allocative efficiency is not Enhanced by privatization. The success of the privatization plan depends on what we plan to do with money earned through privatization programme.

References

Sarvepalli Gopal (1983): Jawaharlal Nehru—A Biography, Vol II, Oxford University Press, Bombay.

Dr. B.D. Kulkarni (1996): Economic Analysis and Business Policy, Everest Publishing House, Pune.

Brecher Michael (1959): Nehru: A Political Biography, Oxford University Press, New York.

K.T. Narsimha Char: Profile of Jawaharlal Nehru: The Book Centre Private Ltd., Bombay.

S.K. Misra and V.K. Puri (1996): Indian Economy—Its Development Experienced, Himalaya Publishing House, Bombay.

11

Socio-economic Ideas of Nehru on Indian Industrialisation

A. Arangasami

INTRODUCTION

When Independence came, India had a slender Industrial base and Stagnant Agriculture. There was widespread want and poverty. Handicrafts were decimated and the colonial administration had created a few islands of domestic conflict and dislocated economic life. Indian economy in Nehru's words, "was in a servile state with its splendid- strength caged up hardly daring to breathe freely; its people poor beyond compare, short lived and incapable of resisting disease and epidemic; illiteracy rampant; vast areas devoid of all sanitary or medical provision and unemployment on a prodigiow scale both among middle classes and mass". The average intake of food was below the accepted nutritional standards; the consumption of cloth stood at less than 12 yards per capita and housing was deficit. On the whole, the Indian economy a typically backward present agrarian low income economy with rigidities in its institutional framework and structural disproportionalities.

Jawaharlal Nehru as the first prime minister of India realized that "the promise of freedom could be greatly strengthened" He squarely put the problem as one of augmenting of standard of living the mass supply them with their needs, give them the *Lecturer (S.S) in Economics, Sir Theagaraya College, Chennai, Tamil Nadu wherewithal to lead a decent life, to help them to progress and advance not only in regard to material things but in regard to cultural and spiritual things also." It was essentials to rebuild the economy, to lay the foundations for industrial and scientific progress, and to expand educational, the social service. The background object and astonishing poverty called for designing a national plan encompassing all aspects of economic and social life.

NEHRU'S IDEAS ON GLOBALIZATION

His ideas are still very useful in terms of Globalization, Liberalization and economic reform. In the context of Globalization makes an attempt to examine the role of the socio-economic ideas of Nehru.

The Globalization implies a regime of comparative markets with no entry or exist barrier. Globalization in the professed goal of the on going economic reforms in India. Globalization means increasing integration of developing countries into the global Economy. It is activated through Liberalization of trade and capital market increasing Dismantling barriers to the international trade ability of goods and services and the ability of capital.

The economic reform programmes with Globalization marketization and Privatization have been launched since 1991. The stress of the programme has been to bring about a real market economy and seek an increased role of Indian economy with global economic system. The core components of reform programmes are.

1. Industrial policy reforms.
2. Trade policy and exchange control reform.
3. Financial sector reforms
4. Public enterprises reforms

5. Fiscal reforms
6. Increased direct foreign investment.

The current economic reform being carried out by Government of India has been described as basically a shift from central planning to the market driven economic system. India has the potential of becoming one of largest common market in the world and there can be great of division of labour freedom of mobility of capital and labour as well as of greater international trade. The implementation of a policy of Liberalization on various fronts was not only a bad step but a challenging one.

The economic policy reforms since 1991 have resulted on some fundamental changes in trade, financial, fiscal, industrial and foreign investment policies, survival stabilization measures have been introduced to tackle the problem of liquidity.

NEHRU AND NEW ECONOMIC POLICY

The New Economic Policy introduced since 1991 made if clear that India can faster as part of the world economy and not in isolation. Our trade policy must therefore create an environment that will provide story impetus to exports and render export activity profitable. The package of trade policy reforms announced in July 1991 aimed at access to high technology and world markets.

The economic reform thus aimed at strengthening export incentives eliminating a substantial volume of import licensing and optimal import compression in view of the BOP situation. The new policy aims at reducing the interference of government if technology by Indian firms particularly in high technology and high investment priority industries.

The new industries-cum-trade policies thus reveal an "input liberalizing-cum- export promoting," or what we can on ODI strategy.

Have always aimed at reduction in the incidence and severity of poverty across masses scattered over different regions and states. It is well known result that the decline in the incidence of rural poverty is very closely associated with the growth in the agricultural sector particularly in the agricultural productivity over the years. The record of poverty alleviation varied significantly across state over India and across rural and urban areas. Education and health care are two important elements in the process of elevation of one's will being and capability in the long run.

Unless the programmes for rural infrastructure development like extension of irrigation facilities and land distribution are accompanied by carefully thought out schemes for taxing the beneficiaries of rural investment and development and investigating the surplus so acquired for the development and investigating the surplus so acquired for the betterment of the true have note in the rural economy, the macro programmes like Jawahar Rojgar Yojana (JRY) and or land distribution, even if meticulously implemented will not be able to eradicate poverty among the bottom layers of income distribution.

The principle of decentralized decision-making has been accepted in the Tenth Five Year Plan to strengthen and effective implementation of rural poverty alleviation programmes in our country. Efforts should be taken to devise institutional mechanisms to pre-empty differentiation of benefits among the rural poor as a consequence of adoption and implementation of poverty alleviation programme in general.

The Indian Economic policy had a complete turn around in 1991, when we had chosen to shift from the phase of the command economy to the phase of the economic Liberalization Privitisation and Globalization (LPG). It is however, worth noting that basic motivation of initiating these reforms has been to make the poor people of the country better off in the immediate run. Some economist feared that the incidence of poverty will shoot up following relaxation of state controls and reliance on market based incentives to drive the forces of growth to the alter neglect of distributive support policies.

Except for the first year after introduction of reforms when the rate of inflation was not still diminished, there has not been any remarkable increase in the incidence of rural poverty, and urban poverty in fact fluctuated, first rising since 1991, and then falling. There is no conclusive evidence of immunization of the living condition of the poor because of introduction of reform package, as the economy experienced good monsoon in successive years. There is no immediate prospect of large scale reforms in our agricultural sectors to step up its growth rate, and hence poverty reduction through the process of Liberalization and Globalization seems unliked. But there are also direct impacts that are possible with globalization and liberalization likely to affect growth and profitability of indigenous industrial enterprises, the renewed dependence on the agrarian economy for further employment creation may have the effects of reducing the rural wage rates in the medium run, which can be circumvented only by raising the productivity of the agricultural sector through diversification and product base.

The socio-economic idea of Nehru's can easily be assessed in terms of Globalization, Liberalization, Privatization and economic reforms. His ideas were mainly consisted of.

A. Laissez—Fair Policy (i.e. Theoretical freedom of each individual to work)

1. Unlimited acquisitiveness or profit motive;
2. Free enterprises in a state of perfect competition;
3. Relationship between state and individual;
4. Democracy under laissez-fair;
5. Joint sector and mixed economy;
6. Position of poor consumer;
7. Position of poor producer or investor.

B. Agriculture and Land Reform and Rural Development

1. Zamindar;
2. Land reforms: objectives evils and measures;
3. Infrastructural development;
4. Agricultural credit and inputs;
5. Co-operative farming;
6. Panchayat raj, rural development;

C. Industry

1. Industrialization-Industrial revolution;
2. Large scale industries;
3. Cottage and small scale industries;
4. Khadi industries;
5. Community service;
6. Co-operation;

D. Capital formation

E. Population problems and Policy

F. Public Finance

1. Taxation;
2. Public Expenditure;
3. Public debt;
4. Deficit budget;
5. Foreign exchange reserves;

G. Stages of Economic Growth

H. Trade and Commerce

1. Balance of Payment;
2. Term of Trade;
3. Direction of Trade;
4. Trade Policy
5. Foreign Exchange
6. Private and Public Investment
7. Multinational Corporation

I. Economic Order

Scientific and Technological progress there role, problems, etc.

J. Socialism

1. Socialism and growth

2. Socialistic pattern of society
3. Problem of inequality and injustice poverty, etc.
4. Problem of unemployment and rural backwardness
5. Regional imbalance

K. Public Sector

Role, objectives working problems, etc.

L. Planning Needs, Objectives, Forms, Evils, Merits and demerits Relevance, etc.

M. Education, Health, etc.

The concentration of poverty in a particular group suggests the decision-makers are not receptive to signals, especially form the fringes and national potential is being wasted. "Governments need to move to non-discriminatory policies and help those in extreme poverty."

The view of Nehru are globally acknowledged. To quote world development reports 2003 (p. 182). Accelerated growth in productivity and income can eliminate poverty and enhance prosperity is developing countries. This growth need to be achieved at the same time critical ecosystem services are improved and social fabric that underpins development is strengthened.

Concern stems from evidence that getting the world on a sustainable part is problematic.

1. In many developing countries, productivity is low, growth is stagnant and unemployment is high.
2. Income inequality is rising. Average income in the wealthiest 20 countries is 37 times that in the poorest 20 countries—Twice the ratio in 1970.
3. Stress on the environment is increasing, Fisheries are being over exploited,
   Soil degraded, coral reefs destroyed, tropical forests lost, air and water polluted.
4. The financial transfers to address these issues one for from adequate, even though the resources are available.

OBJECTIVES OF SOCIO-ECONOMIC IDEAS OF NEHRU

The main socio-economic ideas of Jawaharlal Nehru was to make India, economically strong stable and self-sufficient so that economic and political freedom might be meaningful. His all these ideas and thinking should be viewed in the context of the Indian Social and economic getting. His ideas of mixed economy, planning socialism, Industrialization, agriculture and co-operation, etc., were all directed towards a strong foundation of the shattered economy of India.

India suffered from inefficiency of production, inequality of distribution and instability of economic life at the time of economic planning. The result of his socio-economic ideas during the period ranging from 1950-51 to 1965-66 was an overall strengthening of the Indian Economy and its heading towards desired goals. The national Income of constant (1948-49) prices went up from Rs. 8850 Crores in 1950-51 to Rs. 14930 crores in 1964-65 and the per capita income from Rs. 247.5 to Rs. 314.4 (both at constant prices). During 15 years index number of agricultural production of all commodities (1949-50=100) rose from 95.6 to 157.6 and index of industrial production (1956=100) increased from 73.5 in 1951 to 174.8 in 1964-65.

Similar progress was register in the power generation, construction of road and development of other means of transport and communication. In addition to there material achievements, consequent upon his economic ideas and their execution, there was a change in the motivation pattern and wage of thinking and doing of the Indian people. In fact, the Indian economy changed from a position of stagnation and tradition of dynamism and modernity.

UN-FLICTING FAITH IN CO-OPERATION

Jawaharalal Nehru had an unflicting faith in co-operation because to him co-operation helps actively in effectuation of democratic socialism and peaceful economic change. According to him," I have no doubt theoretically in co-operation. Co-operation working is good in every single department of human activities. It is a better way of life like a true and veteran co-operator he stood for a principle of voluntaryism and self-help through mutual help."

CONCLUSION

Several Third World Nations including India as passing through a rather difficult and painful transition. The package of economic reforms constitutes a sharp turn around in policy thinking compared to the licence-permit raj built up during 1960s and 1970s. The main purpose of globalization and Jawaharlal Nehru's socio-economic ideas has been to make India economically strong stable self-reliant and economic and political freedom more relevant and meaningful. The deviation from the thinking and ideas of Jawaharlal Nehru is present global perspective has also resulted insufficient production, unequal distribution and unstable economic and political situation. After completion of decade of globalization and liberalization a critical comparative and analytical analyses has compelled everybody to give top priority to Nehruvian models along with economic reforms and globalization for sustainable, balanced economic growth and stronger ceremony and to achieve socio-economic and welfare in the new millennium.

Nehruvian ideas are still quite relevant and useful. These cannot be overlooked and neglected in India and other developing nations. Nehruvian ideas compel policy-makers to rethink the role of state in the new millennium.

References

Govt. of India Eighth Five Year Plan, 1992-97, Vol. 2, Planning Commission, New Delhi (1992).

Datt, Ruddar (1994), "Jobless Growth Implementation of New Economic Policies", *Indian journal of Industrial Relation,* Vol. 29, April 1995.

Govt. of India Act, 1935.

Maheshwar, Neerja (1977), Economics of Jawaharlal Nehru, Deep & Deep Publications, New Delhi.

Nehru Speeches, Vol. 4, Speech in Bangalore, February 1962.

Kaushik P.D. 1964 Congress Ideology and programme, Allied Publishers Pvt. Ltd., Bombay, 1964.

Desai, P.B., 1979, Planning in India, Vikas Publishing House, New Delhi.

12

Nehrujee and Industrialisation

ANIL THAKUR

Pt. Jawaharlal Nehru was fully conscious of the fact that industrialization, establishment and encouragement of large scale industries *vis-à-vis* small scale and cottage industries were fundamental to the economic development and modernization of the Indian economy. In his First Note to the National Planning committee on Dec. 21, 1938 he said, "It is clear, therefore, that not only is it open to this Committee and to the Planning Commission to consider the whole question of large-scale industries in India, in all its aspects, but that the Committee will be failing in its duty if it did not do so. There can be no planning if such Planning does not include big industries. But in making out plans we have to remember the basic Congress policy of encouraging cottage Industries."[1] His other note read, "It is equally clear that the rapid development of large scale machine industry is an urgent need of the country, without industrialization no country can have polish or economic freedom.....witnout industrialization also the rapid and effective raising of the standard of the people is not possible. Key industries, Defense industries and Public utilities must be developed on a large scale...."[2]

After the attainment of political independence in 1947 the A.I.C.C. which met at Delhi in Nov. 1947 passed certain resolutions and at its instance the Economic programmer committee was appointed under the chairmanship of Pt. Jawaharlal Nehru. The committee recommended that a quick and progressive rise in the standard of living of the people should be the primary consideration governing all economic activities. It outlined a programmer of industrial development in which industries producing articles of food and clothing and other consumer's goods should constitute the decentralized sector and large-scale and small- scale industries should be developed on a supplementary-complementary relationship pattern."

In the collection of Nehru's speeches (1946-64 in V Vols.) his emphasis on industrial development of the country is quite discernible. In a talk broadcast from New Delhi, on Aug. 15, 1947 he said, "And we have also to promote industrialization country and thus to the national dividend which can be equitably distributed."[4] To his mind the industrial development was not only a step towards economic development but a great bulwark of national defense. One of the portions of his speech delivered at the Industries conference, New Delhi, Dec. 18, 1947 read, "In fact, in war, weapons and all manner of things are necessary. If you are industrially strong, you can build up your army and navy and air force at short notice. If you depend on buying your warships and everything else in a foreign country and that source dries up, it is quite useless to have only a few thousand men shouting about war. So that in the ultimate analysis, even this war business bring you back to production and the growth of industries, small and big."[5] According to him industrialization was a must for the country both form internal and external viewpoint.

As the years rolled by and economic problem of the country increased in number and intensity, Pt. Nehru's zeal for industrializing India was sharpened. While making speech at the Twenty fourth Annual Session of the Federation of Indian Chambers of Commerce and Industry, New Delhi on March 31, 1951 he remarked, "The very things that have growth of technology, industrialization and the rest—and may I say in passing that I and all in favor of the industrialization of India."[6] On March 21, 1956 he said in the Lok Sabha, "Let us admit for the moment that we are proceeding along right lines—those right lines being the industrialization of the country which is good from the economic point of view as well as for defence."[7]

Pt. Nehru knew in fully well that there should be a balance between heavy industry and other categories of industries, In a speech to All-India Congress Committee, In doer, January 4, 1957 he said, "we believe generally that the industrial progress of India will depend and must depend on the growth of heavy industry." There will be on industrial progress unless machines are made here, unless iron and steel are manufactured here. At the same time we have always to remember that unless we balance heavy industry with the growth of village industry, we shall produce and unbalanced structure which may crack up and fall to pieces. Therefore, the importance of village industry, household industry, cottage industry and small industry is very great."[8] In his opinion this sort of balance and coordination between heavy and light industries was conducive to a increasing balanced production and large employment opportunities.

During the Chinese aggression there were some people who wanted to scrap the Third Five Year Plan. Pt. Nehru opposed them tooth and nail and made this fact clear that planning went a long way in industrializing and strengthening the country and there by kin driving the hostile forces back. In a speech made at the meeting of the standing committee of the National development Council, New Delhi, on Jan. 18, 1963 he said, "In fact you know that the big and powerful countries, and thereby, gained strength, whether for war or for peaceful progress."[9]

The above brief survey of his views on industrial development reveals to us that he was enthusiastic to maintain equilibrium between basic, heavy and machine building industry and light industry. But in spite of this fact it remains incontrovertibly true that basic industries and their development merited his attention most. In view of India's backwardness especially industrial, his love for heavy and large scale industries was natural and understandable. Had it not been so, the Indian economy would have remained depressed, unbalanced and colonial for years to come.

From his boyhood to the end of his life Pt. Nehru remained interested in science and technology. As already stated, in his view the growth of science and technology was essential to liberate the Indian masses from the shackles of outdated dogmas, social taboos and superstitions and to convert the Indian economy from stagnation too self-generation and dynamism. Addressing the Indian Science Congress he expressed, "Politics led me to Economics, land this led me inevitably to science and the scientific approach to all out problems and to life itself. It was science alone that could solve these problems of hunger and poverty, of insanitation and illiteracy, of superstition and deadening custom and tradition, of vast resources running to waste."[10] Panditji was fully convinced of the fact that development of science and its offspring technology would improve methods of production in all types of industries and agriculture. During the course of his Inaugural Address of the Azad Memorial Lectures on Feb. 22, 1959 he said very clearly, "There is no future for us without science and technology."[11]

The above view of Pt. Jawaharlal Nehru was responsible for the enunciation of the First and the Second Industrial Policy in 1948 and 1956 respectively. No all-around and balanced industrial development was possible without announcing the Industrial Policy as there was an atmosphere of panic and uncertainty in the world of investors and industrialists especially foreign industrialists. It had to be made favorable and congenial.

Notes and References

1. Report: National Planning Committee, p. 37. (Appendix Chairman's Note on Congress Policy).
2. *Ibid.*, p. 46.
3. Resolution on Economic Policy and Programmer (1924-54), pp. 30-34, A.I.C.C., New Delhi.
4. Independence and After, p. 8.
5. *Ibid.*, p. 152.
6. Jawaharlal Nehru's Speeches (1949-53), p. 565.

7. Jawaharlal Nehru's Speeches (1953-57), p. 42.
8. *Ibid.*, p. 46.
9. Jawaharlal Nehru's Speeches (1957-63), p. 161.
10. Jawaharlal Nehru, the Unity of India, pp. 175-77.
11. Jawaharlal Nehru, India Today and Tomorrow, p. 4.

13

Economic Policy of Pandit Jawaharlal

S.R. Jagtap and C.S. Jagtap

INTRODUCTION

Until 1947, India was ruled by kings and dictators. No Indian king was self sufficient and powerful enough to give the nation wide unifying power. As there was no unifying Indian power to rule the country it effected the progress of the country in each and every field, i.e. political, economical, social, Technological, educational, etc. All the invaders foreigners adopted the policies which were not in favour of India. We can imagine the poor condition of India in each and every field.

PANDIT NEHRU'S IDEOLOGY OF THE SOVEREIGN COUNTRY

From ancient times India has been a staunch follower of peace. It did not bound itself to any of the International groups of the countries such as America, Russia and also kept loof itself from NAATO, SEATO, VERSA, etc. nor did it allow any country to use its ground for military campaign

It is said:

> "India did not belong to any power blocks, India's non alignment is a positive, dynamic, neutralism in which a country acts independently and decides its position on each international issue on the merits of the cause."

In 1950 India accepted China as a communist country though America was against this policy of India.

In 1950—For the peaceful economic development of the country Pandit Nehru and China's Prime Minister Chau-n-Li followed the joint panchsheel (Five Principle plan) plan, i.e.

(1) To Respect the sovereignty and unity of the nation.
(2) No interference in internal politics of the country.
(3) No invasion policy.
(4) To fellow the principles of equality and economic co-operation.
(5) Economical and Political Cooperation to each other.

CONSTRUCTION OF BASIC PRINCIPLES OF ECONOMIC POLICY

After the Second World War the world was divided into two groups. Under the leadership of America, the countries which followed 'Open economic policy' were united and were called NAATO. The another group followed the policy of organised economy. The World's economic and Technical dominance were divided into these two groups and these two groups were trying to influence India. But Pandit Nehru who had lop sided study of India though both policies dangerous for the country. On the contrary he initiated to organise the another group of the countries having some ideology and this group followed the 'policy of loofness'

At the same time he kept good relationship with both the groups, i.e. America and Russia. At this time America and its followers refused to help "Iron and Aluminium" projects of India. At that time Russia and its followers were agreed to help these projects on the condition that this project should be of public sector Russian group' was looking dominant and powerful so Pandit Nehru in 1954 included the words socio-democracy into the Indian constitution.

NEHRU'S POLICY OF INDIAN ECONOMY AND PUBLIC SECTOR

Nehru had deep study of Indian Economy. After independence India had to progress in many fields. It was a backward country. India is agricultural country and it's industrial development was very poor. The problem of unemployment people was a big question. The level of investment and saving was decreased. There was a dearth of supporting facilities. At such time Indian economy was in urgent need of some support (Big support). The private sector were unable to support the problems because.

(a) Private sectors did not have sufficient capital.
(b) Private sectors did not have Administrative system.
(c) Private sectors did not have power to take risk of investing for long-term.

So it was a times demand to increase the speed of Agricultural and industrial production by proper planning and investment.

When Pandit Nehru was a prime minister of India (1947-62) many social and public sectors projects were established. Like public sector, Pandit Nehru felt the need of centralize network of invention.

PANDIT NEHRU AN EXPONENT OF PLANNED ECONOMIC DEVELOPMENT

The economic development of India was very poor. To develop the economic condition of India. Pandit Nehru followed the policy of planned economic development, inspired by Nehru, National planning committee (1938) had started its efforts of planned economic development.

This committee had decided that:

(a) Private property
(b) Industries of national interest
(c) Railway
(d) Waterways
(e) Air ways transportations

SHOULD BE UNDER GOVERNMENT CONTROL

Industries and factories in which there is danger of monopoly. Should be under Government control.

In 1950 Pandit Nehru had established planning commission. First Five Year Plan was applied in 1951-56 by the commission. Gradually and Nehru established principles of planned economic development by creating various plans.

Nehru wanted economic development by establishing basic facilities. For it he appointed committee under the guidance of Prof. Mahalanobis heavy plants had given priority from the Second Five Year Plan. There was much difference between the development concepts of Mahatma Gandhi and Nehru. Mahatma Gandhi was in favour of agriculture and small industries but Nehru was in favour of Modern Technology, Modern Industries. But these two divergent concepts were collaborated for the development of the country.

OBSERVATIONS

Pandit Nehru started 'On age of revolution' by establishing public sector and centralize network of invention. But this public sector was failure because of the following reasons:

(1) It was administrated by the formal rules and laws.
(2) Only 20% of the servants workers were working sincerely.
(3) As there was no personal interest of the administrators and workers in to the sectors so

they did not have any interest in profit and loss. They did not struggled for profit of the sector. Because the total investment was Indian Government.

Because of the failure of Public sector countries like, Russia, China who believed in Public Sector turned towards private sectors. Here one point should be noted that because of the public sector other business industries, etc. of private sectors were flourished so the importance of public sector can not be ruled out. Public sector has a lion's share in the development of India.

References

N.S. Dixit Modern Europe (1780 to 1965).
Prof. N.B. Vaidya, Economy of Vidarbha.
M.J. Akbar, Nehru the making of India.
Dr. Suman Vaidya, History of Russia 1860-1964.
Daily News Paper *Lokmat* of 24 Oct. 2007.

14

An Insight into the Economic Philosophy of Pt. Jawaharlal Nehru

I.D. SINGH

Pt. Jawaharlal Nehru is regarded as one of the architects of modern India. In reality, since the ancient times, economic ideas and activities throughout the world have been guided by the economic philosophies and concepts propounded developed and popularized by a number of economists, philosophers, social reformers, scholars and political thinkers. The economic philosophy and concepts have been basically based upon the philosophy of life. The philosophy of life is based either on idealism or on materialism. So far as India is concerned, it is believed that the economic thoughts of the country have since long been guided more by idealism than by materialism. Whatever might be the economic philosophy and thoughts in past, the Indian economy was the largest one in the world for the entire thousands of years of the first millennium, contributing nearly 30 per cent of the world GDP. But under nearly 200 years of colonial rule India's contribution to global GDP reduced to merely 4.2 percent in 1950. After gaining independence, undoubtedly, India had enormous challenges to face by any standards.

At the dawn of independence, therefore, a consensus was evolved on the broad strategy of all-around development, known as Nehruvian consensus. The salient features of the consensus were that India was to embark upon a path of rapid, multi-pronged, allround development based on its political and economic sovereignty backed by rapid industrialization with equity and justice. In this way, growth, sovereignty, equity, democracy and secularism were to be the corner stones of the advancement of resurgent India.

As a matter of fact, Pt. Jawaharlal Nehru was not only a great patriot, thinker and statesman, but he was also a citizen of the world with a passion for science and technology as also modernity. The basic contributions of Pt. Nehru are democracy, secularism, planning and socialism followed by civil liberty.

Pt. Nehru was an ardent believer in democracy. He believed in equity, social justice, free speech, civil liberty, adult franchise and the rule of law. Pt. Nehru was fully aware that in our country there are numerous religions, such as Hinduism, Islam, Christianity, Buddhism, Jainism, Zororianism, Sikhism, etc. Hence, he was a firm believer of secularism. Apart from democracy and secularism, he took keen interest in science, technology and modernization. The concept of mixed economy is believed to be propounded and implemented by Pt. Nehru. He, with a view to rapid industrialization and growth, adopted medium term plan (five year plan) suitably divided into annual plans. The creation of public enterprises as model employers was the gift of Pt. Nehru. In fact, Pt. Nehru considered plan as an essentially integrated approach to rapid socio-economic development of the country. Similarly, Pt. Nehru believed in democratic planning where all the citizens, the poor and the rich, equally may take the benefits of development.

With a view to evolve plans, the National Planning Commission was setup. Pt. Nehru was the firm supporter of heavy, basic and mother industries whereas Gandhiji believed in small and cottage industries. Actually, Pt. Nehru was highly impressed and influenced by the strategy of planning followed by the then Soviet Union.

Another important contribution made by Pt. Nehru was socialism. He believed in socialistic pattern of society for which he worked till his last bread. Later on, socialistic pattern of society became an act of policy.

Finally, it may be concluded that the policies followed by Pt. Nehru proved right for our country. His emphasis on democracy, human dignity, civil liberty, secularism, Planned development, socialism, national integration, world peace, science and technology became the guiding force for the allround development of the country.

15

Economic Philosophy of Jawaharlal Nehru

BHARTI SHAH

On 15th August 1947, India became an independent country. After the independence the pride and joy of India's attainment of independence and statehood was marred by pain and suffering.

Nehru as a statesman of that time. Could gave a practical shape to the dreams and has played a key role as a leader of mass. He had infinite faith in humanity and its capacity to survive every disaster. He inspired confidence and led people on the road to sanity. He helped congress to define its goal, objectives and spell out a political and economic philosophy. In all the circumstances he remained the symbol of tolerance and season and tried successes to shape the dreams of India.

In his own wards....

> "Every epoch has its own economic structure and the characteristics of its depend upon for the country has progressed"

Along the economic scale the colonial societies were integrated in the capitalize system. The classical Marxism postulates gave rise to he social Formation, in which there are more than one mode of production. In non-colonised society its creates and constitute principal contradiction.

As a philosopher he conceived, fathered and instituted large scale social and economic planning in India, which besides western science and technology, happens to be a most important source for the social changes in the country.

From 1932 and afterward he was attracted by the communist ideas of economic equality and a classless society. Due to this he drafted a election manifestoes for 1937 and 1945 with the socialist intent. He instituted planning as a tool of socio-economic changes. And laid a foundation for democratic state and culture. His ideas were tempered by the compulsion of a backward economy. After all these it was a challenge and burden to find nationalism, an ideology which could hold the various together. Nehru was interested the deeper philosophical aspect of history and his view was "It is future that is important". The history provides preamble.

Nehru was the architect of India's industrialization. His fascination for socialism material progress through forced industrialisation. With transition from Gandhi to Nehru becomes material well-being of the society and more specially for the poor. He had soft corner for Fabian socialism and was a romantic socialist. The German model of development also impressed him. His thinking for the role of power was philosophical and trusting for power, which was needed to achieve socialism.

He believed that,

> "Power was powerless without the knowledge." The fundamental problem of 20th century and the legacy of the 19th century were to use to power. The knowledge was totally related to "Science and the aim were to abolish poverty and to rise the production."

He writes in "Discovery of India" 'it can hardly be challenged that the context of modern world no country can be politically and economically independent. Ever with in the framework of international independent, unless it is highly industrialized and developed its power resources to up most. A country cannot achieve or maintain high standards of living and liquidate poverty without the aid of modern technology in every walk of life. Industrially back ward country will disturb the equilibrium of the world and will help to be more aggressive of developed economics. The economy largely on the basis of cottage and small-scale industries will not solve the problems and cannot maintain the freedom. It the technology demands the big machine it must be accepted.

After 1948 the government of India brought out the first industrial policy resolution under the stewardship of Nehru. In his view India as an underdeveloped economy with limited capital and skill, both public and private sector's development has to play an important role for increase in production and higher standards of living of masses is to achieve.

Thus Nehru was conscious of the potentials of the industrial technological civilization and its capacity to transform an economy of scarcities in to that of abundant.

> "Those who lean too much on others tend to become weak and helpless themselves"
>
> —*Nehru*

In 1947 we got political freedom but only political freedom is meaningless unless there is economic freedom. The man who is starving required economic freedom. And mixed economy was a golden path to achieve the economic freedom. Nehru was a strong supporter of mixed economy.

In capitalism the rich people are those who have plenty of surplus and the poor have none at all. A person who does not work at all gets the surplus and the worker who works hard gets no part if its. Nehru believed that this is a very silly arrangement and the inequality craves so many problems. Poverty becomes a challenge problem and curse for human being.

As the foremost modernist and leader Nehru was the first to emphasized on the need to provide an economic dimension to the freedom of India. He emphasized for a clear assessment of India's resources and its capacities.

The situation created aftermath of partition made Nehru cautious and led him to propound a novel variation of socialism and economic planning. He tried to socialization of the vacuum and the concept of mixed economic was enunciated.

Mixed economic seemed to him to offer optimum economic organization for the development of country. After 1947 he immerged as major propounded at the philosophy of mixed economy and according to him both public and private sector have important role to play. His choice of mixed economy was based on four considerations.

1. A classless society based on co-operative effort with opportunities for all.
2. To refashion the social and economic structure so that they may promote the happiness for our people.
3. To establish a system which could release economic growth and social justice and the democratic rights of common citizen.
4. Fair distribution of political and economic power.

Nehru believed that Idealism is the realism of tomorrow and while we would be idealistic, we have to be realistic also mixed economy alone possessed the flexibility and resilience to accommodate changes in human activates. The democratic method of change would release a vast amount of hidden psychological resources of the people and would proud a great asset to promote economic development. He confessed that economic that hurt moral well-being of a nation immoral and sinful.

The first three five year plans of India's bore and indelible print of his thinking and personality. His definition of planning as to exercise of intelligence to deal with facts and situations as they are and find a wag to solve the problems.

Because of his thinking in Awadi resolution 1955 he told that planning should take place with a view to establishment of socialistic pattern of society. He emphasized on producing more wealth. Nehru played a revolutionary role in providing dimension and a progressive thrust to the process of social changes in India.

Being a great socialistic image of the world democratic socialism and a messenger of world peace he devoted whole life to realize the dream. To give reality to our dream we have to work hard and will be resulted in peace. Freedom prosperity and humanity. The people will come closely to knit together. Non-violence would enable India to be a role model of world peace and prosperity. The non-alignment policy served India's interests in more tangible terms and provided free access to capital and technical skill of industrial power.

The major element of international outlook was "Panchshila" as a policy of international relations and it will provide co-existence, peace and tolerance. The attitude will be "live and let live" to avoid a co-destruction the peaceful co-extended is inevitable format. Thus the general since of non-alignment became an integrated part of inter national pattern and entered in to the climate of world thought.

Nehru wanted the educational system with the aim of to promote the values of socialistic society and to weaken the desire of property and gain. He had the foresight for democratic socialism is feasible in under developed society and the ability to frame a model which this practical. He started India on the right and proper road and set it on the path. Of a peaceful development and growth. His effort was pioneering one India's nation building an he wrote that "realize we present and look at future... to change the rhythm of life and make it an tune with this present and future.

Thus democratic socialism was his creed and for him socialism was an extension of liberal values the areas of human rights widened. It allows increasingly larger section of the people to become beneficiaries of continue socio-economic transform.

In Indian economy's overall performance a sharp contrast to what would have been expected from Nehru's design to growth with the framework of mixed economy. No such development has take place as Nehru dreamed. In fact it resulted in under utilization of resources on a scale. Eventhough he was an architect of "future India." His permanent achievement have started out after his death more clearly.

The philosophy and ideology at Nehru were shaped by number of national and international events, personal contacts, wide reading and introspection. He was a philosopher, entrepreneur and spokesman of India's towards the outside world. He provided an economic orientation and fused the element of modernity, a radical social economic programme in the mass movement.

He was a gardener who cultivated a growth by providing the appropriate environment.

References

"Discovers of India", Jawaharlal Nehru, Penguin Books, India, 2004.

Wit and Wisdom of Gandhi, Nehru and Tagore, By N.B. Sen., New Book Society of India, 1968.

Nehru in His Own Works, By Ramnarayan Chaudhary, Navajivan Publication House, Ahmedabad, 1964.

Jawaharlal Nehru, "A Study in Ideology and Social Change, By R.D. Dube, Mittal Publication, 1988.

The Eight, Dr. D.T. Lakdawala Memorial Lecture, By Dr. Anil Patel, (Feb. 2000).

16

An Analysis of Economic Philosophy of Nehru

R.S. NANDAL

Jawaharlal Nehru was a great leader and statesman and guided the destiny of India, as the first Prime Minister of our India for fourteen years. As a result of his vision and dynamic personality, India came to occupy a coveted position in the comity of nations. Nehru evolved his own approach of democratic socialism for putting the backward and exploited country on the path of progress. Although Jawaharlal Nehru denied his place to be called a political philosopher, yet we cannot overlook his contribution to the theory of democratic socialism. Though Nehru was not an economist, but as a Prime Minister and Chairman of the Planning Commission, he guided his economic ideas and economic policy to the policy-makers for the socio-economic development of the nation. His economic philosophy has been discussed in this paper.

Meanwhile, Jawaharlal saw in his 1952 electoral victor an affirmation of popular support for the principles of socialism and anti-imperialism that he had begun articulating publicly in 1939 campaign. Though not formally a Marxist,

Jawaharlal had revealed a susceptibility to Marxian analyses of historical forces in his early writings. At the Lucknow Congress in 1936 Nehru had gone further, declaring: I am convinced that the only key to the solution of world's problems and of India's problems lies in socialism. I see no way of ending the poverty, the vast unemployment, the degradation and the subjection of the Indian people except through socialism. That involves vast and revolutionary changes in our political and social structure, a new civilization radically different from the present capitalist order. Some glimpse we can have of this new civilization in the territories of the USSR. If the future is full of hope it is largely because of Soviet Russia.

But Nehru was not in favour of orthodox socialism. Nehruvian socialism was a curious amalgam of idealism (of a particularly English Fabian Variety), a passionate if somewhat romanticized concern for the struggling masses, a Gandhian faith in self-reliance, a corollary distrust of western capital and a modern belief in 'scientific' methods like planning. Nehru was too much of a Gandhian to be a fellow-traveller of the Soviet Union, though he shared the admiration for triumphs of the 1917 revolution commonly felt by leftists of his generation. But he always put nationalism before ideology: convinced that the communists' loyalties were extra territorial, he demanded of a band of communists waving their hammer-and-sickle banner during the 1952 campaign, 'Why don't you go and live in the country whose flag you are carrying?' (They replied, in staggering ignorance of their critic: 'Why don't you go to New York and live with the wall street imperialists'?

Jawaharlal saw Indian capitalism as weak and concentrated in a few hands, to him the state was the only guarantor of the economic welfare of ordinary people. Some degree of planning was probably unavoidable; even the Bombay business community drew up a plan in 1944 (called the Bombay plan) for India's rapid industrialization. There was certainly a need for the state to invest some resources where the private sector would not particularly in infrastructure and in agriculture. The economist Jagdish Bhagwati suggested that what India needed at the time was probably socialism on the land and capitalism, Nehru prompted the Government of India to adopt an Industrial Policy Resolution in April 1948 that granted the state monopolies over railways, atomic energy and defence manufacturing as well as reserved rights relating to any new enterprises in a host of vital areas from coal and steel to ship building and communications.

Nehru's economic assumptions demonstrated that one of the lessons history teaches. is that history often teaches the wrong lessons: since the East India Company had come to trade and stayed on to rule? Nehru was instinctively suspicious of every foreign businessman, seeing in every western briefcase the thin end of a neo-imperial wedge. The Gandhian equation of political nationalism with economic self-sufficient only served to underscore Nehru's prejudice against capitalism, which was in his mind equated principally with the slavery of his people. Protectionism was inevitable result in Jawaharlal's mindset the essential corollary of political independence was economic independence. That this meant a far slower release from poverty for the Indian people he never understood.

In December 1954 the government, under Jawaharlal's prodding, formally adopted the goal of 'a socialistic pattern of society' of national economy. Within a year of the Second Five Year Plan enshrined industrial self-sufficiency as the goal, to be attained by a state controlled public sector which would be financed by higher income, wealth and sales taxes on India's citizenry. India would industrialize, Indians would pay for it, and the Indian government would run the sow. This approach was enshrined in an Industrial policy Resolution in 1956 that enshrined state capitalism in India while calling it socialism. Nehru placed bureaucrats rather than entrepreneurs upon the commanding heights, stifled initiative and investment, and spent the rest of his years in office presiding over a system that sought to regulate stagnation and divide poverty.

Nehru, like many third world nationalists, saw the imperialism that had subjugated his people as the logical extension of international capitalism, for which he therefore felt a deep mistrust. As an idealist profoundly moved by the poverty and suffering of the vast majority of his countrymen under colonial capitalism, Nehru was attracted to non-capitalist solutions for their problems. The idea of Fabian socialism captured an entire generation of English-educated Indians, Nehru was no exception. As a democrat, he saw the economic well-being of the poor as indispensable for their political empowerment, and he could not entrust its attainment to the rich. In addition, the seeming success of the soviet model which Nehru admired for bringing about the industrialization and modernization of a large, feudal and backward multinational state not unlike his own appeared to offer a valuable example for India. Like many other of his generation, Nehru thought that central planning, state control of the 'commanding heights' of the economy, and government directed development were the scientific and rational means of creating social prosperity and ensuring its equitable distribution.

Self-sufficiency and self reliance thus became the twin mantras: the prospect of allowing a western corporation into India to 'exploit' its resources immediately revived memories of British operation. 'Self-reliance' thus become a slogan and watch word: it guaranteed both political freedom and freedom for economic exploitation. The result was a state that ensured political freedom but presided over economic stagnation; that regulated entrepreneurial activity through a system of license, permits and quotas that promoted both corruption and inefficiency but did little to promote growth; that enshrined bureaucratic power at the expense of individual enterprise. For most of the first five decades since Independence, India pursued an economic policy of subsidizing unproductively, regulating stagnation and distributing poverty. Nehru called this socialism.

The logic behind this approach and for the dominance of public sector, was a compound of nationalism and idealism the conviction that items vital for the economic well being of Indians must remain in Indian hands-not the hands of Indians seeking to profit from such activity, but the disinterested hands of state, the mai-baap of all Indians. It was sustained by the assumption that the public sector was a good in itself, that, even if it was not efficient or productive or competitive, it employed large numbers of Indians, gave them a stake in worshipping at Nehru's 'new temples of modern India' and kept the country free from the clutches of profit-oriented capitalist who would enslave the country in the process of selling it what it needed. In this kind of thinking, performance was not a relevant criterion for judging the utility of the public sector. Its inefficiencies were masked by generous subsidies from the national exchequer, and combination of vested interests socialist ideologies, bureaucratic management, self protective trade unions and captive markets-kept it beyond political criticism.

But since the public sector was involved in economic activity, it was difficult for it to be entirely exempt from economic yardsticks. Yet, most of Nehru's public sector companies made losses, draining away the Indian taxpayers' money. Several of the state-owned companies even today are kept running merely to provide jobs less positively, to prevent the 'social costs' (job losses, poverty, political fall out) that would result from closing them down. All this we owe to Nehru. Since economic self-sufficiency was seen by the Nehruvians as the only possible guarantee of political independence, extreme protectionism was imposed: high tariff barriers (import duties of 350 percent were not common, and the top rate as recently as 1991 was 300 per cent), severe restrictions on entry of foreign goods, capital and technology, and great pride in the manufacture within India of goods that were obsolete, inefficient and shoddy.

The mantra of self-sufficiency might have made some sense if, behind these protectionist walls, Indian business had been encouraged to thrive. Despite the difficulties placed in their way by the British Raj, Indian corporate houses like those of the Birlas, Tatas and Kirloskars had build impressive business establishments by the time of Independence, and could conceivably, have taken on the world. Instead they found themselves being hobbled by regulations and restrictions, inspired by Nehru's socialist mistrust of the profit motive, on every conceivable aspect of economic activity, whether they could invest in a new product on a new capacity, where they could invest, how many people they could hire, whether they could fire them, what sort of expansion or diversification they could undertake, where they could sell and for how much. Initiative was stifled, government permission was mandatory before any expansion or diversification and a mind boggling array of permits and license were required before the slightest new undertaking. It is sadly impossible to quantify the economic losses inflicted on India over decades of entrepreneurs frittering away there energies in queuing for licenses rather than manufacturing products, paying bribes instead of hiring workers, wooing politicians instead of understanding consumers, getting things done' through bureaucrats rather than doing things for themselves. This, too, is Nehru's legacy.

The combination of internal controls and international protectionism gave India a distorted economy, under productive and grossly inefficient, making too flow goods of too low a quality at too high a price. Exports of manufactured goods grew at on annual rate of 0.1 percent until 1985, India's share of world trade fell by four fifths. Per capita income with a burgeoning population and a modest increase in GDP, anchored India firmly to the bottom third of the world rankings. The public sector, however, grew in size thought not in production, to become the largest in the world outside the communist bloc. Meanwhile, income disparities persisted, the poor remained mired in a poverty all the more wretched for the lack of means of escape from it in a controlled economy, the public sector sat entrenched on the 'commanding height's and looked down upon the toiling, overtaxed middle class, and only bureaucrats, politicians and small elite of protected businessmen flourished from the management of scarcity.

India's curse, Jagdish Bhagwati once observed, was to be afflicted by brilliant economists. Nehru had a weakness for such men: people like Mahalanobis, who combined intellectual brilliance and ideological wrong headedness in equal measure, but who was given his head by Jawaharlal to drive India's economy into a quicks and of regulatory red tape surroundings a mirage of planning. Nearby three decades after Nehru's death and long after the rest of the developing world (led by China) had demonstrated the success of a different path, a new Congress Prime Minister,

P.V. Narsimha Rao, launched the country on economic reforms. In place of the Nehruvian mantra of self-sufficiency, India was to become more closely integrated into the world economic system. This repudiation of Nehruvianism has survived and became part of the new conventional wisdom. Though there is no doubt that economic reform faces serious political obstacles in democratic India, and change is often made with the hesitancy of governments looking over their electoral shoulders, there is now a definitive rupture of the Nehruvian link between democracy and socialism: one is no longer the corollary of the other. The bogey of the East India company has finally been laid to rest.

Jawaharlal's approach to the economy was in many ways characteristics of the great flaw that afflicted many freedom fighters under Nehru, socialism (as he practiced it) became a national dogmas, to which his successors stayed loyal long after other developing countries, realizing the folly of his ways, had adopted a different path. Rajaji abandoned him to establish the Swatantra Party in 1959 explicitly in protest against Nehru's economic policies. Charan Singh was against the co-operative farming policy of Nehru and left the congress party. Later on this Nehruvian policy of co-operative farming in India was totally failure and the policy had to be abandon by the congress party. But Jawaharlal was able to resist tendencies in favour of promoting gradual change land reforms legislation. Some would point also to the development of India's industrial and intellectual infrastructure the dams, steel mills and institutes of technology that are the most visible result of Jawaharlal's leadership of India's economic policy. Yet others could argue both that these could have come through the private sector and that most of India's public sector industries were so inefficient that the country would actually have been better off without them. (Certainly the most successful steel plant in India was one set in the private sector by the Tatas-under British rule).

And yet there is no denying one vital legacy of Nehru's economic planning the creation of an infrastructure for excellence in science and technology, which has become a source of great self-confidence and competitive advantage for the country today. Nehru was always fascinated by science and scientists and he gave free rein to scientists in whom he had confidence to build high quality institutions. Jawaharlal's establishment of the Indian Institute of Technology has produced many of the finest minds and India's extraordinary leadership in the software industry is the indirect result of Jawaharlal Nehru's faith in scientific education.

While massive investments were made in the public sector enterprises under the Nehru's Economic Policy, no serious effort was made to run them on commercial lines. Their socio-economic character was used to plead for continued losses in some and very poor level of profits in others. Consequently, the Government contained to meet the losses out of the general exchange. Three serious mistakes were committed in their administration. First the positions at the top were given to general administrators rather than to professional experts. Thus the administrative bureaucracy of the country took charge of the PSU's as their chiefs. The second costly mistake was the failure to develop work-ethics among the employees. As a result, the PSU, developed huge wage-bill without commensurate increase in productivity. Thirdly, to satisfy certain lobbies big farmers, urban, consumers, etc. irrigation, fertilizer and electricity charges were kept below costs and huge subsidies were paid and as a result the state level public enterprises incurred heavy losses and these losses mounted further as year rolled by Nehru model of growth exhibited other weakness too. It failed to provide a national minimum level of living despite five plans. Nearly 40 percent of the population lived below the poverty line. The number of unemployed and under-employed was quite high and was increasing continuously. Inequalities of income and wealth had worsened and there was a growing concentration of economic power in the hands of a few. Land reforms were not properly implemented. It was in this context that the Janta party in 1977 adopted Gandhian model of economic growth which laid emphasis on the development of agriculture and rapid growth of cottage and village industries.

Nehru's mistrust of foreign capital kept out much needed foreign investment but paradoxically made India more dependent on foreign aid. This applied not just to industry, the First Plan's necessary emphasis on agriculture (essential following the loss of the 'national granary', West Punjab, to Pakistan) was so faulty in conception that by 1957 the country's agricultural output had dropped below that of 1953 and the government was soon importing food grains in a country where four out of five Indians scraped a living from the land.

The modest size of that economic pie was itself a Nehruvian legacy. Other countries put authoritarian political structures in place to drive economic growth, in some cases, notably in South-East Asia, this worked, and political liberalization has only slowly begun to follow in the wake of prosperity. Nehru recognized from start that prosperity without democracy would be untenable, for him the Central challenge in a pluralist society was to order national affairs to give everyone an even break, rather than to break even. In the process Nehru's India put the political before the economic horse, shackling it to statistic control that emphasized distributive justice above economic growth, and discouraged free enterprise and foreign investment. The reasons for this were embedded in the Indian freedom struggle: since the British had come to trade and stayed on the rule. Nehruvian nationalists were deeply suspicious of foreignness approaching them for commercial motives.

To conclude it is wrong to indict the Nehru model of growth on the ground that it had neglected agriculture and the small sector. It would be wrong to ignore the development of heavy industry and let us not forget that it is inadequate investment in the power development programmes and the insufficient generation and distribution of power which has led to the failure in agricultural sector. In fact there is no conflict between the heavy industry and the agricultural sector in the use of human and material resources. Both can be developed simultaneously. If the approach of balanced growth was valid in 1950's it is all the more so in 1990.

References

Shashi Tharoor: "Nehru The Invention of India", Viking Penguin Books India (P) Ltd., New Delhi-110017, India, Ed. 2003, pp 173-78, 240-44.

Rudar Datt and K.P.M. Sundarm: "Indian Economy", S. Chand and Company Ltd., Ram Nagar, New Delhi-110055, Ed. 2004, pp 169-70, 173.

17

Economic Thoughts of Jawaharlal Nehru

C.B. Sharma

INTRODUCTION

As the first Prime Minister of India Jawaharlal Nehru was famous for his economic thoughts and Social views. Since the man was a great freedom fighter he was well acquainted with the existing economic and social scenario of India on the eve of independence. He had seen the basic problems of Indian peasants particularly of Pratapgarh (U.P.)[1] and fought for their problem during British rule. In course of thinking and fighting for the miserable condition of peasants Nehru became influenced by marxian thought partially. However he was a critics to the behaviour and approaches of the leftist forces.[2] Zamindari system was highly criticised by Nehru and he tried a lot for its elimination and finally succeeded in its abolition just after getting independence as in his observation this system was highly injurious and exploiting to the people of peasants class of the then India. Besides it Pt. Nehru propounded a number of economic and social ideas which are discussed below.

IDEA OF DEMOCRATIC SOCIALISM

Just after independence Nehru propounded the idea of Democratic Socialism in India. The Philosophy of socialism given by Karl Marx and Fredrick Engles, who believed that eradication of private ownership from the means of production is an essential condition for eliminating exploitation from the world. Marx was of the opinion that private, property is considered to be a major cause behind the existence of social and economic evils. In soviet Russia Economic planning based on total nationalisation of private property was adopted as the means to expedite economic growth. For the first time in the economic history of the world soviet government made this sincere effort to end poverty, hunger and unemployment from its territory. The economic progress achieved by didn't of this economic policy in Russia compelled the capitalist countries of the world to follow the economic policy of soviet Russia.[3]

When India became independent it was facing the problem of mass poverty and unemployment along with the problem of under employment and even seasonal unemployment. That was the time when our country was suffering from untrained and illiterate labour force, static agriculture and semifeudal relations and a comparatively less developed industrial sector and poor infrastructure in the form of inadequate facilities of transformation and communication, energy, power, banking, finance, health and education. Hence India's development required a powerful national effort and was compelled to adopt planning as a lever of social and economic change.

Jawaharlal nehru, the great architect of Indian planning and chairman of the "Planning Commission of India" was the real admirer of the soviet planning and followed the concept of socialism for the development of national economy, but the credit should be given to the same personality that he never discarded the democratic values of the capitalist society as an essential factor for the alround development of a nation.

Thus in his economic thoughts to take advantage of the virtues of two extreme societies which were them selves passing through a phase of radical changes Nehru's vision of the New India was described as "Democratic Socialism". Hence in view of the economic philosophy of Jawaharlal Nehru Socialism and democracy are the two major tools for the creation of a society in India in which every people have equal opportunities to education, healthcare, and employment etc. and exploitation of depressed people by affluent class shall be abolished. The supreme goal of democratic socialism is to foster free and fuller growth of human personality.4

POLICY OF MIXED ECONOMY

In course of streamlining the hard need of democratic socialism for promoting economic development Jawaharlal also advocated and finally adopted the policy of mixed economy. This type of economic policy is the out come of the compromise between the two diametrically opposite schools of thought. One champions the cause of capitalism and the other strongly pleads for the socialisation of all the means of production and control of the entire economy by the government.

India as adopted the same policy may be considered as the good example of mixed economy. In the economic field, the state is to direct its policy to secure a better distribution of ownership and control of the material resources of the community and to prevent concentration of wealth from the hands of few along with the exploitation of labour. It was also admitted that there is no possibility for the state to attain these ends implied in the directive principles unless the state it self enters into the field of production and distribution. This mention the rationale behind the deliberate policy of expansion of the public sector to promote rapid industrialisation and self reliance. In India in view of adopting the policy of mixed economy the government demarcated the area for the promotion of industries in the public and private sector which was specified in the second industrial policy of 1956.

Although the public sector was conceived of as a senior partner in the process of economic development the private sector was permitted to exist and cope up with the same efforts of the public sector within the overall framework laid down for the economy. In other words we may say that the two sectors are supposed to function as parts of single organism.

FEATURES OF MIXED ECONOMY

In India the policy of mixed economy adopted during the leadership of Pt. Nehru has salient features to the combination of the capitalism and socialism. For example individual freedom of business initiative and capital accumulation along with investment are allowed to function. But it is not a free capitalism rather a controlled capitalism since the system of self interest and private property are all limited in the interest of society. On the other hand the public sector industries are managed and operated on the basis of the welfare of community or in other words with a view to execute the policy of maximum social advantage.

Therefore in India the government was pledged to the establishment of a socialist order of society in which the present in equalities of wealth are sought to be reduced to the minimum level. How ever the state would not eliminate the system of private management which is supposed to do a good job in the field of growth and production in spite of having a lot of shortcomings in itself. There fore the adoption and execution of the policy of mixed economy is the result of Nehru's commitment of democratic socialism.

NEHRU MODEL OF DEVELOPMENT

Since Pt. Nehru was a well read Statesman, he was famous for his fundamental ideas of economic development. As also discussed above he was the pioneer and an ardent supporter to the philosophy of democratic socialism and conclusively adopted the policy of mixed economy for energing the speed of economic and social development of India. In spite of his above thoughts Nehru was a big supporter of rapid industrialisation in the nation. He was of the opinion that establishment of large scale industries in the public sector may help our economy to achieve its goal in a faster speed.

Nehru, Mahalonbis model of development emerged as the driving force to the strategy of development adopted in the mid fifties while the Second Five Year Plan was going to be formulated. The policy was found to be continued right up to the eighties with a short interruption of 2-3 years when Janta Party was came in to power, i.e. 1977-80. This model was based on long run developmental strategy which accorded greater preference to the long-term goal of development. Their strategy emphasised on the points given below.

(i) A high rate of saving so as to boost investment to a higher level.
(ii) It preferred a heavy industrial bias for the development of industrial base of the economy.
(iii) It opted for the protectionist path so as to safeguard infant industry.
(iv) It encouraged import substitution so as to achieve self reliance and
(v) Last it aimed at enlargement of opportunities for the less privileged sections of the society.

Growth with social Justice was thus the goal of Nehru-Mahalanobis model since it entered to foster a self generating path of development with an assurance to the common man that poverty, unemployment, disease and ignorance would be removed so that individual could realise their potential with the extension of social and economic opportunities.[5] During fifties marmot mechanism cold not be able in making judicious allocation of resources to meet the objective of growth with social justice and in this way a greater role was imparted on the state. In the economic field the principle functions of the state was to improve economic and social infrastructure. The economic infrastructure was concerned with the development of irrigation, power, transport and communications so as to expand markets and remove constraints existing on the path of economic development. By improving social infrastructure by way of health and education, the state wanted to develop skilled manpower so that it could provide the necessary skills needed for the functioning of the new industries. To channelise investment in to socially desired lines of production the government nationalised major commercial banks in to different phases.

Hence through the public sector the state controlled the commanding heights of the economy under the guidance of Nehru and Mahalanobis model.

REGARDING HEAVY INDUSTRIES

Nehru wanted to give prime importance to heavy industries while his political preacher Gandhi was having a different view and tried to prefer agriculture supported by handicrafts and cottage industries. Nehru model of growth based on heavy industries was probably the most suitable model in the 1950's and 1960's as the development of such industries was proved to be instrumental in making the country militarily strong to face external aggression and internal disaster. For laying the foundation for further industrial expansion and freeing the country from foreign dependence. Now due to the development of heavy industries our defence has been sufficiently developed and thus enable our economy for getting a path of self sustaining growth.[6]

COTTAGE AND SMALL SCALE INDUSTRIES

The Nehru Mahalanobis model also gives importance to cottage and small scale industries. But in the process of implementation of the Nehru-Mahalanobis model, small scale and cottage industries were given a step motherly treatment by the government as large scale and medium sized industries were allowed to make production of consumption goods and created a situation to block the prospect of small industries.

However the Janta government wanted to correct this mistake by the industrial policy of 1977 which was latter on reversed by the congress government in 1980. Thus Nehruvian policy in favour of large scale industries was continued and multinational are being invited in the pretext of rapid economic growth and required to promote export oriented manufacturing.

REVENUE SYSTEM OF MUNICIPALITY AND DISTRICT BOARD

Jawaharlal was once given chance to act as the chairman of Allahabad Municipality. In this way the revenue system of Municipality and District Board were seen in practice by the person concerned. Nehru was against the then existing system of revenue collection by these autonomous bodies as there was a lot of disparities and injustice in the collection of municipal taxes from the people residing within the service area of the same body. He found that people of affluent class residing in big Bungalows with a large area of land are paying less tax in respect to general people residing in ordinary houses. It was also observed by him that this body could not function properly in the concerned town due to lack of fund and no attention was being paid by the government on their financial suffering. The government was not careful towards the quality of service rendered by municipality and system of defective revenue collection was also ignored by the government. As Pt. Nehru was not satisfied with this economic system of municipality he resigned from the post of chairmanship of Allahabad Municipality just after completing one year of his service. He was of the opinion that tax charged by the municipality should be in respect to the service rendered by the body to different persons. One who is getting more service should pay more tax and the man in general availing normal service should pay minimum tax to municipal body.[7]

REGARDING LAND REFORMS

In course of his action and observation as a freedom fighter Nehru was well aware with the role of Indian peasants in accelerating the development of India. While struggling for independence Jawaharlal had seen the real and miserable condition of the peasants and decided to take a number of steps for the betterment of their lives was taken at the time.

It was decided that Land Reforms is an essential condition for improving the working condition and economic situation of peasants in major part of our country. The Indian National congress in 1935 in a Resolution on Land Reforms stated unequivocally. "There is only one fundamental method of improving village life namely, the introduction of a system of peasant proprietorship under which the tiller of the soil is himself of the owner of it and pays revenues direct to the government without the intervention of any Zamindar or Taluqdar. This resolution was initiated by Jawaharlal to a great extent as he had seen the exploitation of peasants by Zamindars by his naked eyes.

The purpose of land reforms is there fore two fold. One the one hand it aims to make more rational use of the scarce land resources by affecting condition of holdings, imposing ceiling on holdings so that cultivation can be done in most economic manner. On the other, it is a tool of redistributing agricultural land in favour of less privileged class and of improving the terms and conditions on which land is held for cultivation by the actual tillers, with a view to ending exploitation.

As expressed above Nehru along with his other associates was of the opinion that existing problem at the time of independence can be solved with the help of land reforms. It aims at redistributing ownership holding from the view point of social justice and reorganising operational holdings with a view to the optimum utilisation of land. Besides this, there was the problem to the condition of tenancy, i.e. the rights and conditions of holding land. The entire concept of land reforms aims at the abolition of intermediaries and bringing the actual cultivator in direct contact with the state. The provisions of security of tenancy and Rent Regulation provide a congenial atmosphere in which the agriculture feels sure of reaping the fruits of his labour. The scope of land reforms which was initiated by Nehru to a great extent was related with the following aspect:

(a) Abolition of Intermediaries
(b) Tenancy Reforms, i.e. regulation of rent security of tenure for tenants and conferment of ownership on them.

(c) Ceiling on land holdings.
(d) Agrarian reorganisation including consolidation of holdings and prevention of subdivision and fragmentation of land holdings and
(e) Organisation of co-operative farming.

Thus on the eve of independence there were two fold problems to be fought by the government leaded by Nehru. On the one side there were large number of landless labourers and tenants and on the other were big landlords holding vast area of land in their possession. Such problem were shot out by the then cabinet under the policy of "Land Reforms Programmes" which was initiated with a thunderous enthusiasm, but soon the vitality of this enthusiasm was lost and the implementation of land reforms became a very tame affair. There is no doubt that land reforms programmes were adopted broadly in a proper perspective but being riddled with a number of loopholes it could not succeeded properly and proved to be failed in brining required justice to the poor peasants. Professor M.L. Dantwala rightly observed "By and large land reforms in India enacted so far, and those contemplated in the near future are in the right direction, and yet due to lack of implementation, the actual results are far from satisfaction."[8]

Thus under the mission of land reforms programmes the steps taken by the government during the Prime Ministership of Pt. Nehru could not be executed in a powerful way and found to be partially effective in solving the different forms of problems existing in India.

CONCLUSIONS

As discussed earlier Jawahar Lal Nehru was famous for his economic thoughts and social attitude from the very beginning of his political life. Since the man was a great freedom fighter of India he was well acquainted with the economic and social scenario of its different regions. He had seen the basic problem of Indian peasants particularly of Pratapgarh (U.P.) and fought much for the betterment of their lives during British Rule.

Nehru was partially influenced by the Marxian thoughts and conclusively propounded the idea of "Democratic Socialism" Just after the freedom of India. He also saw the effect of Economic Planning in the economic development of Soviet Russia by way of socialistic model of planning. He was of the opinion that economic development can be made through the policy of Democratic socialism as these two factors are the main tools which can establish peace and prosperity in an undeveloped country like India. The idea of Democratic Socialism forced Nehru to adopt the policy of mixed economy within which the government demarcated the area for promoting industries through public and private sector in which public sector was considered as a senior partner.

Nehru by the advice of Mahalanobis adopted a model of development which emerged as the driving force of the development policy adopted in the mid of fifties while the Second Five Year Plan was going to be started. This model intends to initiate a self generating path of development with an assurance to the common man that poverty, unemployment, disease and ignorance would be removed so that individual could get their potential with the extension of social and economic opportunities. Jawaharlal wanted to promote heavy industries in the country. The establishment of Iron and Steel companies in Durgapur, Bhilai and Rurkela are the result of the same policy and it helps our nation to turn in to a military and industrial power of the world.

Nehru was an ardent supporter to the idea of the development of science and technology. He was of the opinion that these two factors are the important base for healthy economic growth of a country. For changing Indian Economy in to a developed economy the above noted two factors must be energized in India.

Regarding land reforms in India Nehru had taken a lot of initiative like Abolition of Intermediaries, Tenancy Reforms, Ceiling on land holdings, etc. and brought a lot of changes in the basic condition of Indian peasants. All such reforms introduced in the field of agriculture sector was really the call of the days of his time.

In our above discussions we find that Jawaharlal was a

most practical leader and a man of social and economic thought of his time. But one thing I would like to add in my discussion that his idea of mixed economy and land reforms can not be escaped from criticism. Nehru's idea of mixed economy was not proved to be conducive in eliminating poverty and unemployment and even in promoting required industrial development. The new economic policy of 1991 which is quite different from the policy of mixed economy is definitely a more favourable policy for the industrial and economic development of India and solving the problem like poverty, unemployment and even underemployment in the country.

Similarly Nehru was partially right in supporting the idea of land ceiling with a view to maintain economic and social justice in the rural sector of India. But he never bother for solving the problem of economic and social disparities existing in the urban sector of India. Really the suffering and discontent of a major part of urban people was not lesser than the people of Rural India. Hence for maintaining social and economic justice allover the country the idea of "Property Ceiling" must be championed and passed by parliament during his Prime Ministership. His idea of land reforms proves that he was in favour of developing the basic condition to the people living within the Rural India or depending on agriculture for getting their loaves and fishes but never try to minimize or eliminate the disparities exiting in the urban sector and specially in the big cities of India.

SUGGESTIONS

After going through above discussions regarding the different economic thoughts of Nehru I would like to suggest that an act like "Property Ceiling" must be proposed by Nehru in order to establish maximum and Justiciable equality in the society and avoid the increasing tempo of corruption and concentration of wealth from the urban sector. Perhaps ! Nehru did not prefer to propose "Property Ceiling Act" which may be proved to be the real crusader to bring economic and social justice, feeling it to be a complete communistic approach and difficult to be passed from parliament and it will go against the interest of capitalist class residing mostly in urban sector and may hammer on his popular and political personality and even lastly on the vote banks of his political party. How ever if such an act would be passed during his leadership it may proved to be a panacea for preventing every sorts of malignant problem developing into the economic and social body of India in a very perpetual manner.

How ever the economic ideas propounded by Jawahar Lal Nehru are of great use and has its own relevance even for the present society and we the people of India should follow and adopt his economic ideas in general with a great devotion and powerful enthusiasm so that our country may enjoy a peaceful and prosperous future.

Notes and References

1. Nehru, Pandit Jawaharlal, Meri Kahani, Sasta Sahitya Mandal, Conaught Circus, New Delhi, 1999, 14th edition, p. 93.
2. *Ibid.*, p. 239.
3. Datt Ruddar and Sundram, K.P.M., Indian Economy Democratic Socialism in India, S. Chand & Company Ltd., New Delhi, p. 159.
4. *Ibid.*, p. 161.
5. *Ibid.*, p. 169.
6. Charan Singh, India's Economy Policy, p. 105.
7. Nehru Jawaharlal Meri Kahani, p. 277.
8. M.L. Dantwala, Report of the Tokyo Seminar on "Problems of Economic Growth", Congress for Cultural Freedom, p. 2.

18

Jawaharlal Nehru as an Economic Philosopher

R.R. Gawhale and R.B. Bhandwalkar

Jawaharlal Nehru was born in a wealthy and aristocratic family in Allahabad on 14th November 1889. He was a complex man, visionary, man of peace and pragmatist. Nehru was statesman, Philosopher, author, prophet, politician and economist all rolled into one. The political career of Nehru was started after his meeting with Mahatma Gandhi at the Lucknow session of Indian National Congress in 1916. In 1946 he formed the interim government of India. India became free from British rule in 15th August 1947. Jawaharlal Nehru was the first Prime Minister of India. When he become Prime Minister of India he grappled with economic, political and social problems courageously.

Jawaharlal was a great socialist. Socialism means different things to different people. Many people thinks that socialism means equality. His socialism was economics and scientific it also involved revolutionary changes in economic structure. It means ending of vested interests in land, industry, private property. Socialism was the key solution of world's problems and of India's problems. Socialism was a philosophy of life to put an end to poverty, unemployment, degradation and subjection of Indian people. Socialism was devised to reconstruct free India by abolishing Zamindari system, untouchability, communalism and casteism. The goals of five year plans were set or framed according to the desire of Nehru, so as to increase production in agriculture and industrial factors, to raise national income and to raise the standard of living of Indian people thereby to achieve rapid economic development of the nation. His socialism in 1955 was converted into a democratic socialism and became it's votary. It was ever-changing and also ever-evolving. He believed in scientific socialism. He advocated Mixed Economy. His goal was socialist pattern of society. He advocated co-operative farming and the establishment of service co-operatives. His approach to economic development was pragmatic. He believed in peaceful democratic method. He did not treat democracy and socialism in two separate compartments. He was firmly wedded to democratic way of life. Nehru believed in representative Government based on parliamentary institution.

He said, "Democracy as a structure of society in which social and economic equality was gradually attained." Nehru considered capitalism and democracy are two contradictory terms. He stood for classes and casteless society. Democracy functions in an atmosphere of peace. Problems however, difficult are persuasion. Thus Jawaharlal Nehru was a perfect and genuine democrat. He thought that both socialism and democracy meant removal of disparities or establishment of social and economic equality in the society. Such a society must provide every man and woman with equality of opportunity and freedom to work for the unfettered development of his or her personality. It aims at the provision for everybody of a national minimum in terms of housing, clothing, food, education and health at the reduction of inequalities and checking of monopolies, at the provision for equal opportunities to all without any distinction. It also recognises that vital role of private sector and the significance of collage and small scale industries. It does not advocate the nationalisation of everything, it is not merely an economic concept but a philosophy of life.

Nehru was deeply attached to the concept of planning as a techniques for solving India's grave economic problems of unemployment, mass poverty, food shortage, etc. and for the advancement of productivity. Nehru first visited Moscow in 1927 and Russia's planning created a strong impression on his mind. In 1938 Nehru became the chairman of the National Planning Committee set-up by the congress. Nehru became Prime Minister he found of halting approach of senior officials towards planning. Towards the end of February, 1950 the Planning Commission was established with Nehru as Chairman and Gulzari Lal Nanda as Deputy Chairman assisted by other distinguished person. Nehru re-wrote a considerable part of the draft Resolution of terms of reference of the Planning Commission and linked the work of the Planning Commission directly with the Fundamental Rights and with the Directive Principles of state policy embodied in the constitution. Nehru and a long line of national leaders before him from Dadabhai Naoroji to Mahatma Gandhi brought bear on the movement for national freedom their impact is not easy to measure nor can it yet be fully assessed.

Nehru presented each of the three Five year plans to parliament. To him the beginning and the end of a Five year plans were vital dates in the country's history. In the first plan, the emphasis was on agriculture. Nehru set great store by community Development Projects. There was little or no provision for the basic industries in the first plan. He soon realised this weakness. He also felt that the first plan was lacking in the perspective for the future. First plan did not lay sufficient emphasis on basic objectives and was also weak in its scientific and industrial content. Nehru initiated joint studies by the Planning Commission, the Finance Ministry and the Indian statistical institute, which helped in the formulation of the Draft outline of the second plan in 1955.

Nehru's ideas and influence provided a new approach to and outlook on the formulation of the second plan which may be summed up in the following four points.1) Emphasis was placed on the rapid development of basic and heavy industries. 2) Cottage and small scale industries were thought vital for producing consumer goods and for providing more employment. 3) Close inter-locking and inter-relationship between agriculture and industry was clearly recognised. 4) Emphasis was also placed on increasing the supply of scientific and technical personnel and hence on the need for expanding facilities for training it.

In the formulation of the third plan Nehru emphasised that the basic approach of building up a strong industrial base and an economy of self-sustained growth was to be retained. He laid accent on increased production of steel, coal, power and on rural electrification. Secondly the inter-dependence of agriculture and industry was also made plain. Thirdly, he expressed his concern over insufficient progress and lags in education, slum-clearance and housing improvement the need to ensure certain minimum amenities to the people in rural area, the welfare of children, etc. The third party placed stress on these aspects owing to Nehru's insistence.

Nehru maintained that planning was continuous process and perspectives planning was the essence of the planning process. He advised that investment in men is most fundamental. Even during the period of Chinese aggression he was firmly of the view that the plan was 'the warp and woof of our national life' and it was the war effort itself that required the plan. Nehru had a flexible approach in all matters. He was against foreign capital before independence but after independence in the changed context he advocated foreign aid and foreign loan for rapid economic development of the country provided. They were given in such a way as not to influence Indian affairs. He welcomed economic aid from all friendly countries. He was also conscious of the fact that Indian is a vast country with great diversity National unity is a must for economic, political and social advancement of the country. He was a staunch believer in democracy and as such he ascribed great importance to persuasion and involvement of people to secure a National consensus in support of the plan.

Nehru was fully conscious that industrialisation, setting up of basic industries and big industries in addition to cottage and small scale industries, was fundamental to the rapid, economic progress of the country Prof. Mahalanobis classifies problems of planning from the point of view of implementation in two parts. One he calls the concentrated sector and other he calls the Diffused sector. After dwelling on such classification He says that Nehru was generally more effective in decisions in planning in the concentrated sector in regard to industrialisation. Nehru were responsible for the revision of the industrial policy Resolution of 1948 and the adoption of the new Industrial policy Resolution of 1956 which still holds sway over the industrial field. Specially for the progress and achievement in the field of steel production and oil exploration are greatly indebted of Nehru's initiative thus production of capital goods will increase to facilitate the country's economy. Further increased production of good and agricultural raw materials in necessary to keep pace with rapid industrialisation. To this end increased production of agricultural implements, machinery for irrigation and fertilisers will be of immense help. Let us, not forget that Nehru never denied the role of cottage and small scale industries in India's developing economy.

Nehru was a lover of India. He was not a narrow nationalist as most politicians and patriots tends to become. Nehru's theory and practice of nationalism had three foundations. First he was against the racial discrimination and arrogance of the British rulers. Second source of Nehru's nationalism was economic in nature. He blamed the British for the rampant poverty and ruthless exploitation of the country. Third foundation of Nehru was a great internationalist. As an apostle of peace, Nehru looked down with war and violence. He was the principal spokesman of Asian and African aspiration for complete political and economic freedom. The Panch-Sheel was the basis of Nehru's foreign policy. According to Nehru Panch-Sheel was a peaceful and constructive strategy. He was the messenger of peace. He had full with in world peace. Nehru wanted to use science and technology for social and economic advancement and national development of the country. He initiated the process of planning influencing it in a great way from time to time, give us a clear direction for the establishment. of a welfare state based on democratic socialism, plunged us into scientific revolution and gave a scientific temper to our outlook, laid the sound foundations of political and economic stability

Nehru was one of the graters figure's in Indian history and an outstanding statesman whose service to the cause of human freedom are unforgettable. He established the parliamentary democracy, he followed the process of planned development. He was a philosopher, writer, historian, political thinker and economist. In his scheme there is no scope for dogma or tradition His contribution to worlds politics in also not forgettable. Nehru gave the message of world peace and world brotherhood. Pandit Nehru was the 'Jewel of India.'

References

Jawaharlal Nehru, The Discovery of India, Calcutta, 1946.

J.S. Bright, Jawaharlal Nehru: Before and After Independence Delhi, 1950.

Jain, K.P., Article on Nehru as an Economist, Sahitya Bhawan, Agra.

Jawaharlal Nehru, An Autobiography, Allied Publisher, New Delhi, 1962.

P.B. Rathod, Vimla Rathod, Indian Political Thinkers, Common Wealth, Publisher, New Delhi, 2006.

19

Jawaharlal Nehru and His Economic Planning: An Analysis of Neo-Liberal Criticism

MANISHA PATHAK

I. INTRODUCTORY

It is now universally acknowledged that if Mohan Das Karamchand Gandhi was prime mover of the independence movement, Jawahar Lal Nehru, is founder of the process of development of India after independence. Jawahar Lal Nehru initiated the development of India by adopting the process of economic planning.

Jawahar Lal Nehru was not a professional economist. He was one of the greatest intellectual giants produced in India during the Indian independence movement. He had studied science and law as a student. By profession he was a lawyer. As a scholar, he was deeply interested in history. Basically, however, he was the leader of the people. He initiated economic planning of India as the leader of the people.

The era of planning in contemporary India, which owes

its birth to him, has always divided articulate public opinion in the country. Nehru the nation builder does not inspire the same uncritical acceptance as Nehru the freedom fighter did before the dawn of independence. One class is of the view that the present progress and prosperity in India, is due solely the results of the economic planning initiated by Nehru. There is another class that puts blame for all economic ills in Indian economy to his economic planning.

The criticism of economic planning of Nehru by public leaders and scholars commenced from the day it was initiated. A few criticisms from this class may be mentioned here as examples.

It may be recalled that C.D. Deshmukh, an eminent administrator and Finance Minister resigned from Nehru Cabinet, because he did not approve the constitution of Planning Commission. Other public leaders of the time like U.N. Dhebar, called Nehru/s planning a golden mean, that is, mix of public and private sectors, A.D. Shroff considered it as the wrong path, Ashok Mehta considered planning without progress and for S.A. Dange it was a plunge in the dark

Criticism of economic planning of Nehru was made by eminent scholars. As an example, one can take the criticism made of the Second Five Year Plan by the professors C.N. Vakil and Dr. P.R. Brahmanand, the eminent economists of the time, in their famous book, "Planning For An Expanding Economy". The central theme of criticism of Second Five Year Plan in this book is that this plan was based on Harrod-Domar model of economic growth. This model refers to economic difficulties faced by the advanced countries on account of consistency in the rate of savings to national income. The authors believe that this model should not have been applied to an underdeveloped country like India. The authors were also critical of the adoption of the economic philosophy that maximum rate of technical progress in the production of consumer goods was not necessary. They were thus highly critical for curtailing the rate of growth of factory reproduced consumption goods and encouraging expansion of employment in cottage and smallest scale industries. They recommended the strategy of development through what they called the production of wage goods.

It is indeed not possible to do justice to any of this class of the critics of the economic planning of Nehru in such a passing reference as made here. The "obiter dicta" references of criticisms of Nehru's economic planning mentioned here of this class of critics, however, clearly show that these criticisms were not against the concept of economic planning as such, but more against the contents of the various plans.

The criticism of Nehru's economic planning, that is emanating after the adoption of the new economic policy from July, 1991, is quite different. These criticisms are based on the so-called now neo liberal ideas propounded in this country, under the impact of the concept of liberalization and globalization after 1991. The purpose of this paper is to analyze neo-liberal criticism of Jawahar Lal Nehru's economic planning.

2. GENESIS OF NEO LIBERAL CRITICISM

The genesis of neo liberal criticism of economic planning of Nehru stems from the central role in economic development that was assigned in it to the state The neo liberal scholars are of the view that in Nehru's economic planning the state was wrongly placed at commanding heights in all economic matters and the role of price mechanism, competition and other economic forces was ignored. These were crippled and badly distorted by undue intervention of the state and thus lead to many ills.

The neo liberal thinkers allege that the insertion of socialistic ideology of Nehru in economic planning further complicated the matter. It may be mentioned here that Nehru had evolved his own version of socialism. It is different from the rigid Marxian version of socialism and milder Fabian socialist thought. Nehru did not want to establish a socialist society, but only a socialist pattern of society through economic planning.

The neo liberal criticism of economic planning of Nehru differs from the criticism made of economic planning of Nehru in pre liberal era in the sense that it negates the very concept of economic planning and the role in it of the state.

It insists that price mechanism, competition, and free play of economic forces, and not planning through state was the right panacea for economic development of India after independence.

The views expressed by neo-liberals about the economic planning of Nehru needs an objective analysis and attempt may now be made in this direction. This can commence by analyzing the main events that led to creation of economic superstructure of planning during the period in which Jawahar Lal Nehru was the Prime Minister and undisputed leader in shaping all aspects of India including her economic development.

3. NEHRU'S ECONOMIC PLANNING

Jawahar Lal Nehru was Prime Minister of India from August 15, 1947 to May 27, 1964. First Five Year Plan commenced on 1 April 1951 and by the time Nehru ceased to be the Prime Minister due to his death, Third Five Year Planhad completed only one year, one month, and 27 days. Nehru could guide economic planning process only for a period of two five year plans, and one year of third plan, that is, for about 11 years or so. Nehru's strategy of economic planning in assigning central role to the state in all economic matters continued even when he was not on the scene up to the year 1980. It was only after 1980 that the role of the state in economic matters was gradually reduced and ultimately it culminated in announcement of the new economic policy in July 1991.

It is not that Nehru formulated his ideas about economic planning suddenly after he became first Prime Minister of India. As a matter of fact, he evolved his ideas about economic planning over a long period of thinking and deliberations. As early as 1938, the Indian national congress had taken the initiative, on his suggestion, to appoint the national planning committee to evolve development strategy once independence was achieved. He was chairman of this committee. His ideas regarding economic independence and role of the state in economic matters can be traced in the minutes of the national planning committee appointed by

Indian national congress, his book, "The Discovery of India," and in his speeches made during pre-independence period.

Nehru took first step in implementation of his ideas regarding economic planning, after independence, by establishing a Planning Commission on 15th March, 1950. The Planning Commission was established by a Resolution of the Government of India. It was established after the Constitution of India had already come into existence. It, thus, does not form part of the superstructure that has been created by the Constitution of India for the governance of the country. The Resolution constituting the Planning Commission indicated that the Commission would be an advisory body and make recommendations to the Cabinet and the responsibility for taking and implementing decisions rest with the central government and governments of the states. As a matter of fact, the Commission gets its authority, because the Prime Minister of India is also the chairman of the Planning Commission.

The First Five Year Plan (1951-56) does not contain Nehru's ideas regarding economic planning. The First Five Year Plan only aimed at correcting the disequilibrium which was created in Indian economy by Second World War and partition of India. This disequilibrium in the Indian economy has been aptly described by Professor C.N. Vakil, in his book, "Economic Consequences of Divided India", by saying, that Indian economy, at the time of independence was worn out by the war and crippled by the partition.

Nehru started implementing his ideas regarding economic planning from the Second Five Year Plan. As a leader of the people he first of all codified his ideas about economic planning and then commenced their implementation. He codified his ideas about economic planning in the Avadi session of Indian national congress held in 1955. In Avadi session of Congress, the aim of economic planning was laid down to establish a socialist pattern of society in India. The Resolution for establishment of the socialist pattern of society in India said, inter alias, that in this society, the production will be speeded up, means of production will be owned or controlled by the state and there will be even distribution of economic power. It said further, that in this society, the decisions will not be taken in the interest of individuals, groups or regions, but on the basis of the interest of the society as a whole.

Nehru started implementing his codified ideas about economic planning, named as, establishment of socialist pattern of society, from Second Five Year Plan, which commenced from April 1, 1956. It was made very clear in Second Five Year Plan documents that the purpose of economic planning was to establish a socialist pattern of society in India.

The strategy in economic planning of Nehru was first to develop the basic industries, then capital goods industries and after that consumer goods industries. Simultaneously agriculture sector, infrastructure sector and social services sector will also give due share in the process of development. The main role in this task was assigned to the public sector. The private sector was also expected to play its role in the process. The aim of this strategy was to achieve economic independence. Nehru was promoting a production structure through planning and industrialization that would eliminate the need for imports and free the country from the threat of closure of the world markets.

4. ANALYSIS OF NEO LIBERAL CRITICISM

The genesis of neo liberal criticism of economic planning of Nehru has already been mentioned earlier in this paper. To be fair to Nehru, while analyzing this criticism, one must make a distinction between the economic planning as it was practiced when he was alive, and when he was no more on the scene. The earlier planning can be called the economic planning of Nehru and the latter Nehruvian economic planning. The main contentions of new liberal criticism may now be analyzed.

(a) Role of the State

The role of the state in economic matters has always been a subject of debate since the day economic science was born as a systematic subject of study. There has been a view that free play of economic forces with minimum essential intervention of the state brings the best possible results in economic matters, and lead to optimal use of resources.

There is another opposite view, which says that free play of economic forces lead to exploitation and poverty of masses, as such, the state must effectively intervene in economic matters in the interests of the people as a whole. As to the degree of intervention of the state in economic matters, there are thinkers like Karl Marx who plead for total state intervention in all economic matters, and there are other thinkers who plead for limited intervention only in certain economic activities like production and exchange. Recent historical events, particularly downfall of the USSR has proved that "free play of economic forces view" is near the truth. This has given birth to a new perception and this is named as liberalization and globalization. This perception is that if economic forces are allowed free play by the states of the world and the world is treated as one economic unit, then best possible results will come out in all economic activities including production, exchange, distribution and consumption of wealth. All countries of the world will be benefited by this process.

Neo liberal criticism of Nehru's economic planning is based on liberalization and globalization perception. The critics of this class are of the view that Nehru's economic planning leads to corruption, mismanagement, leak of resources, miss-utilization and miss-direction of resources due to state intervention in economic matters. Inward looking import substitution industrialization strategy further complicated the problem. They are of the view that countries which had adopted liberal policies in economic matters, and had given due place to private sector, like Japan, South Korea and others South Asian countries have done relatively better then India in matter of economic development. They, thus, come to the conclusion that the economic planning of Nehru was not the right course for India immediately after independence.

An objective analysis of the above criticism makes it clear that it does not take into consideration the time factor. The above criticism may appear to be valid if seen from the situation prevailing in India and world today. The economic situation when India was fighting for independence and when it won the independence were quite different in India, as well as in the world. In this period, the Indian economy was at its lowest ebb and the whole Indian economy was carefully redesigned by the British, during their rule, to siphon out the resources from India and for serving imperial interests. In those days, in India, there was dearth of capital, entrepreneurship, necessary infrastructure and an appropriate milieu for free play of economic forces. The world economic scene was then dominated by the British. As such, the role assigned by Nehru to state in his economic planning in economic matters appears apt, if situation prevailing then in India and the world are also taken into consideration. The inertia created in the Indian economy by the imperial power and its domination at global level in economic matters could not have been overcome but only by planned use of the state power in economic matters. Looked with this perspective, the neo liberal criticism of economic planning of Nehru loses its ground.

(b) Nehru's Socialism

Neo-liberal scholars are highly critical of induction of socialist ideas by Nehru in his economic planning. They are of the view that Nehru's socialism has created unwieldy bureaucracy in the country, which is inefficient, corrupt and has mismanaged economic system. This class of thinkers is of the view that the private sector and free play of economic forces would have produced good economic results but because in Nehru's socialism, the role of private sector in economic development was severely restricted by the licensing regulations through industrial policy resolutions and by such restrictive legislations like Monopolies and Restrictive Trade Practices (MRTP) Act, 1969 and Foreign Exchange Regulation Act (FERA), 1973..

A typical criticism of Nehru's socialism can be very much as in words of Gurucharan Das, quoted below from his book, "India-Unbound;"

"One of the great achievements of modern times is the liberal conception of humanity; the view that there are universal and inalienable human rights, and that powers of reason can honour these rights and eradicate poverty and social distress. The problem with liberalism, however, is that in search of freedom and social justice, liberals either get impatient or have to exert power through vast bureaucracies. This leads to experiments of political and social engineering. Nehruvian socialism was one such experiment, carried out in a relatively benign manner. Nehru, the liberal, did not realize that socialism would lead to statism and seriously compromise the very freedom that he had fought so hard to win, suppressing the innovative energies of the people." (p. 354)

It is now gradually being accepted that socialism leads to statism, and thus is not the best economic policy. To criticize Nehru's economic planning and inculcation of his version of socialist ideas in the same does not appear fair if considered in the background of the period in which Nehru had formulated his views about economic planning and socialism. The view that free play of economic forces leads to best results was not universally accepted then and the economic thinkers then were at the crossroads. Some were advocating the journey through the path of free enterprise, whereas others where recommending the path which lead to statism.

Moreover, Nehru's socialism was not doctrinaire socialism. It was a socialism propounded by the leader of the people. He did not want to establish a doctrinaire socialist society in India. He wanted to establish a socialist pattern of society in India of his own version. In Nehru's socialist pattern of society, the production was to be speeded up. There appears nothing wrong in speeding up of production. As a matter of fact, all countries aspire to speed up the production. There also appears nothing wrong in the commitment of the nation that the means of production should be owned or controlled by the state. In ultimate analysis, all means of production are gifts of the nature. Thus the people of India as a whole should be the real owner of the means of production and means of production should be used for the benefit of the people of India as a whole. It is a different matter that for the purpose of exploitation and for the purpose of distribution of the benefits from such exploitation that means of production may be leased out to others. Ultimate owner, however, should be the people of India as a whole. In their capacity as the ultimate owners of the means of production, the people of India should have collectively right to control them.

In Nehru's socialist pattern of society, there was need to have even distribution of economic power. This premise of Nehru is certainly on a weak foundation and cannot stand the test of reasoning. It is indeed not possible to have even distribution of economic power, which manifests in the present-day society in the form of wealth and income. What one can aspire for is the just distribution and not even distribution of wealth and income. Just distribution indicates ensuring fulfilment of minimum basic needs of all in the society. It was also the visualized by Nehru that in his socialist pattern society decisions would be taken keeping in view the society as a whole. This has, however, not happened. On the contrary, as a result of state intervention in economic matters it became possible to take decisions to please the vote banks rather than society as a whole.

5. CONCLUSION

On the basis of the analysis made so for of the neo-liberal criticism of Nehru's economic planning it can safely be said that neo liberal critics are not judging fairly Nehru's ideas about economic planning as formulated when Nehru was on the scene. They are judging Nehru's economic planning on the basis of the situation prevailing in India and the world after the emergence of the concept of liberalization and globalization. Nehru's economic planning needs be judged in the situation that was prevailing at the time when India, won freedom.

An objective analysis of performance of economic system is percentage growth of GDP per annum. Professor Arvind Panagariya, of Columbia University, U.S.A. has worked out in his recently published book entitled, "India—The Emerging Giant," that between 1951-65, the percentage growth of GDP per annum in India was 4.1 per cent. This was the era of economic planning of Nehru. Professor

Panagariya says further in this book, "India—, had grown less than 1 per cent per annum during the first half of the twentieth century. Thus, its growth rate of 4.1 per cent represented a marked improvement over what had been achieved earlier." (p. 124)

No doubt slowing of growth rate latter right up to 1980 and leak of resources due to corruption, miss direction, and miss utilization, the emergence of unwieldy and mostly inefficient bureaucracy, distortion of decision taking process due to vote banks, etc. Are certainly the off shoots of economic planning that the country is facing today. To be fair to Nehru, they emerged in the era of Nehruvian economic planning and not in the era of economic planning of Jawahar Lal Nehru.

References

Nehru Jawahar Lal, "An Autobiography", Allied Publishers; New Delhi, 1962.

Nehru Jawahar Lal, "The Discovery of India", Asia Publishing House, New Delhi, 1961.

Nehru Jawahar Lal, "Letters from a Father to His Daughter", Puffin Books, New Delhi, 2004

Zakaria Rafiq (editor), "A Study of Nehru", *Times of India* Publications, Bombay, 1960.

Gopal S., "Jawahar Lal Nehru- A Biography", Oxford, 1975.

Shenoy B.R., "Problems of Indian Economic Development", Madras University, 1958.

Vakil, C.N., "Planning for an Expanding Economy", Vora and Co., Bombay, 1956.

Vakil, C.N., "Economic Consequences of Divided India", Vora and Co., Bombay, 1956.

Paranjape, H.K., "The Planning Commission", The Indian Institute of Public Administration, New Delhi, 1964.

Panagariya, Arvind, "India-The Emerging Giant", The Oxford University Press, New Delhi, 2008.

Gurucharan Das, "India Unbound", Penguin Books, New Delhi, 2007.

"National Planning Committee of the AICC", AICC, 1972.

"Five Year Plans", Planning Commission, Govt. of India, New Delhi.

Pathak (Dixit) M., "Corruption-A Drag on Economic Growth", IEA Annual Conference 90th, Vol. II, p. 1179.

"*Economic and Political Weekly*", Sameekasha Trust Publication, Bombay.

"*The Economic Times*", Bennett Colemans and Co. Ltd. Bombay.

20

Nehru's Views on Economic Planning and Development

D. RAJASEKHAR

India is a vast country which contains people at various developments the problem it presents are of an extremely complex character. Its social and economic life carries within its folds many contradictions that battle the imagination of even experts. It was a no mean task to outline on the basis of people's consent a new society built upon a new liberal socialistic concept involving vast socioeconomic changes in a people died in centuries of conservation in practically every field of life.

The problem of reconstruction of socioeconomic conditions in India can be tackled from four different approaches. The capitalistic approach which liberates people to do what they desire, and which in turn can make changes in the socioeconomic structures. Another approach is socialistic one which has quite opposite principles than the former and this approach implies negation of individual liberty. Next, Gandhian or sarvodaya approach, which inspires by simple principles but have difficulties in its implication to some extent. Moreover, it is clear that India cannot or should not in her own interest remain unaffected by the great changes that are taking place in the rest of the world in the realm of science and technology.

There is now general agreement that our system should not result in a concentration on wealth in the hands of a few for that the problems of labour and management should be tackled in a more realistic manner. Similarly there is a new approach towards the working of our social system because of the spread of mass education and impact on planned economic development.

Nehru knows that his country is backward but he has faith innate intelligence of his people. He believes that but for the narrow parochial or sectarian attitude of some of her leaders in the past, India would have made great headway in the scientific and technological field. For this reason, he is a believer in unrestricted democracy and considers it as an antidote to narrow sectarian trends. Moreover, scientific and technological advance will greatly help the process.

Nehru technique is simple; he first secures a broad based approach agreement as vital issues setting out the aims in general terms and then proceeds to implement the agreed proposals always remaining conscious of the fact that such an agreement cannot be constructed as an agreement of all in all its details. In this technique which is Nehru's special contribution to the successful working of socialistic policies in a democratic setup. He does not differ from other socialistic in his devotion to a socialistic society. But he believes that a good socialist should also be a good democrat not only in his approach but in his functioning.

Nehru however strongly to overcome these handicaps as best he can. One way of doing it is to inculcate among the people the urge and consciousness for great scientific and technical knowledge and among those who have the knowledge, greater competence and efficiency. It gives time to the people to assimilate the broad objectives and to understand their implications and the policies based upon them. It ensures people support and at the same time leaves them free to workout the details to suit their peculiar circumstances. This process is deliberate and continuous so far has Nehru is concerned.

He is clear that no amount of shedding of crocodile tears on the part of vested interest and their sympathy for the 'have-nots' can make on jot of difference to the prevailing maldistribution of wealth, the situation demands not a charitable but a realistic approach. A self generating economy in the direction in which Nehru was to lead India can be operated only to the extent that it has a sound agriculture and industrial policy.

Nehru has been thinking about the working on a new economic pattern under the same time creating a consciousness in its supports among people. But Nehru thought the problem could be resolved by the people in an organised or planned manner so that it may be possible for India to adjust them to her tradition and genius. It is no mean achievement to have brought them about in a democratic and planned manner. For this purpose, it became essential to adopt a proper technique. Nehru devised that technique with result that India today is marching ahead irrespective of many obstacles that she has to face and the many drawbacks from which she suffers.

As India marches, however, along the new path we notice some gaps, some of them wide, some narrow. Nehru remains an optimist he is an enthusiast for rapid industrialisation but also realise that there must be immediately adequate provision for peoples food and assured supply to them of raw materials at economic cost. He realises that the supply of agricultural goods—food for the industrial wage earners and raw material for industry at economic cost—is an inseparable part of a successful industrial plan. He is clear however that there is no option for a backward nation but to try and plan on both industrial and agricultural sides simultaneously. So that there is a balanced economic development.

The practical experience of the two plans has given us a good idea of India's economic needs; these cannot be fulfiled unless her agriculture is properly regulated and organised. Agriculture depends upon the caprice of nature which often brings about floods and droughts. Further, there is the pressing problem of burgeoning population with escalating birth rate and decreasing death rate. Rural indebtedness, fragmentation and uneconomic holds or other factors are acting as barriers of progressive economy.

There is no question of compulsion or pressure on the agriculturist. It is a purely a voluntary arrangement. The government will no doubt help in the process but there is no question of direct or indirect coercion. Once a farm become uneconomic it can only produce indebtedness, low productivity and finally liquidation. During that period land becomes neglected. Nearly half of our agricultural holdings are less than five acres each. A continued increase in population threatens to make the situation worst.

Nehru's main contribution has been more in broadening the outlook of giving greater vision to his people. Organisational work always received secondary attention at his hand and his forte has been to offer fresh, evocative objectives, to take the vision a notch higher every time. Even now, for instance, when the community development programme begins to lack lustre, he plays as before the country the objective of cooperative farming. He is ever a step forward, but he rarely attempts to discover where the earlier effects have gone wrong or how to overcome the inadequacies in a situation. His effort has always been to take his country in those directions may be more by the force of his ideas than by action.

Nehru is undoubtedly Asia's outstanding democrat no one can gainsay the fact that Nehru's leadership has provided the anchorage for stabilising democracy of India. Here again one notices his inability to function organisationally while some of his own ideological assumptions have begun to foster erosive forces despite the fact that it is his charismatic leadership which is providing the foundations of democracy.

The driving 'orces of planned economy cannot be bank directors, industrialist, foreign business houses, and landlords. But it is thus these forces which control the economy, sit in the government hold its strings. Born and bread in private capital, how can one expect them to do those things which eliminate capitalism, is a profits and power? Out of every productive activity, they must extract the surplus for themselves and give less to the real producer the worker on the fields and in the factory. That is the source of economic crisis that every now and then engulfs our society. Even Keynes realise it but could not cure it because the cure meant taking away the sources of productive wealth from private capital.

The disciples of Nehru in the economic field are trying to apply Keynesian theories to our economy. A chronic crisis and unemployment will ever be with us, declare their leaders. Nehru the humanist and liberal disagrees with these pessimistic conclusion but finds no other means to make his plan work better than the same Keynesian outlook.

Nehru intellectual clear and honest because it is honest he makes many reservations in his formulation. These reservations weaken implementation, introduce intractable knots in execution. The intellectual sensitivity somehow weakens the homeness of will. Nehru can fail to figure out the sources of his policies which are par from pragmatic; they are essentially the outcome of his dynamic thinking. The changes the modifications and even the shifts in his policies are the result of his thinking aloud. In every act of Nehru's, one notices a deep concern for the people; he dedicates himself to their betterment with a devotion which has few parallels in his history. He is always more interested in his conveying to others a feeling of willing or voluntary participation. Because of this technique of his, India has been able to secure basic agreement on so many intricate socioeconomic problems.

References

1. Nehru, Jawaharlal, Discovery of India.
2. Nehru, Jawaharlal, Autobiography.
3. Nehru, Jawaharlal, Glimpses of World History.

21

Nehru's Ideas on Economic Planning and Industrial Development

Ved Prakash Dubey

Nehru, a great economic eclectic, was aware of significant concepts contributed by different schools of economics. His economic thinking was based on western doctrines. His economic thoughts stand midway between Gandhism and Marxism. He partly differed and partly agreed with Gandhi regarding socio-economic perspective of India. Nehru's perception centered round his aspirations to increase wealth of India and elevate the standard of living of Indian people. He advocated planning based on the charter of economic progress initially adopted by U.S.S.R. He was strongly aware of Soviet achievements, which proceeded from the implementation of the charter of economic progress. Hence Pt. Nehru aimed at taking India along the path of progress by introducing the system of planned economic development. In Nov. 1947, Nehru formed an Economic programme committee under his supervision. On the basis of the reports submitted by this committee in 1948, a permanent

Planning Commission was established in 1950. This committee aimed at removing socio-economic stagnation persisting in the country after Independence. Nehru was of the view that economic planning was the only way to remove the poverty and abolish the demon of unemployment in the country. He devised five-year plans to achieve different targets. He said, "Two things are necessary, the first is long-term planning and the second is contracted planning for relatively short period." Nehru laid stress on the continuous process of progress through planning carried on in a balanced and dynamic way. In Nehru's opinion, agricultural and industrial progress should march together in the broad perspectives of international political and economic conditions.

FIVE YEAR PLAN

The First Five Year Plan (1951-56) prepared under Nehru's supervision was presented to parliament for final approval and came into operation from first April, 1951. Its main objective was to promote agriculture and lay emphasis on private investment. It aimed at increasing agricultural production as well as raw material required for industrial development. Inspite of its defects, it was a successful plan. As a result, there was an increase in the national income which was more (17.5%) than the target (11%) and the per capita income increased by 10.5%.

The Second Five Year Plan was formulated and implemented during Nehru's Primeministership. It reflected Nehru's ideology. In the second plan, there was more emphasis on industrial progress. Nehru pleaded for the application of science and technology in order to increase the spirit of economic development. In second plan there was shift in emphasis. Nehru vehemently advocated in favour of rapid industrialization. As a result, three steel plants were set-up at Durgapur, Bhilai and Rourkela. The first and second plan were instrumental in bringing certain structural changes in the Indian economy.

The Third Plan was also formulated under Nehru's supervision and guidance. In this plan equal importance was attached to industry and agriculture. It failed to achieved the designed targets. The performance was not satisfactory.

Nehru's ideas of economic planning had a lot of relevance for Indian soil. He simply added economic thought-pattern and applications regarding industrialization, agriculture and socialistic pattern to the meaning and spirit of swaraj. It was due to the implementation of the first plan that national income increased by about 17.5%. Per Capita income recorded an increase of 10.5% as against the target of 10%. Thus the first plan as expected by Pt. Nehru was a remarkable success. IInd and IIIrd plans were not satisfactory simply because these plans could not achieve the real targets. The country continued to face food shortage, unequal distribution, poverty and the problems of unemployment. The problem of economic inequality persisted much between 1951 and 1968. Nehru's planned economy could not remove the problem of inequality in distribution as well as the grim situation arising out of unemployment. But this does not mean that Nehru's thoughts on policies were insignificant. The main purpose of his economic ideas was to make India economically strong and self-reliant. His ideas of planning, agriculture and industrialization were of paramount significance in the sense that his planned efforts led to the establishment of economic pattern in India. As a result of his economic ideas, there was an overall strengthening of the Indian economy. Nehru's ideas of economic planning proceeded from the sense of democratic socialism. There was lot of emphasis on development of basic and heaving industries, Land reforms and co-operations for agricultural reorganization. Nehru pleaded for scientific research and technological progress. His ideas were well recognized and fully appreciated even during his tenure as P.M. His economic ideas as reflected in the five year plan had a very sound impact on the Indian economy as well as industrial development.

INDUSTRIAL DEVELOPMENT

According to Pt. Nehru industrial establishment and encouragement of large scale industries and cottage industries were fundamental to the economic development and modernization of the Indian economy. Nehru was of the view that there will be no industrial progress unless machines are used. In Nehru's opinion, the country should havé heavy industry along with the growth of village industry. He introduced the first and second industrial policy in 1948 and 1956 respectively. His industrial policy gave due importance to the role of the cottage and small scale industries in the national economy. Moreover, he stressed the need of foreign capital and enterprise. Importance was given to foreign capital and enterprise under the first industrial policy. Further he adopted the principle of mixed economy as the basis of industrial policy. He laid emphasis on the inclusion of large scale industries in the public sector and other industries in the private sector.

Chief objectives of the new policy announced by Nehru in 1956 were as follows:

1. acceleration of the rate of economic growth and speeding up the industrialization.
2. expansion of public sector.
3. reduction of existing disparities in income and wealth.

Moreover, Pt. Nehru aimed at creating basic facilities like power, transport, communication and finance. Besides a number of finance corporations were set-up during his period.

1. The industrial finance corporation of India (1948).
2. The state finance corporation.
3. The national industrial development corporation.
4. IDBI (1964).
5. UTI (1964).
6. LIC (1956).
7. National small scale industries corporation (1955).

All these financial institutions were helpful to enhance the speed of industrial development.

CONCLUSION

Nehru was well aware of the problems of Indian economy. His view was that Indian poverty can not be removed unless there was proper and continued growth of large scale and small scale industries as well as the proper application of science and technology. He strongly advocated the cultivation of scientific temper and setting up of research laboratories. He thus stressed the importance of the combined growth of large and small scale and cottage industries as well as the enhancement of the agricultural productivity. His policy of agricultural and industrial expansion was strictly in accordance with the traditional Indian economy on the one hand and global situation and formulation on other.

22

Had Jawaharlal Nehru any Role in Planning for India's Economic Reconstruction before and after Independence?

ANATH BANDHU MUKHERJEE

False Publicity, sycophancy political motivation and dishonesty are the only epithets which have clouded history of Indian planning for economic development. A man devoid of pragmatism and sense of propriety and will Fabian ideas was put up as a man of India's destiny. It is a great lie and distortion of history to state that the National Planning Committee was set-up in 1944. There had been deliberate attempts by a handful of self employed and paid pseudo economists and historians to paint the history of Indian Planning in a wrong way. Jawaharlal Nehru had nothing to do with the formation of the National Planning Committee—the truth and history being that the National Planning Committee was set-up by Netaji Subhas Chandra Bose in 1938 and not in 1944 or earlier. It was with a view to placate and please Gandhiji—who was a strong opponent of industrialisation and modernisation of Agriculture—that the name of Jawaharlal Nehru, who was in London at that time, was proposed by one of the famous Indian Scientists Dr. Meghnad Saha in place of Dr. Visvesvaraya because when the National Planning Committee was formed after a prolong discussion in the industry Ministers meeting 1938, Delhi—the name of the famous Engineer Dr. Visvesvaraya was proposed for the chairmanship of the committee. But Dr. Saha thought that the planning Committee's proposal for industrialisation would Gandhiji and he would not allow it to function. So to ensure his support the name of Bapuji's most obedient man Jawaharlal Nehru's name was proposed to chair the committee. This decision of the Committee was conveyed to Nehru—who was then in London. And as a gullible person—he did not hesitate to accept the proposal. But he was so ungrateful and vindictive that he tried his best to obliterate the name of the man who was responsible in founding the National Planning Committee to take up future development plan for independent India. When the discussion on the formation of the National Planning Committee was on nobody thought of Jawaharlal's name. Why? Because it was clear to most of the members that a man who lived in the world of ideas and dreams and a man who talked too much and used to delve in ambiguity could not be of any help to a committee of experts. But as a tactical move Dr. Saha in consultation with the President of the Subhas Chandra Bose, proposed the name of Jawaharlal Nehru, though his science background posed problems about his ability to head the National Planning Committees. It is also highly regrettable that some psycophants went to the length of calling the 2nd Five year Plant 1956 model as Nehru Mahalanobis model! A man who knew very little of and economics is being popped up as the co-author of plan model which was itself not original but a borrowed soviet model! But who can stop political bankruptcy and intellectual dishonesty? There is another issue, i.e. the question of mixed Economy—it is also claimed by the same brand of people but the idea of mixed economy came out of the brain or Jawaharlal Nehru. This is also a false and tall claim, history tells a different. All these and other issues have been discussed and analysed in this paper. Dr. Lohia, summed up Nehru's continuation in the following line. "Hegave cash to his family, ashes to the nation and gas to me."

I. NEHRU'S BACKGROUND AND THE HISTORY OF INDIAN PLANNING COMMITTEE

Jawaharlal Nehru took his "National Sciences Tripos in science from Cambridge University. His subjects were "chemistry geology and botany, but (my) interests were not confined to those". We also took interests like "many of the people at cambridge about books and literature and history and politics and economics. Continued "I felt a little at sea at first in this semi high brow talk", but by reading a few books and soon got the hang of it and could at least keep my end up and he being shy and diffident and would seldom speak or lecture in the 'Majlis' debates—and for this he had to pay fine. But such a diffident person—all of a sudden turned out a critique of his 'moderate' father. He wrote, "it is curious that inspite my growing extremism in politics, I did not then view with any strong disfavour the idea of joining the I.C.S. then becoming a cog in the British Government's administrative machine in India." But to prove his maturity in politics he wrote, "Such an idea in latter years would have been repellent to me." But his role in Congress and Indian politics at crucial times had been self defeating and opportunitistic.

He posed to be a radical socialist and used all sorts of flowery and idealistic words about socialism—but in practical life he was of feudal mentality and nature. He was intolerant arrogant, impractical, vindictive and an autocratic person. He believed in dynastic rule and did everything in his power to make his daughter the future ruler after his death. He wanted his daughter to be the leader of the congress party and as he thought he made her President of the AICC in 1958-59—when the Communist party of India was ruling in Kerala. The Congress Presidentive Report on the situation prevailing in Kerala was prepared in such a way that President's rule could be imposed on Kerala and actually President's rule was imposed in that state on 31st August, 1959. This clearly showed that Nehru was neither a liberal democrat nor a socialist but an autocratic to the core of his heart. Again he very skillfully initiated the famous "Kamraj Plan" just to make way for his daughter.

Corruption and Nehru

Jawaharlal Nehru was the Kingpin and fountain head of corruption in Independent India. The Jeep Scandal and the Rs. 114 core INA fund were only the two of the many scans that rocked Independent India during his regime.

He was very much vindictive. He could not tolerate his political opponents. This was clearly evident when one looks at his attitude to one of the greatest patriots of India Netaji Subhas Chandra Bose. He was so envious of Netaji Subhas Chandra Bose that he did not even recognize his role in setting up the National Planning Committee. He was so naive and dishonest that he did not even mention the name of Nataji Subhas Chandra Bose in his Autobiography as the founder of the National Planning Committee. He wrote in his Autobiography (p. 607). "My other activity was the chairmanship of a National Planning Committee which was formed under Congress auspices with the cooperation of the Provincial Governments." He mentioned the formation of the National Planning Committee but did not mention the name of its founder. Some people say he was a historian. Is it? Then why did he not tell the truth? He was afraid of facing the truth. From this statement it might appear that the NPC (National Planning Committee) dropped from the sky and he sprang up as its chairman. Not only in his Autobiography but also in his 'Discovery of India' he took some nine pages (pp. 418-27) to explain his activities as the Chairman of the Planning Committee—but as an 'honest' 'discoverer of India" failed to discover the name of its founder. It is a deliberate calculated and immoral attempt by him to eraze an important page from Indian National movement. But history abhors lies and vacuum. Now the time has come to unmask the 'new Discoverer of India' and the role of his entourage or cohorts. The cycle of truth is moving fast to put the last nail in the coffin of lies that his men built up so assiduously. He is now being denigrated as a humbug, a chatterbox an arrogant intolerant, ill tempered feudal lord. He is a failed politician and statesman. All his activities as a political leader are being questioned today and he has been made responsible for all the failures of India in the political and economic fields. From the Kashmir problem (1948) to brazen chinese invasion 1962. He died a shattered disappointed and disheartened man.

He was so jealous of Netaji Subhas Chandra Bose that crossing all limits of civility went to write a letter to England Prime Minister. Attlee in 1948—requesting him to take action against the Patriots of Patrot Netaji Subhas Chandra Bose. He also tried to remind Attlee that Netaji Subhas Bose was a war criminal—so he should be treated as such! Could this man be called an Indian politician or be condoned of his shameless lust for political power and fame? But history is very cruel and exacting. The big lies and falsehood which kept Nehru's true face and role in Indian politics after Independence marked are now falling apart and the tattered skeleton of a pseudo socialist and notorious power hungry face of an opportunist politician is coming out.

II. THE HISTORY OF NATIONAL PLANNING COMMITTEE

In this section an attempt has been made to unravel the history of the formation of the National Planning Committee. It has long been a practice with the persons who were close to Nehru to show and laud him up as an outstanding statesman an crudite scholar, a pragmatic politician and as a visionary or idealist and a litterateur of eminence. I shall take up all these issues one by one and show that most of the epithets used by his coherts are far from the truth. The history will show the place where he actually belongs.

At first I shall discuss the history of the formation of the National Planning Committee. Let us take a look at Pattavi Sitaramaya's History of the Congress. He wrote, "Early in August, 1937—hardly a month after the congress had formed ministries in the six provinces, the working Committee contemplated the formation of an Expert Committee to explore the possibilities of an All India Industrial Plan and to this end as a preliminary step, the

President of the Congress was authorised in July 1938 to convene a conference of the Ministers of Industries and called for report of the existing industries operating in different provinces and the needs and possibilities of new ones. Such a conference was held at Delhi on the 2nd and 3rd October 1938. In the Premier's Conference convened in May 1938 by President Subhas Chandra Bose, problems of Industrial Reconstruction, Power resources and supply as well as general question of co-ordination amongst the provinces had come up for consideration. At the Conference of Industrial Ministers. Netaji Subhas Chandra Bose delivered an instructive inaugural address in which he foresaw the details of national reconstruction in an Independent India." Here Pattavi has willingly forgotten to mention the name of Subhas Chandra Bose as the leader who was responsible for forming the Planning Committee. One should not forget him because it was he who being Gandhiji's Presidential candidate, supported by almost all the stalwarts of the Congress Committee, lost to Subhas Chandra Bose in 1939. Tripuri Congress election by a big margin.

Pattavi, it is clear, has created a confusion by Jumbling up 1937 and 1938 events from his writing it must appear that the Congress Working Committee of 1937—whose tenure ended in January 1938—virtually had no authority to dictate or authorise the new President elected in AICC Conference 1938 (Feb), to convene a conference of the industry ministers. Yet it did. Secondly, he said that the working Committee 'Contemplated' but did not give effect to the idea of convening Congress Industry Ministers meeting. He tried to conceal the fact that the new President Subhas Chandra Bose, formed the National Planning Committee in 1938 and he made it clear in his famous Haripura Congress Speech that "To solve the economic problem agricultural improvement will not be enough. A comprehensive scheme of industrial development under state ownership and state control will be indispensable.

One cannot fail to note that the working Committee resolution spoke of the formation of an expert Committee for industrial development, hydo electricity generation, state planning and what not? But what was missing in that resolution was the question of priority. The basic question being which path India should follow for economic reconstruction, the Gandhian cottage industry or Industrialisation through heavy industry was not raised. Because the working Committee did not have the courage to go against the wishes of Gandhiji. So, it was Subhas Chandra Bose who took the Challenge and boldly spoke for India's reconstruction through industrialisation. He did not believe that India's economic reconstruction could be done by 'Charka' and cottage industries.

Jawaharlal Nehru, on the other hand in the Bombay Esplanade Maidan meeting on 19th May, convened to felicitate the Congress Ministers, congratulated the Congress President on his "having called the Conference of Prime Minister, which he said was necessary not only to find out what the Congress Ministers had achieved but also to find out what still remained undone." (*Times of India*, May 16 1938) Subhas Chandra Bose as the convenor of the Industries Minister's Conference (held in May) said, in October meet of the Industrial Ministers. "In May last I convened in Bombay a Conference of the Premiers of the seven Congress Provinces. On that occasion, we discussed, as some of us will remember, the problems of industrial reconstruction, development of power resources and power supply, as well as the general question of co-ordination and co-operation among the Congress Provinces."

Subhas Chandra Bose after his election as President of the AICC took immediate steps to form National Planning Committee. He convened four important meetings and conference within a span of seven months. In may 1938 the first meeting of the Congress Working Committee was convened and along with this the Prime Ministerand Congress Ministers meeting was held in Bombay. In July the Working Committee meeting was the second meeting. The third meeting was that of Industry Ministers (Congress) Conference in Delhi in October. And at the fourth conference in Bombay in December the Planning Committee was formally Constituted.

In Constituting the National Planning Committee the third Conference (October) had a very important role. *The*

Times of India reported on 4th October 1938, "Declaring the conference open Mr. Bose emphasised that Congressmen today had not only to strive for liberty but also to devote a position of their though and energy to problems of national reconstruction." Again on October 17th, *The Times of India* wrote, "In formulating a comprehensive Plan (Mr. Bose said), India would be treated as one economic unit and efforts would be put forward to make India self-sufficient, as far as possible, in the matter of her particular requirements, subject to the fundamental laws of economics. The task was undoubtedly a formidable one, especially as the co-operation of the Central Government which was essential for its success would not be for the coming." He was aware of the challenges before the National Planning Committee. He knew that the opposition to the Planning would come from two fronts—the home front and the Government. The role of Congress leader led by Gandhiji was clear to one and all. The Charka and cottage industry brigade would not allow the committee to talk about industrialisation was a foregone conclusion and to overcome this obstacle it was necessary to device a tactic and plan a strategy to deal with this congress attack. So to remove the apprehension of the Gandhite Congress—Subhas Chandra Bose along with Dr. Meghnad Saha applied the master stroke in naming the Chairman of the Planning Committee. Here we will take help from Meghnad Saha's own writing. Let us see what he had to say. 'The resolution to form a National Planning Committee was adopted earlier and Sir M. Visvesvaraya was requested to accept the Chairmanship of the Committee. After having talk with Sir Visvesvaraya, I was able to convince him refraining from accepting the said post. I convinced him unless a front ranking Congress leader was made the Chairman the resolutions of the National Planning Committee would remain as theoretical issues and would have no importance or value to the Congress. That great old man at once acceded to my request. And as per my advice Pandit Jawaharlal Nehru (then in Europe) was requested to Chair the National Planning Committee." (Rethinking our future.....). Even the members of NPC did not think taking Jawaharlal Nehru on the Committee. Why? Perhaps they thought him to be an impractical and good for nothing person. This was not a whisful thinking could be proved from the reminiscences of the architect of the planning report. Satya Ranjan Bakshi an able associate of Subhas Chandra Bose—wrote in 1961, "There was apprehension whether the Resolution of National Planning would be accepted by the Charka following Congressites. That is why the Political statement on the Planning had to be toned down. That task was done by Subhas Bose and myself. The original draft on the Planning was prepared by P.N. Ghosh and Meghnad Saha. P.N. Ghosh's contribution in this respect was imvaluable. So with a view to making it (the Planning Committee) acceptable to the Congress authority it was decided by us that the name of Jawaharlal Nehru an obedient disciple of Gandhiji would be proposed as the Chairman of the Committee and it was readily accepted by Nehru. But to make the Planning Committee really effective experts from all over India were made members of the Committee and they were Dr. Visvesvaraya, Dr. Meghnad Saha, Prof. K.T. Saha, Prof. P.N. Ghosh and others. Yet the meetings of the Planning Committee had to bear with the irrelevant useless flamboyant speeches of Jawaharlal Nehru and for this Dr. Visveswaraya and others were very much annoyed and dismayed. (Satya Ranjan Bakshi wrote these to Sankari Prasad Bose in 1961).

Jawaharlal Nehru had no clear ideas about comprehensive Planning. So, when he received the letter requesting him to accept the offer of Chairmanship of the newly set-up Planning Committee, he frankly wrote, "I have been thinking of Planning for Indian for a long time. Unless some sort of Planning is taken up it is not possible to make real progress. I was alarmed very much having seen the range and comprehensive nature of Delhi resolutions of this committee. Still then the range and far reaching content of these resolution, have made me extremely glad." Now we have the admission that Jawaharlal Nehru "has been thinking of Planning for India for a long time." So it was in his mind and did never come out in reality. So the Credit for constituting National Planning Committee could not be bestowed on him. It must be admitted nobody with the exception of Nehru and his entourage of psycophants did claim this honour for him.

A. National Planning Committee Constitution. How did the Press React?

Before taking up the press reaction it is important to note that a big difference had taken place between the 1937 (August 14-17) working Committee Resolution and July 1938 Resolution of the new Working Committee. The 1937 resolution had some lines on inter provincial planning—but it did not spell the modalities of The Planning. It was the handiwork of Jawaharlal Nehru. But the July 1938 resolution spelt out clearly that the Planning Committee would be constituted for the industrialisation of the whole of India. And this was done under the Presidetnship of Netaji Subhas Chandra Bose. He was a man of action and a visionary. So he could visualize the future reconstruction of India through industrialisation though he knew that his efforts in this move would not be acceptable to Gandhiji and his followers and ultimately he was forced to resign being a victim of Gandhiji and his famous clique from the post of Congress Presidentship in 1939. This episode clearly exposed the reactionary and undemocratic nature of the AICC. A man who was not even a member of this grand organisation had the last say in the working Committee. The tragedy of Indian National Congress is this that the so called protagonist of socialism and a self-styled liberal democrat Jawaharlal Nehru did not have the guts or courage to raise his voice against the worst deplorable and totally unethical move of a handful of Gandhi followers. He as an opportunist as ever took a so called neutral stand but in reality betrayed Netaji in those critical and epoch making days of Indian freedom movement.

Now we will review the role of the Press in those momentous days. It was quite natural that the Nationalist papers like Amrita Bazar Patrika. Hindusthan Standard, Marhatta, Madras Mail etc would quite normally support the moves taken by Netaji Subhas Chandra Bose. To these papers this was a major achievement. Unlike *Amrita Bazar Patrika*—the *Hindusthan Standard* expressed a bit doubt about the real achievement of the Industrial Planning. The paper said: "there are great hassels on the road to success. It would not be easy to remove these hackles and to do so one needs the highest quality of Eco-political intelligence." This paper pointed out the problems of industrialisation. A balance must be there between Agriculture and Industry. Russia had to suffer for the lack of this balance, there are the hurdle of Government rules and laws—yet he the paper wrote, "The direction of the way has been found and it has been resolved that vibrant activity would replace idle and loose talks and the life force would find right and definite direction for expression (7th October 1938 Economic Planning for India—Editorial in the *Hindusthan Standard*).

Amrita Bazar Patrika in its editorial on 18th October 1938, wrote, "The Industry Ministers Conference has ended achieving tremendous success. The programme of the conference has been followed in disciplined manner. The conference has passed many a resolution as a result the National Planning Committee has been Constituted.

Marhatta, a famous newspaper of Pune in its editorial wrote, "Subhas Babu has been responsible for the reorientation of the Industrial policy of the congress and the Delhi conference of the Industries Ministry of the Congress provinces which he called and successfully guided, is an historic event for the first time during the last eighteen years, the attitude of the Indian National Congress towards the industrialisation of our Mother Country has been definitely formulated and National Planning Committee has been appointed which will soon commence its work, under the Chairmanship of Pandit Jawaharlal Nehru. In order that the work of the Planning Committee which the former has to constitute, should take a definite shape on this lines laid down by him, it is essential that Bose should be at the helm of this Organisation for at least one year more (quoted by Amrita Bazar Patrika 14th Nov. 1938). It is seen that Marhatta expressed happiness that Subhas Bose would be in charge of the Congress for one year more. The paper also mentioned that the Planning Committee was constituted by Subhas Chandra Bose and not any other person. Nehru was never clear in his mind about his course of industrialisation of India. We will take up Nehru's views on industrialisation later in this paper. The paper also wrote that the congress had been non commital for over 18 years on its attitude on industrialisation of India. Because Congress was bound by

Khadi clause and Gandhian philosophy of Charka and cottage industry. *The Indian Economist* a weekly from Calcutta in an editorial on 17th October, titled, "Industrial Planning" wrote, "at least industrial Planning embracing the whole of India is going to be launched. Economic Planning is the order of the day. Extreme economic nationalism is at the root of it. For the sake of a new base of economic life each and every country has accepted some sort of Planning. India too cannot remain indifferent. At the same time the paper cautioned that India should not imitate any country or model blindly. We will take note of another paper in the following paragraph.

Commerce—A weekly of Indian Financial Commercial and Industrial Progress—was a very important magazine—it was published from Bombay and it supported the British Commercial interests. This weekly highly applauding the move on Industrial Planning wrote, "There has been in the country so long a certain amount of loose thinking in certain quarters regarding future economic policy. It has been stated by some that only cottage industry should be developed and that large scale industries should be avoided. Others have maintained that India is essentially an agricultural country and that the economic improvement of the people should and could be brought about only through developing agriculture. We are glad to note that the conference has come to definite conclusion that the problems of poverty and unemployment, of national defence and economic regeneration cannot be solved with out Industrialisation. Editorial—Delhi Conference and Industrial Planning. Commerce clearly exposed the "loose thinking" that had been going on among the charka brigade and pointed to the views of two dominant groups in this Congress. The Gandhi followers did not like industrialisation of economic development—they believed this move would kill cottage industry and other group thought that India being predominantly an agricultural country—she should make economic development through agricultural development. But the *Commerce* was happy because the conference thought otherwise and put stress on industrialization in a big scale. In another editorial—Industrial Planning for India—Commerce wrote, "we presume that the (British business) community will only be too glad to extend its co-operation to all genuine attempts to improve the economic prosperity in India on the basis of stimulating private enterprise and ensuring equal opportunities for all those engaged in the process"—22nd October, 1938, *Madras Mail.*

Madras Mail is more or less a liberal newspaper. In the editorial The Industrial Conference' 3rd October, 1938—the paper openly praised Subhas Chandra Bose for his boldness in announcing the industrialisation plan and went to the extent of pointing out that Bose's policy would usher in a progressive line for India. "The speech of Subhas Chandra in the industrial Ministers' Conference need serious observations and it is crystal clear." The paper continued, "The speech is important because it indicates that in the Congress there are men including the one now occupying the office of President, who do not share Mr. Gandhi's thoroughly retrogade economic ideas, who see that this country cannot possible revert to a village economy but must advance in Company with the rest of the world and even if necessary, by forced marches." It is to be noted the paper has the guts to call Gandhiji's economic ideas as retrogade and reactionary. One should keep in mind that Gandhiji's Congress has made it mandatory for all Congressmen to obey the Congress Constitutional provision of the Khadi clause. The formation of the All India Industrial Committee and the steps taken by the Congress President make the Charka brigade of Gandhiji jittery. Gandhiji, though not a regular member of the Congress (he did not renew his membership by paying the usual fees of members since 1934). Yet he was the last word in the Congress organisation! Now the followers of Gandhiji came out of their torpor. The reaction of Subhas Chandra's policy on planning came in for sharp and virulent attack from expectedly the Gandhiji followers and Gandhiji himself.

It is now more or less evident that the press representing diametrically opposite ideas, views and interests did come out in supply of economic reconstruction through industrialisation. But this is not the end of the story.

B. The Discordant Notes

Though most of the newspapers and magazines wrote editorials and articles favouring industrialisation, still some papers expressed doubts and were apprehensive of the moves of the Planning Committee. *The Times of India* in an article "Plan for Industry" showed nervousness reading the speech of the Congress President regarding the nature of industrialisation. The paper advised the Planning Committee not to go beyond limit. They wrote, "Are we now to go beyond this, to commit ourselves to a system of national Socialism in which onus of risk could be taken over from the private investor, and Government will virtually guarantee such large scale schemes as the manufacture of motor cars and power alcohol? If so, let us define our attitude at the outset. Let the taxpayer know whether he is to be called upon to shoulder the burden of potential loss in these and other direction, and that the consumer be told frankly that India's aim is self sufficiency and he must be prepared to pay the price. If the state is to assist industry, let us be assured that it will share in the profits as well as indemnify industrialist, against loss. Is the object in view—totalitarianism as the German model or State control of the Soviet Type? If neither of these two extremes is desired, the Planning Commission (Committee) should lay down limits beyond which possibly uneconomic schemes will not go...... Economic realism is an essential element in economic planning." The paper so far as to advise the Planning Committee not to be totalitarian in its approach and should share the industrial loss if any under its activation. But the question of economic realism which the paper had pointed to should not be missed while planning for development. But the paper could not stomach the speech of the Congress President Subhàs Chandra Bose. The paper in another article published on 20th December, 1938, wrote, "with the general sense of their (Bose and Nehru's) remaining there will be no disagreement. But Mr. Bose was somewhat wide of the mark in the accusation about money being "Squandered" by Governments of the past of hydro electric development and in his criticism of "foreign" concerns which have taken the initiative in putting India's natural resources to practical use." The *Times of India* was critical of Bose's remarks and so made their views clear and tried to "rectify" Bose's comments.

The attackers—Gandhiji and his followers:

So long as there were loose talks about industry, industrialisation, Planning, socialism Gandhiji and his lieutenants did not place much importance on those issues. But after the Industrial ministers' conference in October, when it was clear that Congress was going for industrialisation leaving aside the Charka and Cottage industries—it was too much for them to lie down and kill time. First we will take up Gandhiji's reaction. Having heard the negligence shown to Khadi in the Congress leadership—Gandhiji reacted furiously and in a hard hitting article he wrote, ("it should be remembered that at the same time Subhas Chandra Bose had taken up the task of addressing the nation in favour of industrialisation), "I have not hesitated to say, and I make bold to repeat now that without Khadi there is no Swaraj for the millions, the hungry and the naked and for the million of illiterate women.

"I have letters from Bombay, U.P., Bengal and sind bitterly complaining that the Khade clause of the congress constitution "is honoured more in the breach than in the performance".

"Is there no connection between Swaraj and Khadi? Were Congressmen who made themselves responsible for the Khadi clause in the constitution, so dense that they did not see the fallacy which is obvious to some critics?

"But my argument has perhaps no force with many Congressmen when anarchy reigns supreme among them." Gandhiji advised wholesale "purge" of these who fail to obey constitution. The irony is that Gandhi himself was not a member of the Congress at that time—still he demanded the "wholesale Purge" of these violators of Khadi clause of the Congress Constitution! (*Amrita Bazar Patrika,* 20 Nov., 1938). Not only that the Gandhi followers apprehended that henceforth Congress would neither encourage cottage industries nor new education system or *'nai talim'*. After a heated discussion in the Congress working Committee in its meeting (July 1938) adopted the following resolution. "It was emphasised that the wrong impression in the public mind should be removed. Ultimately it was decided that the matter be referred to Mr. Gandhi before any resolution is passed." (*Madras Mail,* Dec. 12, 1938). Most of working Committee members did not have the courage to stand up against Gandhiji's retrogade economic policy. Subhas Chandra Bose in his Indian Struggle (1935-42) wrote: "Later in the year (1938) he (the writer) launched the National Planning Committee for drawing up a comprehensive plan of industrialisation and of national development. This caused further annoyance to Mahatma Gandhi who was opposed to industrialisation." We will show how Gandhiji reacted to the issues of industrialisation and an all embracing Planning economic reconstruction of India. But here in the next section we will take a look at Jawaharlal's views on Planning and industrialisation of India.

C. Jawaharlal's Views: Planning—Industrialisation

Jawaharlal Nehru was always a man of doubtful nature. He was a man of split personality. Though he was a Gandhite in letters but not in spirit and practice. Gandhiji eulogised him as his heir apparent—but he did not believe in Gandhiji's philosophy and economic ideas. Still he put up an image of a middle roader. He tried to keep everybody in good humour. He in a letter (29th Sept. 1938) to Krishna Kripalani Wrote "Personally Speaking I am in favour or heavy industry. .... I cannot think that a country or a nation can advance/progress without the help of heavy industry. Unless there is heavy industry there can be no improvement in the living standard of the people. And there will be every possibility of loosing economic and political freedom. For the Defence system of the country heavy industry is a must. Besides this, for a large scale development of the cottage industries, a political and economic force is required that could not be built up without the base of heavy industry.

2. But heavy industry had bred many a blemish or defects. According to Kumarappa (a Gandhite theoretician) the generation of the huge industrial wealth that has sprang up under the present day capitalist system, has been built up on the basis of violence and this has ignored the question of distribution. So Kumarappa wants to tell that along with the progress and improvement of the cottage industry the issue of distribution will be properly solved and that will have less of violence. Jawaharlal more or less assented these (words).

But his main point is that the case of violence and injustice the responsibility should not lie on the heavy industry—the responsibility lay entirely on the private ownership of the means of production. He believed that if private ownership of the means of production could be abolished by the introduction of Socialism—in that case the bad effects of the heavy industry could be prevented and better results could be enjoyed.

3. Jawaharlal wanted cooperation between heavy cottage industries. It was desirable to introduce and promote heavy industry and move towards industrialisation but still then the necessity of promoting and developing cottage industries would not be lost. He said further that "he is not a votery of cottage industry. He can co-operate with them but he can not accept their views. From the above lines one might find see a sort of similarity between the statement of Subhas Chandra Bose and Jawaharlal Nehru. But the only difference was in their approach—where Bose's statement was forthnight and clear—but this very element is missing in Nehru's statement. But Nehru tried to defend an undefendable issue—where he said, "Congress never expressed it opinion against heavy industry. But for a number of reasons I accept the justification that too much weightage had been put on the cottage industries. Personally speaking in favour of heavy industry, yet for the sake of political, social and economic reasons I have been supporting the Khadi gramodyog movement. But I never had any doubt the fundamental difference between the large scale or cottage industries—still from time to time the ways the two were developing had cast doubt in my mind. In this matter, perhaps I will not be able to represent the view's of Gandhiji's too far, but in reality there did not develop any contradiction between the two." Now we will take up the views of the Congress.

"It is true that Congress took it for granted that the large Scale industry would be able to stand up independently on its own without any support, so cottage industries stole all the attention. This issue should be judged against this perspective. Our organisation was a non official one and the economic structure of the state was beyond our control. And to provide support to large scale industries would have meant providing support to vested private interest and this even included foreign vested interest. Our goal was not only to generate jobs for the idle and inactive youths to increase production but also to utilise the leisure time of the millions of human beings, to develop self-confidence among the Indian people. Congress has attained some success in this field."

Now we will examine these statements. Nehru was speaking here for himself and not for the Congress. But the truth is this that the theory of Swaraj or freedom through Charka expresses anti large scale industry mentality. Did not Gandhiji suspending non cooperation movement, in 1932, proclaim that publicity for Khadi and removal of untouchability—the twin ideals of Congress? Did any Congressman speak against this move or lodge any protest against this proclamation? What was Jawaharlal Nehru's stand then? Jawaharlal Nehru said that he did not find any fundamental difference between the large scale and cottage industry. If so? The fact must be admitted that in 1932 afterwards till 1936 the Congress could not muster strength to allow a race between the two. But the confrontation between the two had started in 1938 when he was writing this letter. He did not have the courage to go against the wishes of Gandhiji.

The other statement of Jawaharlal Nehru should be challenged. He said that Congress took it as granted that the large scale industries would be able to stand on their own without any help and that was the reason for supporting the cottage industries. Then we might ask—did the large scale industires have not strength to stand up on their own? How many large scale industry had really stand up on their own in the pre independence era? The reality was most of the large scale industries—before and after independence had to be brought under protection for their survival. So the statement of Jawaharlal Nehru could be taken seriously.

One more point need classification. Nehru said to encourage large scale industries before attaining political power would mean giving impetus to vested interest (native and foreign). If that be so then it would be better not to think of economic development.

D. Gandhiji's Reaction Relating to National Planning

Gandhiji took Charka (Khadi) and Cottage industry in religious seriousness. His reaction to the talks of National Planning and large scale industry—etc. could be asessed from the letter he wrote to Jawaharlal Nehru on 9 Aug. 1939. He wrote "Dear Jawaharlal, I was thinking due to busy schedule of talking to you something about the planning Committee in the Working Committee meeting. This morning after my talks with you Sankarlal came here. He brought with him a copy of Kripaloni's letter (written to him) on this subject. I am one with the objection raised by Kripalani on this matter. Truly speaking, I have never been able to make out the utility of the activities of the Committee. And I do not know whether the activities of the committee are duly reported to the working Committee. I am also unable to understand the usefulness of the existence of its numerous sub-committee. I am of the view that huge amount of money and time are being spent on such a work the result of which is either going to be nought—or will yield very insignificant result—this is my apprehenion." (A Bunch of letters—J.N.). Those who were acquainted with Gandhiji's views this letter would surely not surprise them. But Kripalani role in this case is really annoying. Because he being the Secretary of this working committee was present in the Delhi Industry ministers meeting conference and the decision to constitute a National Planning Committee was unanimously adopted. But Kripalani's role surprised Subhas Chandra Bose. He did not express his disension. Yet he spoke against National Planning, etc. It is clear that the Gandhiji's followers did not have the guts to go against the Gandhian development plan strategy of Charka. So it was Subhas Chandra Bose who had the courage and strong will to stand up against the 'retrograde and reactionary' policy of Gandhiji and take initiative to lead India to a new road to development.

IV. MIXED ECONOMY

Subhas Chandra Bose while inaugurating the All India National Planning Committee at Bombay Dec. 17, 1938, said, 'I divided industries into three classes: Cottage, medium—

scale and large scale industries and I pleaded for a plan which would lay down the scope of each of these industries." "Among large scale industries mother industries are the most important because they aim at producing the means of production." He continued, "If the power industry and the machining manufacturing industries are controlled by the state for the welfare of the nation, a large number of light industries like, the manufacture of bicycles, fountain pens and toys can be started in this country by men of the artisan class, working with the family as a unit. "On mother industries he said, 'It (the National Planning Committee) will have first to direct its attention to the mother industries, i.e. these industries which make the other industries run successfully—such as the power industry, industries for the production of metals, heavy chemicals, machinery and tools and communication industries like railways, telegraphs, telephone and radio." He did not fail to point out, "whatever little industry there is, is being controlled by foreigners, with the result that there is a lot of wastage." So this should be brought under state control." He wanted to stop this wastage of resources and expressed hope that Planning Committee should have to control this industry. Here again we see that Subhas Chandra Bose spoke of a mixed economy for India.

Mother industries should be brought under government control, i.e. State Control. But the toy industry, cottage industry, bicycle industry, fountain pen should be let to the private sector. But his farsighted outlook prompted him to take a look at the "communication Industries like Railways, telegraph, telephone and radio" which would ensure the control of the Government on this Industries. The importance of these industries cannot be over estimated. He visualised that communication would be vital in this future. And the transport industry need serious attention otherwise this sub continent could not be brought under one banner and flag. So he gave a clarion call to the planning committee to the Planning Committee to nurture and develop the transport and communication industries such as the railways, steamships, electrical communications, radio, etc. In the 21st Century everybody perceives the importance and utility of these industries. He foresaw this in the thirties of the last century. He thus sowed the seeds of Mixed economy for India's economic reconstruction. The concept of Mixed economy was thus born and it was taken to a logical conclusion by Jawaharlal Nehru that is all.

In the same address he stated clearly—"A comprehensive scheme of industrial development under state ownership and state control will be indispensable. A new industrial system will have to be built up in place of the old one, which has collapsed as a result of mass production abroad and alien rule at home." He was well aware of the evils of modern industries but still he favoured industrialisation hence said, "However much we may dislike modern industrialisation and condemn the evils which follow in its train, we cannot go to the pre-industrial era, even if we desire to do so. It is well, therefore that we should reconcile ourselves to industrialisation and devise means to minimise its evils and at the same time explore the possibilities of reviving cottage industries where there is a possibility of their surviving the inievitable competition of factories. In a country like India, there will be plenty of room for cottage industries, especially in the case of industries, including hand spinning and hand weaving, allied to agriculture." In this speech one call find a socialistic touch in the words, "under state ownership and state control." He simply expressed the reality of that period. Because at that time there were not many national industrialists—who would take the initiative in setting up core or mother industries and that is why he put stress on the state ownership and control. But he was not a blind follower of Soviet or any other country. He made it clear in his speech at Sonepur—fifty miles away from Lucknow, while inaugurating the first socialist school for the Congressmen, "Socialism is a modern philosophy of life. The age of individualism with its resultant capitalism was over. I consider socialism good for humanity. When I say good, I accept the principle, but its application in India depend on history and psychology of other factors. For free India, however, social reconstruction must be on socialistic lines." (*A.B.P.*, Nov. 22, *Pioneer*, Nov. 22) He made it clear that India would develop socialism in her own way keeping in mind the objective condition of the country. But Jawaharlal Nehru was too vocal in his liking for socialism. But nobody knew—what he actually meant by Socialism. A man who had no link between his word and work—who lived in a world of fantasy far from the real life could not be a man of India's destiny. Propaganda can not make a colossus with feet of clay can not walk on a hard surface. Nehru tried to save his image but history has proved him wrong.

V. MAHALANOBIS MODEL?

Now the story of Mahalanobis model: The union Cabinet had three plan drafts before it. The economists' panel's memorandum (drafted mainly by D.R. Gadgil, Mahalanobis's draft frame and Planning Commission's own draft. As was expected the model (Mahalanobis model) was rejected outright by the Planning Commission. But Mahalanobis approached Jawaharlal Nehru and aroused his enthusiasm. This changed the attitude of the Planning Commission overnight and the Second Five Year Plan (1956-61) was based on this model." Bhabatosh Datta continued further, this model first a two sector and then a four sector model largely of the Soviet type. To him whole thing was basically a matter of choice between two alternatives. Under the first alternative, there would be an immediate improvement in consumption standards, but this would restrict long-term investment in capital goods and thus slow down the rate of growth. The second alternative was to restrict consumption currently and use the resource available for investment in the infrastructure required for long-term growth, e.g. in steel, electricity, in multipurpose river projects, in basic chemicals and fertilizers—Mahalanobis convinced Nehru that the Second alternative would be desirable for our economy and Nehru went on inaugurating the "New temples of India" all over the country". Bhabatosh Datta clearly stated that "Mahalanobis was deeply impressed by his association with the Soviet economist Feldman and gave a two sector model and then a four sector model largely of the Soviet type."

"Mahalanobis was criticised for not giving adequate importance to wage goods. He himself felt that fertilisers and irrigation water would improve agricultural production and that the other basic needs of the low income groups would be met by small and cottage industries. Problems arose in the 60's. Mahalanobis believed that anything which would be physically practicable would not be constrained by the lack of finance. He did not forsee the financial difficulties that arose in the late 60's and he was practically at a loss in realising the basic factors behind inflation."

BRAHMANADA'S CRITICISM OF MAHALANOBIS STRATEGY

P.R. Brahamananda had doubts about the theoretical knowledge of those economists who supported the strategy of the Second Five Year Plan. He wrote, "Macro model at the back of the Second Five Year Plan abstracted from relative prices and there was no way by which a desirable set of relative prices as wanted by the proponents of the Second Five Year Plan. Strategy could have been part of the policy frame to sustain the Second Plan's Strategy. The Feldman strategy treated agriculture, and farmers as simply instruments for development of heavy industries. The Soviet experience of the 30's of the last century had demonstrated this very clearly. There was heavy food shortage in the USSR. The farmers had to bear the brunt of this experiment." He also said, "They were not theorists, that was the tragedy of the plan and I think of India at the time. Probably if Gadgil had been a theorist, specially at the Macro level, he might have realised that the expectation from the Second Plan's Strategy had no foundation in its structure." Gadgil was neither a capitalist roader nor a communist—yet he strongly advocated regulated licences, imposition of ceiling and permits all around. This sort of regulation required an honest and patriotic bureaucracy and a political system. The Second Plan's strategy demanded a strong Central authority to control, guide and intervene off and on in the implementation of the policies of the plan in every step. He did not realise that this was not possible in the Indian set-up."

CRITICISM OF THE MAHALANOBIS MODEL

Mahalanobis followed the Soviet model with all its limitations.

Firstly, it was a model for a closed economy followed the Soviet model with all it limitations. It was a model for a closed economy which had to build-up an industrial base depending on its own resources.

Secondly, this model depended heavily on foreign help and technology. This was a major negative point of the planning strategy.

Thirdly, the Mahalanobis model had neglected the demand side of the economy and considered only the supply side of the economy. No attempt was made to know whether thee demand for out put of different sectors would be equal to supply.

Fourthly, the strategy led to a heavy shortage of consumer goods and economy was open to an alarming inflationary situation. This could not be controlled duly that time.

Fifthly, the strategy of building a self-relient economy with heavy dependence on foreign aid, capital and technology was itself self defeating.

Sixthly, Domer's observation on Feldman's model is relevant here in this connection "closed economy" without well developed metal, machinery and subsidiary industries is unable to produce a sizeable quality of capital goods and thus to invent a high fraction of its income, however high as potential saving pro may be.

Seventhly, the emphasis on public sector units gave birth to a very were top heavy system. And very soon most of the public sector units turned out to be the most inefficient and loss making units of the country.

Eighthly, on plus point of the 2nd plan strategy must be admitted—that is one of the objectives of the Second Five Year Plan was the extension and expansion of public sector industries. In this case the Second plan made a significant move. It laid the foundation of a well not public sector in Indian economy.

Lastly, I submit that the model and strategy the Second

Five Year Plan was neither original nor did it pave a new path for Indian economy and it makes me sad to think that even someone of the stature of Mahalanobis could be a victim of the serious fallacy of viewing all economic plan purely as a piece of "Social Engineering".

VI. CONCLUSION

(a) The Planning Committee was constituted by Subhas Chandra Bose and no other person. Jawaharlal Nehru was made Chairman in place of Dr. M. Visvesvarya, as a tactic to please Gandhiji—so that he would allow the Planning Committee and the Commission to go for economic reconstruction of India through industrialisationand modernisation of Indian agriculture.

(b) The concept of Mixed Economy was to be found in the Presidutial address of Subhas Chandra Bose defined Haripara Congres in 1938, of the AICC. It was used by Jawaharlal Nehru in independent India.

(c) The Second Five Year Plan model is known as Mahalanobi's Model but it was desired from the Russian economist Feldman's model for Soviet Union. So it has not nothing to do with Jawaharlal Nehru a man with very little knowledge of economics and mathematics. He was a never student of pure science.

His subject for tripos were—Chemistry, Geology and Botany and not Physics, Chemistry and Mathematics. It is regrettable that his followers became so much survive that they shamelessly called the Mahalanobis model as Nehru—Mahalanobis model.

References

Jawaharlal Nehru (1986)—A Autobiography.

Jawaharlal Nehru—The Discovery of India (1956). Signet Press—Calcutta.

Sankari Prasad Basu—Subhas Chandra O National Planning (1992)—Jatiyo Prakashani—Calcutta (in Bengal).

Pattavi Sitaramiya—History of the Congress (1960).

Times of India—May 16, 1938.

Times of India—Oct. 17, 1938.

Times of India—Dec. 1938.

Amrita Bazar Patrika—Editorial 18 Oct. 1938.

Marhatta—Quoted in Amrita Bazar Patrika, 14 Nov. 1938.

Commerce—9th Oct. 1938, Editorial.

Madras Mail—22nd October, 1938.

Times of India—Plan for Industry, Oct. 1938.

Subhash Chandra Bose—Indian Struggle, 1935-42, Netaji Research Bureau, 1975.

Subhash Chandra Bose—Selected Speeches of Subhash Chandra Bose. Introduction S.A. Ayer—Public Divisions, 1992. Government of India..

Bhattacharyya, Dhires (1996) ed.—Science, Society and Planning Forward by Bhabatosh Datta, pp. v-vi, Progress Publishers, Calcutta.

Brahmananda, P.R. (2001)—Dr. Gadgil Birth Centenary Memorial Lecture Delivered at the 84th Annual Conference of IEA held at Vellore during 28-30 Dec. 2001, pp. 7-9.

Friedman (1956)—Mahalanobis Nehru and the Second Plan—The Statesman 22, Nov. 2006.

Sengupta, Ajit (1996)—The Mahalanobis Strategy in retrospect pp. 65-65 in Science, Society and Planning, *op. cit.*

Mukherjee, Manish, *op. cit.*, pp. 9.

Mukherjee, A.B. Strategy of Second Five Year Plan How Original it was? Arthabeekshan, Sept. 2007.

Friedman, M.—Mahalanobis Nehru and the Second Five Year Plan—The Statesman, 22 Nov., 2006.

23

Socialistic Economic Philosophy of Jawaharlal Nehru

BISWAJIT GUHA

I. INTRODUCTION

Pandit Jawaharlal Nehru, the 'Gentle Colossus' was the architect of modern India. He had a different vision about the future of Indian economy. He was both a nationalist as well as an internationalist. He was a socialist, but not a Marxist as he was a liberal democrat who advocated the philosophy of democratic socialism. Though being a socialist, Nehru did not believe in violent class struggle. Instead, he believed in the idea of peaceful transition to socialism—a new idea of non-capitalist path of development. Nehru dreamed of a self-sufficient economy of India that would be based on the heavy and basic industries—the 'temples' of the modern age as he called them. He was opposed to the idea of joining either the imperialist, i.e. the capitalist bloc or the socialist bloc. Instead, he was a strong advocate of the non-aligned movement of third world countries, i.e., of the countries of Asia, Africa an Latin America. Nehru vehemently opposed the Nazis, Fasci and their allied forces as he sincerely believed in World pe and in the principle of 'PANCHSHEELA'. He was very much impressed by economic measures adopted by the British Labour Party government that came to power immediately after the end of the Second World War. Their measures contained the wave of nationalization of banks and different public utility services, introduction of welfare state, etc.. He was simultaneously impressed by the rapid growth of the Soviet economy that was possible mainly by assigning priority on the development of heavy and basic industries. Though being a follower of Gandhiji, Nehru tried to strike a compromise solution or to arrive at a mixture of British and Soviet models of development. He believed in the idea of peaceful co-existence, i.e. in the idea of keeping equidistance from both the imperialist or capitalist bloc and the socialist bloc or that of keeping similar peaceful relation with both. He was in favour of using foreign aid in a very careful manner. This research paper is an attempt to explain different aspects of Nehru's Socialistic economic philosophy and their reflections on policies of India's economic development.

II. NEHRU—A MAN OF DOWN-TO-EARTH REALITIES

Jawaharlal Nehru proved himself as one of the greatest historians of India through his narration and analysis of events of history in different books, specially, in his books, 'The Discovery of India' and 'Glimpses of World History'. He was aware of the fact that the evolution of society and culture of all the different communities in India was sharply different from the same in the countries of west, i.e. of Europe and America. So, if we are to develop India, we have to take care of special social and cultural features of India and hence it would be disastrous if the models of development as practiced in the countries of the west are blindly followed in India. Indian communists were vehemently criticized by Nehru who pointed out their failure to understand the realities of Indian society. Indian communists always based their arguments on the experiences of Soviet Union and China though Indian realities are different. Nehru believed, therefore, that each country should plan out its way of life in accordance with its own circumstances and national genius. India is wedded to the democratic way as against the authoritarian methods. Nehru pointed out that Indian communists became antiquated in their ideas. While referring frequently to the experiences of Russia and of different countries of Europe, the Indian communists failed to understand that the conditions in India were entirely different and hence we had to find our own solutions to our problems. Due to their lack of understanding of the 'down-to-earth realities', Nehru alleged that Indian Communists "were constantly pulling the country backwards". Speaking at a meeting of the Congress Parliamentary Party, Shri Nehru observed: "I was one time a student of Marx. I was much influenced by him, although when I read him, he did not impress me enough to accept him as the guide for action here in India. . . . We have to understand the conditions in our own country, our own people and their background." (Narayan, Shriman p. 56).

III. SOCIALISTIC ECONOMIC PHILOSOPHY OF NEHRU

Shri Nehru repeatedly made it clear that the policy of the Congress and the government of India was to establish 'a socialized economy' through peaceful and democratic means. The word 'socialism' is, surely, not the monopoly or 'copyright' of the socialist party of any country. Nehru did not use it in any dogmatic or rigid sense. He felt that our Indian economic system needed to be moulded and shaped in such a manner that the interests of the individual and the society could be properly harmonized and that economic inequalities between man and man are reduced to the minimum. This could be possible only if the economic pattern attempts to achieve full employment, more production and greater social and economic justice. Nehru argues that Indian Socialism should aim at providing gainful employment to all able bodied citizens, irrespective of any kind of distinction and also reduce glaring economic and social disparities in standards of living. But this should be achieved through democratic and peaceful means and not through totalitarian and violent methods.

It was Nehru who was the main architect behind the resolution on the 'socialistic pattern of society' adopted at the

Avadi Session of the Indian National Congress. It was based on the seven following principles:

(i) Right to work and full employment;
(ii) Maximum production of national wealth;
(iii) Maximum national self-sufficiency;
(iv) Social and economic justice;
(v) Use of peaceful, non-violent and democratic methods;
(vi) Decentralisation of economic and political power through the establishment of village panchayats and industrial co-operatives:- and
(vii) Implementation of the ideal of 'unto this last', that is, the last man should be our first concern.

All these principles are in conformity with the great teachings of Mahatma Gandhi and these could be summarized as the philosophy of 'Sarvodaya'.

A study of history, practical testimony of the socialist revolution in Soviet Russia and an objective assessment of the Indian condition led Nehru to have firm conviction to socialism as the panacea for the solution of the problems of Indian poverty, feudalism and social backwardness. He always remembered that socialism to be effective and successful in India would have to appear in the Indian grab and mingle with the spirit of India. Precisely, this objective reality led him to combine scientific socialism with what Nehru called the Indian genius.

Nehru starts with Marx, but goes much farther and adds to it new dimensions to make it relevant for the present, though he retains his orientation towards scientific socialism. Thus by making Marxism free from its rigidity and dogma and thereby makes socialism a progressive ideology.

Nehru accepted the objective of Marx's socialism of equality and social justice, but preferred to adopt different techniques for achieving the same. While accepting the presence of class struggle in the society, he refused to accept class-war and violence as the only solution. Nehru believed that the class contradiction could be resolved through class cooperation in a co-operative way rather than threatening or through the concept of war.

Nehru felt that in a democratic framework, many ideas of Marxism became redundant. The expansion of adult franchise and thus election by democratic means, growth of trade union movements and adoption of a series of comprehensive measures for labour welfare and social security, land reforms and several other measures caused considerable diffusion of wealth and economic power. This diffusion intensified further as a result of regulations of both monopoly business, and Economic malpractices of the capitalist class, nationalization of public utility services and many other key enterprises of the economy. The introduction of the system of mixed economy alongwith gradual expansion of the public sector was considered by Nehru as a path of peaceful transition to socialism.

"It was precisely for this reason that Nehru never defined socialism in exact words when he talked of socialism, it may be remembered that he had used various expressions both in his speeches as well as in his writings such as 'Economic Democracy', 'Socialist Democracy', Socialist State' and 'Socialistic Pattern of society'. When he used these expressions, he used them as synonymous with one another and not as distinct expressions. Nevertheless, he deliberately refrained from giving a definition". (Mishra, Neelam, p. xiii). A human democratic Socialism is Nehru's specific brand of socialism. Freedom of the individual and the equality of opportunity can be attained only in a democratic Socialist Society.

The socialist economic philosophy of Nehru was clearly evident when, as the Prime Minister, he played the role of pioneer in introducing economic planning in India. Countering the mischievous propaganda that planning meant regimentation and the rise of totalitarianism, he declared that planning meant the most rational use of available resources to achieve certain nationally accepted goals which could bring about an improvement in the standard of living of the people and strengthen political independence of the country. He was opposed to the idea that planning was a road to serfdom. Instead, he cleared much confusion about the meaning of planning. The requirement was primacy to basic and heavy industries and infrastructural facilities like generation of electricity, setting up of multipurpose river valley projects, etc. which alone could lay down the foundation of a self-reliant economy. Nehru reiterated: "Let us have as great a measure of self-sufficiency as possible. If we are not self-sufficient, we are dependent on other countries, may be for food, may be for other thing. If we are dependent, we may get into conflicts while we may avoid them if we have a large measure of self-sufficiency.,,,,,, Self-sufficiency does not mean cutting the international trade which will increase but not in the basic things that we require". (Selected works of Jawaharlal Nehru, Second Series, Gopal, S., Ed., p. 371).

The Industrial Policy Resolutions of 1948 and 1956, introduction of public sector and its gradual expansion and thus introduction of mixed economy, adoption of measures for regulation of monopoly, assignment of priority on the development of heavy and basic industries in the Second Five Year Plan (1956-61) and several other related measures reveal the application of socialist economic philosophy of Nehru. All these were directed towards realization of following goals:

(i) Acceleration of the rate of growth of the economy,
(ii) Reduction of social and economic inequalities,
(iii) Provision of social security and social justice,
(iv) Attainment of economic self-sufficiency, etc.

Nehru asserted his faith in socialism as 'the only key to the solution of the world's problems and of India's problems'. He considered socialism as not merely an economic doctrine. It was a 'vital creed' to him which he held with all his 'head and heart'.

References

Gopal, S. Selected Works of Jawaharlal Nehru

Maheswari, Neeraja: Economic Policy of Jawaharlal Nehru, Deep & Deep Publications, New Delhi; 1997.

Martyshin, Orest: Jawaharlal Nehru and His Political Views, Progress Publications, Moscow, 1989.

Mishra, Neelam: The Socialist Orientation of Jawaharlal Nehru, Gian Publishing House, New Delhi, 1989.

Mukherjee, Hiren: the Gentle Colossus—A Study of Jawaharlal Nehru, Manisha Granthalaya Pvt. Ltd. Kolkata, 1964.

Narayan, Shriman: Towards A Socialist Economy, Indian National Congress, 1956.

Nehru, Jawaharlal: The Discovery of India, OUP, 1988.

Nehru, Jawaharlal: Glimpses of World History, OUP, 1995.

24

Jawaharlal Nehru: Socialism and Planning

BINOD CHOUDHARY AND UMESH PRASAD

INTRODUCTION

Nehru, a great leader of humanity, understood the call of steady economic expansion of India. He for one was seized of the problem of breaking through economic stagnation so that India could take its rightful place amongst the comity of progressive, prosperous and peace-loving nations. He often said that the Indian people were awakening from their long slumber under colonial rule. This slow process of regeneration could not be smooth nor sweet for every one. This regeneration and reconstruction alone could bring the real meaning of freedom to the vast and sprawling population of India for whom the primary meaning of independence would constitute of freedom from want, freedom from hunger, freedom from exploitation and emancipation from socioeconomic disabilities.

A great historian, a nationalist par excellence, the noblest lover of humanity, a phenomena pulsating the call of peace amongst men and nations, and a practical visionary of socio-economic reconstruction for India- that was Nehru. Today his spirit and ideas are helping the nation shape its destiny.

Jawaharlal Nehru was initially responsible for creating an awareness and laying the foundation for social planning in India. It was at his initiative that the All-India Congress Committee passed a resolution, as back as 1929, that "in order to remove the poverty and misery of the Indian people and to ameliorate the condition of the masses, it is essential to make revolutionary changes in the present economic and social structure of society to remove gross inequalities". Continuing his Presidential address to the same Congress he described himself as a socialist. "I must frankly admit that I am a socialist and a republican. We must realize that the philosophy of socialism has gradually permeated the entire structure of society the world over....." He stated further: "India will have to go that way too, if she seeks to end her poverty and inequality...."

NEHRU AND SOCIALISM

Nehru's interest in socialism dates back even prior to his interest in planning. It is perhaps, during his visit to Europe in 1926-27, Nehru realized, for the first time, that 'political independence' was only a step towards the attainment of "social freedom" and also to speak about the importance of socialism. Nehru and Gandhiji drafted the resolution passed at Karachi Session of Congress in 1931, which recommended the owning or controlling of key industries, etc. This resolution was regarded by Nehru as "a step, a very short step, in a socialist direction". During the great world depression of 1930s when there was all-round misery, Nehru regarded socialism as the way to end poverty, unemployment. Addressing the 1936 Lucknow Session of the Congress he stated, "I am convinced that the only key to the solution of the world's problems lies in socialism." He, however, was sure about the implication of what he spoke as he said, " When I speak this word I do so not a vague humanitarian way but in the scientific, economic sense... I see no way of ending the poverty, the vast unemployment, the degradation and the subjection of the Indian people." He, thus, even regarded socialism as a way to achieve freedom. He considered the theory of *laissez-faire* as to be 'verging on absurdity' because only few were benefited under it at the cost of many. Moreover, 'free-enterprise....means inevitably growth of monopoly and monopoly inevitably leads to the restriction of the spirit of enterprise of individuals, except a few. He was never ambiguous about his socialism which he practised during his life time. He stated: "the picture I have in mind is definitely and absolutely a socialistic picture of society. I am not using the word in a dogmatic sense at all but in the sense of meaning largely that the means of production should be socially owned and controlled for the benefit of the society as a whole". His socialisation, however, did not mean 'nationalisation of industries, banks and allied undertakings, because in adopting such an easy and short-range course, there were many pitfalls. Socialism, to him 'meant increase in national income, increase in national investment, expansion of the judicious public sector and equality of opportunity for all."

SOCIALISM AND INDUSTRIAL GROWTH

These trends in thinking influenced the formulation of the Second Five Year Plan and indeed became an organic part of it. In retrospect, it is possible to see why, without being committed in detail, Shri Nehru was greatly attracted to the scheme of development outlined in the Draft Plan Frame prepared by Professor P.C. Mahalanobis. Shri Nehru saw the approach in this document as marking a turn towards acceleration in economic growth, towards basic changes in the industrial and technological structure, application of science and scientific methods on a larger scale and promise of a self-reliant economy which itself possessed the means to achieve rapid economic progress and solve urgent social problem.

This was a period of intense debate and criticism, but Shri Nehru adhered throughout to all his fundamental propositions. He expressed them most completely in two important addresses, one delivered to the Standing

Committee of the National Development Council on January 7, 1956, and the other to the National Development Council on January 20, 1956. In these he declared that it was our firm policy to go towards a socialist structure of society. "Taking India as it is," he said, " I think we have the background here, the urge and the necessity for going in that direction." This would be a long-term process. For this purpose, long-term planning was essential, so that we have some clear idea of what in 15 years' time we hope to achieve. Shorter plans must be fitted in with the broad general scheme. "Ultimately, we should develop that structure of society which encourages the right impulses and not the wrong impulses, the right tends and not the wrong trends." Shri Nehru believed in our capacity in India in winning over people rather than fighting them. He said:

> "We can bring about social changes and development under pressure of events, by the pressure of democracy and also by friendly co-operative approach rather than the approach of trying to eliminate each other and the stronger party winning. I think, we can do that even in the industrial field."

Perhaps it is this phase that Shri Nehru's views on the general concepts of planning came to be most clearly defined. He emphasised that planning and, specially democratic planning, meant consultation with as large a number of people as possible from all consultation with as large a number of people from all over India, but the approach to planning not only depended more and upon the broader objectives, but had to be a statistical approach. Hence, the growing importance of statistical data, sample surveys and calculation at every stage of the results of the action we contemplate. Planning meant the interlocking of production, consumption, employment and a large number of other things, like transport, social services, education and health. In seeking the objective of Socialism, there should be some precise content about the goal, about the methods and about the means by which you seek to achieve the goal.

Shri Nehru did not wish merely to nationalize and

waste resources in compensating private parties, but certain fields of activity should be sacrosanct for the State, and the public sector should be given much greater scope. Subject to these, there should be every opportunity and freedom for private enterprise to grow and we should increase and encourage every element to produce and help in nation-building. There should be much greater stress on the heavy machine-making industry as that was to be the basis of industrial growth. He declared:

> "You must go to the root and base, and build up that root and base on which you will build up the structure of industrial growth. Therefore, it is heavy industries that count, nothing else counts, excepting as a balancing factor which is, of course, important. We want planning for heavy machine making industries and heavy industries; we want industries that will make heavy machines and we should set about them as rapidly as possible because it takes time."

These thoughts led directly to the revision of the Industrial Policy Resolution of 1948 and the new Industrial Policy Resolution of 1956, which has since held the field. The approach to industrial development set out in this Resolution was applied successively to steel, coal and oil, in each case after a degree of controversy. In steel and oil, in particular, without strong personal support from Shri Nehru, it would have been difficult to proceed very far. These trends were helped by what was at the time a new technical aid by the Soviet Union.

NEHRU AND PLANNING

This was Nehru's mind as at was attuning itself to the needs for economic planning of the country. Nehru's scientific socialism was taking on a definitive form during this period and it was largely because of his dynamic pragmatism that many a socialist remained with him in the Congress. During his Chairmanship of the National Planning Committee, he worked for clear political and economic goals that he considered to be the right ones for the nation. Although, as he himself said, "Marxism lighted many a dark corner of his mind," yet he knew it could not provide a proper answer for India's ills because the seed of Marxism could answer to the problem of the day. But planning could inasmuch as it provided a pedestal from where to look at the real problems and to plan the efforts of the State and the people to attain the objectives that the nation set before it.

With the advent of Independence the basic hurdle to conditioning and gearing up of the State machinery towards the new economics objectives were overcome. Nehru the democrat and Nehru the socialistic combined into one and began to lead the country towards its goal of democratic socialism.

After the country adopted its Constitution which is a hallmark of perfection of democratic values in practice, Nehru took up the task of planned development of the country. Proper background to this effort at planning was provided the 1948 Industrial Policy Resolution. Today, the Five Year Plans of the nation constitute the best memorial to Nehru. A network of national laboratories, large-scale public sector industries, highly decentralized small-scale and village industries, a multitude of hydro-electric power and irrigation projects, growth of key industries both in the public and private sectors and the development of undeveloped India into the one which has long back broken through the stagnation-are symbols of Nehru's India under planning.

The post-independence are upto a year ago, dominated as it was by Nehru had a distinct feature. This period was marked by gradual transformation of the society Among other features, Nehru's ideas of socialism and equality have created amongst the Nehru's ideas of socialism and equality have created amongst the vast mass of the Indian people a consciousness towards their democratic rights and equalitarian justice. Looking narrowly at this resurgent consciousness, some people may term it as a sort of growing resentment. But is it not, thinking objectively, a remarkable achievement of the nation since it denotes a specific growth of awakening amongst the people at large from the age-old slumber and God-bewilled staticism. It is this consciousness which would become a force and if directed properly into the body polite, it would ensure a rightful approach to the developing society.

Nehru regarded planning as an ever-flowing stream, because only then there was a rhythm of expansion in the development of the people. He stated, "Planning is a continuous process and cannot be isolated for short periods. Thus, the Third Five Year Plan is a projection and combination of the first and the second Plans, and projection and combination of the first and the second Plans, and it will lead to the Fourth and the subsequent plans. Planning is a continuous movement towards desired goals.. Indeed, perspective planning is of the essence of the planning process. As this development of the people, and a sense of enterprise and achievement comes to them….." Nehru was never deterred by the problems, however, severe they may be, which came in the implementation of the plans. Before the National Development Council in May 1956, he stated, "The new problems, which arose at every step gave confidence in ourselves and the ability of the people to achieve development." Then at the time of the massive Chinese attack on India, When there was confusion even in the high circles about the continuation of the plan, Nehru was strongly against any pruning of the Plan. Just two day after the attack he said, "We are at the cross-roads of history and are facing great historical problems on which depends our future. The plan was the warp and woof of our plan. The basis of the plan is to strengthen the nation, to increase production……the basic objective of the plan was to strengthen the nation and, therefore, the plan should be looked upon as an essential part of the national effort." It was, alone, his determination and support which was responsible for the continuation of the plan.

CONCLUDING REMARKS

Nehru's socialism and his concept of planning were scientific instruments meant to be employed by man to subserve humanity and not to crush it. Nehru was, above all, intensely human and it was this intense feeling for the human-beings that created a new economic philosophy for the country under Nehru's leadership. But his economic philosophy of democratic socialism did not suffer from any narrowness of vision. For the wrote: "I do not see why under socialism there should not be a great deal of freedom for the individual; indeed, far greater freedom than the present system gives. He can have freedom of conscience and mind, freedom of enterprise and even possession of private property on a restricted scale. Above all, he will have the freedom which comes from economic security, which only a small number possess today." This architect of modern India who kept the man as his upper most objective of service, always looked upon socialism and planning as hid tools. And it was for this reason that he talked of planning in the following terms: "Planning by itself has little meaning and need not necessarily lead to good results. Everything depends upon the objectives of the plan and on the controlling authority, as well as, of course, the Government behind it. Does the plain aim definitely as the well-being and advancement of the people as a whole, at the opening out of opportunity for all and growth of freedom and the methods of co-operative organisation and action?...An attempt to preserve old and vested interests cuts at the very root of planning. Real planning must recognize that no such special interests can be allowed to come in the way of any scheme designed to further the well-being of the community as a whole."

Nehru loved the freshness and richness of life and nature, and as such, he never subscribed to the materialistic concept of the society, not to the materialistic interpretation of history. His democratic and planned socialism was to be a tributary to the national river-never to be dry, never to be overflowing, always to enrich it with its pure ingredients of transparent values and enriching qualities and yet, to serve only as a tributary and never becoming river.

REFERENCES

Gandhiji wrote to him, "it appears to me that much money and labour are being wasted on an effort which will bring forth little or no fruit."

See, Jawaharlal Nehru: A Bunch of Old Letters, 1958.

Address to meeting of National Development Council, September 1960.

Lok Sabha Debate, Part II, December 11, 1963.

Jawaharlal Nehru, An Autobiography, 1962.

Address to Federation of Indian Chambers of Commerce and Industry, March 27, 1960.

Address to National Development Council, November 1954.

Address of All Party Consultative Committee on Planning, April 15, 1961.

25

Nehru's View on Socialist Planning: An Evolution

CHANDRA KANT SINGH AND A.S. MOHAMMAD

The reason for the claim of the Congress leaders and the violent reaction to it in opposition circles lies in the assumption that the concepts of planning, industrialisation, role of the state, etc., are inherently socialist and that their adoption has made the Congress a party wedded to socialism. It will therefore be pertinent to note that the economists and politicians of Indian nationalism refused to subscribe to the theory that the state stood above the practical policies concerning economic management. As a matter of fact, the pioneers of Indian economic thought who rose to prominence in the closing decades of the 19th century—Naoroji, Ranade and Dutt- were highly critical of the *laissez faire* theory which is said to have been the basis of the British colonial rule in India. They in fact charged the British that in the name of "free trade", they were running India's agriculture, handicrafts and trade and preventing the growth of modern industries. As the freedom movement grew, the demand that India's indigenous industry should be protected from foreign competition became more and more insistent.

Naturally, therefore, the first experiment in world history for the development of a country's economy on the basis of planned intervention by the state—the First Five Year Plan in the Soviet Union—attracted India's economists, publicists and politicians. All the more so when it was found that the USSR which until then was a relatively backward economy was able to industrialise itself rapidly, making it possible for that country to catch up with the developed capitalist countries as well as to face the mighty challenge of the anti-fascist war.

This gave rise to exercises in India for planned economic development undertaken first by the eminent engineer-statesman of Mysore, M. Visvesvaraya, who published a volume under the title *Planned Economy for India* (Bangalore, 1936). This was full two decades before Nehru took the initiative to reorient India's planning process, earning for his exercise the name "Socialist Planning". It should, however, be noted that M. Visvesvaraya was an ardent advocate of the development of capitalism through his model of planning.

That plan prepared on the initiative and under the leadership of Nehru thus turned out to be the practical implementation of what had been envisaged by Visvesvaraya to begin with, and the authors of the Bombay Plan subsequently. The difference was that the authors of the two earlier plans were frank enough to state that they were planning the development of capitalism in India in which the state was assigned a key role, but would assist the private sector. The authors of the latter were on the other hand making the tall claim that they were preparing, through planned economic development, to take the country to socialism.

It will be useful in this context to compare the extent of industrialisation in general and the establishment of heavy industries in particular contained in the 15-year Bombay Plan and the first 15-year period covered up to the completion of the Third Five Year Plan.

The total investment during the three Five Year Plans (1951-66) was nearly double what was visualised in the Bombay Plan (Rs. 18,400 crore in place of Rs. 10,000 crore).

Against this, however, should be set the rise in price level. If this is taken into account, the total investment in the three Five Year Plan periods will not in real terms be more than what was visualised in the earlier Plans.

More important, however, was the role assigned to industrialisation in the first three plans (implemented during Nehru's life). This was much less than in the Bombay Plan. The latter had envisaged 44.8 per cent of the total investment to be in the industrial sector, while in the former, it was only 33 per cent. The total percentage of investment in all industries in the three Five Year Plans in fact was even less than the investment in basic industry as per the Bombay Plan.

Although thus closely following the lines laid down by the authors of the earlier Plans (who were the self-confessed advocates of capitalist planning), the Second Five Year Plan (together with the perspective plan for the long-term development of the country) gave the appearance of preparing the country for advance towards socialism—a point which supplied ammunition to Nehru's critics from the right. It also bred illusions among sections of the left that the Second Five Year Plan was being written on a clean slate—socialist slate. It helped Nehru and his colleagues in their twin political objective to launch a frontal attack on opposition from the right and to create confusion among those in the left.

Nehru and his party in other words were able, through the formulation of a more outspoken anti-imperialist foreign policy, the forthright declaration of socialism as the national objective and the preparation of the Second Five Year Plan to be followed by similar Five Year Plans, to convince the people that they constituted a move to the left. As a matter of fact, however, they were all in line with the objectives and policies of the bourgeoisie as a class, though section of that class were opposed to this move because of their close links with internal and international reaction.

The adoption of socialism by the Congress as the national goal was followed by the formulation of the Second Five Year Plan. The Congress leaders from Nehru downwards claimed that this was the practical application of the concept of socialism into the field of economic development.

The right opponents of the Congress opposed this "left-ward shift". Rajagopalachari who for the first few post independent years was Nehru's colleague turned against him and took the initiative for the formation of the Swatantra Party.

Even within the left a section thought that, with the adoption of new policies, the Congress has ceased to be what it had so far been a party of landlords and capitalists. For the Communist Party, in fact, this was the beginning of a serious ideological and political struggle between two groups within the party (one of which proposed the political line of united front with the Congress) leading to the final split of the Party a decade later.

The reason for the claim of the Congress leaders and the violent reaction to it in opposition circles lies in the assumption that the concepts of planning, industrialisation, role of the state, etc., are inherently socialist and that their adoption has made the Congress a party wedded to socialism. It will therefore be pertinent to note that the economists and politicians of Indian nationalism refused to subscribe to the theory that the state stood above the practical policies concerning economic management. As a matter of fact, the pioneers of Indian economic thought who rose to prominence in the closing decades of the 19th century—Naoroji, Ranade and Dutt were highly critical of the *laissez faire* theory which is said to have been the basis of the British colonial rule in India. They in fact charged the British that in the name of "free trade", they were running India's agriculture, handicrafts and trade and preventing the growth of modern industries. As the freedom movement grew, the demand that India's indigenous industry should be protected from foreign competition became more and more insistent.

Naturally, therefore, the first experiment in world history for the development of a country's economy on the basis of planned intervention by the state—the First Five Year Plan in the Soviet Union—attracted India's economists, publicists and politicians. All the more so when it was found that the USSR which until then was a relatively backward economy was able to industrialise itself rapidly, making it possible for that country to catch up with the developed capitalist countries as well as to face the mighty challenge of the anti-fascist war.

This gave rise to exercises in India for planned economic development undertaken first by the eminent engineer-statesman of Mysore, M. Visvesvaraya, who published a volume under the title *Planned Economy for India* (Bangalore, 1936). This was full two decades before Nehru took the initiative to reorient India's planning process, earning for his exercise the name "Socialist Planning". It should, however, be noted that M. Visvesvaraya was an ardent advocate of the development of capitalism through his model of planning.

"Having regard to the conditions prevailing in India, it is safe for this country", he opined, "to proceed along the lines practiced in such capitalist countries as France and the United States of America... We have yet to build up some measure of moderate industrial prosperity, and for the present, capitalism is best suited for that purpose. Only the monopolies incidental to capitalism should be minimised; and wherever they are inevitable, a watch should be maintained and special modifications made by legal enactments and otherwise in the direction of service to the public."[1]

Giving "a picture of reconstructed India" as he conceived it, Visvesvaraya continued: " "The country will have been industrialised in the sense that the United States of America, Canada, Japan and Soviet Russia are today. Two or three new heavy basic industries, owned by large public companies or firms or by local governments themselves, will have been established in every province. Many medium-scale industries and a great variety of minor and cottage industries will have sprung up."[2]

The line adopted by Visvesvaraya was that of industrialisation in which the state would play and active role, though the main purpose was to develop private capitalism. This line was subsequently taken up by a group of big businessmen headed by two of the biggest capitalists in the country, Tata and Birla. Like the earlier Visvesvaraya Plan, the Tata-Birla plan or the Bombay Plan envisaged rapid industrialisation. On the role of state in industrial development, they said:

> "State control appears to be more important than ownership or management. Mobilisation of all the available means of production and their direction towards socially desirable ends is essential for achieving the maximum amount of social welfare. Over a wide field, it is not necessary for the state to secure ownership or management of economic activity for this purpose, Well directed and effective state control should be fully adequate."[3]

They went on: "in exceptional cases where the state finances an enterprise which is important to public welfare or security", or where, "in the public interest it is necessary for the state to control an industry but the circumstances of the industry are such that control is ineffective unless it is based on state ownership", this has to be done. Even in such cases, however, "if later on private finance is prepared to take over these industries, state ownership may be replaced by private ownership."[4]

State control is recommended in the case of "public utilities, basic industries, monopolies, industries using or producing scarce national resources and industries receiving state aid", but such control should be exercised "without unduly hampering the initiative of the management.[5]

The final suggestion is far more revealing: "It does not invariably follow that all the enterprises owned by the state should also be managed by it. There are three alternative methods of management open in such cases: By the state, by private enterprises and by *ad hoc* public corporations. It is necessary to take into account the wider and more fundamental questions or the extent to which public welfare and security will be safeguarded and promoted under each system. It is not possible to lay down a general rule as regards this aspect of the question and each case must be decided on its merits. In the ultimate decision, the governing issue will be whether the state control is not sufficient to safeguard the public interest but in addition to it, state management also be provided."[6]

Big business in the country was thus demanding that the state should so intervene in the development of the country that the state control—even state management in some cases—should subserve the interest of the private sector. In the other words, just as the British rulers were using their control over the state and government of the country to serve their (foreign monopoly) interests, so should the national government of free India use the newly-acquired state power to serve the interests of the Indian bourgeoisie. Nobody could have accused the big business planners of the mid-1940s of preparing a plan for developing the country's economy along socialist lines. And yet, they wanted state control—even state management in some cases—since that alone would help the development of the private sector as it developed in the U.K., the U.S.A., France, Japan, etc.

A mutual comparison of Visvesvaraya's Plan and Bombay Plan and also with the Second Five Year Plan framed on Nehru's initiative would show that they were broadly along the same lines. The Visvesvaraya and Bombay Plans, however, remained on paper; they could not be put into practice during the first decade of independence. The struggle for political power which was on upto 1947; the partition of the country into two new states, the Indian Union and Pakistan; the inclusion of East Bengal, West Punjab and Sind in the new state of Pakistan; the deterioration of the food situation in the new state of the Indian Union that followed the partition and several other problems made it impossible for the leaders of independent India to apply their minds to the problem of translating into action the ambitious goals and objectives which had been set in the national plans drawn up in the days of freedom struggle. They were preoccupied with such problems as refugee rehabilitation, food deficit, deficit of raw material to the two manufacturing industries of the country (cotton textiles and jute) and, above all, the ongoing war and disturbances in Kashmir.

They did of course take the earliest opportunity to prepare a plan for the development of the country's economy. Even while drawing up the first plan report in 1951, the new rulers gave some thought to the long-range development of the country. Chapter one of the report had in fact given a graph showing the plan objectives regarding the growth of national income and aggregate consumption expenditure for

25-30 years. The country's income was to be doubled in 21 years; India would, by the year 1971-72, have as much more by way of national income as it had in 1950-51. Allowing for the increase in population that would in the meanwhile take place, it was calculated that per capita income would be doubled in a period of about 27 years, i.e. by 1977-78.

More important than the question of aggregate national income, however, was the direction of the change envisaged in the national economy. Both the Visvesvaraya and Bombay Plans had given the greatest emphasis to industrialisation. That precisely was what was lacking in the first plan. The Bombay Plan, for instance, had envisaged a total investment of Rs. 1400 crore in the First five years, of which Rs. 790 crore was to be invested in the industrial sector. During the first plan period, however, only Rs. 377 crore out of Rs. 1960 crore were invested in industries. That plan obviously was such that it would condemn India to the same backward position as it was in the earlier period and force her to be fully dependent on the capitalist powers.

This failure of the First Five Year Plan should be explained by the fact that the British rulers and their friends from the capitalist countries were not prepared to help India industrialise itself, even though the industrialisation was not to take the course adopted in the Soviet Union. The framework of the first plan in fact had been modeled on what such imperialist agencies as ECAFE and the Colombo Plan had prepared for the newly liberated countries which were expected to continue as the satellites of world capitalism. The foreign "benefactors" of India's ruling classes did not want the latter to develop into rivals which they would become if they succeeded in putting into practice the grandiose plans contained in the Visvesvaraya and Bombay Plans. The first plan had thus envisaged the development of capitalism in India so as to make her continue to be a satellite of world capitalism.

What about the socialist powers ? The Indian ruling classes and their party did not initially take them to be capable of helping countries such as India to develop as their people desired. Devastated as the Soviet Union had been during the of years of the anti-fascist war, they thought that country would not be in a position, even if its leaders wanted to render substantial aid to India. In other words, while the rulers of capitalist countries were interested in keeping India backward, the rulers of socialist countries would be unable to assist them.

That this was a miscalculation, was proved even while the First Five Year Plan was in operation. The Soviet Union had recovered from the destruction caused during the war. Its economy saw a rapid advancement. The success attained by here post-war Five Year Plans showed that for her recovery the Soviet Union did not depend on the capitalist powers as had been expected, but in fact she put herself in a position to help other needy countries. Some of the other socialist countries were also advancing at rates far more rapid than could be dreamed of by the capitalist countries.

Coming to the Asian continent, it was becoming clear that China was setting a new example for all the underdeveloped countries of Asia. The agrarian revolution carried out by the Chinese people's democratic government became the source of inspiration for all the underdeveloped countries. Even the most hardened representatives of India's ruling classes could no longer argue that the socialist countries have nothing to offer to our development plans, either by way of advice or material assistance and cooperation.

The experience made the leaders of the government turn to the socialist countries for help in the diplomatic, political as well as economic fields. The response was encouraging. Experts and advisers from the socialist countries came in large numbers to help our planners to formulate a plan of genuinely independent economic development of the country. They offered technical know how and capital goods to India. All these enabled India's planning authorities to undertake the "bigger and bolder" approach contained in the second Plan.

That plan prepared on the initiative and under the leadership of Nehru thus turned out to be the practical implementation of what had been envisaged by Visvesvaraya to begin with, and the authors of the Bombay Plan subsequently. The difference was that the authors of the two earlier plans were frank enough to state that they were planning the development of capitalism in India in which the state was assigned a key role, but would assist the private sector. The authors of the latter were on the other hand making the tall claim that they were preparing, through planned economic development, to take the country to socialism.

It will be useful in this context to compare the extent of industrialisation in general and the establishment of heavy industries in particular contained in the 15-year Bombay Plan and the first 15-year period covered up to the completion of the Third Five Year Plan.

The total investment during the three Five Year Plans (1951-66) was nearly double what was visualised in the Bombay Plan (Rs. 18,400 crore in place of Rs. 10,000 crore). Against this, however, should be set the rise in price level. If this is taken into account, the total investment in the three Five Year Plan periods will not in real terms be more than what was visualised in the earlier Plans.

More important, however, was the role assigned to industrialisation in the first three plans (implemented during Nehru's life). This was much less than in the Bombay Plan. The latter had envisaged 44.8 per cent of the total investment to be in the industrial sector, while in the former, it was only 33 per cent. The total percentage of investment in all industries in the three Five Year Plans in fact was even less than the investment in basic industry as per the Bombay Plan.

Although thus closely following the lines laid down by the authors of the earlier Plans (who were the self-confessed advocates of capitalist planning), the Second Five Year Plan (together with the perspective plan for the long-term development of the country) gave the appearance of preparing the country for advance towards socialism—a point which supplied ammunition to Nehru's critics from the right. It also bred illusions among sections of the left that the Second Five Year Plan was being written on a clean slate—socialist slate. It helped Nehru and his colleagues in their twin political objective to launch a frontal attack on opposition from the right and to create confusion among those in the left.

Nehru and his party in other words were able, through the formulation of a more outspoken anti-imperialist foreign policy, the forthright declaration of socialism as the national objective and the preparation of the Second Five Year Plan to be followed by similar Five Year Plans, to convince the people that they constituted a move to the left. As a matter of fact, however, they were all in line with the objectives and policies of the bourgeoisie as a class, though section of that class were opposed to this move because of their close links with internal and international reaction.

Notes and References

1. Visvesvaraya, Planned Economy for India, p. 161.
2. *Ibid.*, p. 257.
3. Bombay Plan, pp. 27-28.
4. *Ibid..*, p. 28.
5. *Ibid.*, p. 29.
6. *Ibid.*, pp. 29-30.

26

Nehru's Vision of World Socialism and Economic Co-operation

A. SANGAMITHRA AND JAYASELVI

INTRODUCTION

When Gandhi left the Indian National Congress and Swaraj Party was founded, he decided to revive and recognize the Indian National Congress by reforming the ideology on the basis of an ECONOMIC CREED. He thrived to achieve complete Independence, political and economic both. The method, by which he wanted to accomplish this, was "Democratic Socialism", which was different than that of Marx. This was a logical and scientific approach in democracy to realize equal distribution of income via planned Programmes. He felt that a complete change was difficult as capitalism was deep rooted in the soil; so some form of capitalism and some form of state ownership could benefit the conditions then prevalent in the country.

ECONOMIC THOUGHTS OF JAWAHARLAL NEHRU

His Economic Ideology developed along this line that

the economy of free India could advance progressively if divided into Public and Private sectors to combine and substitute for proper and smooth growth. He had learnt from the past records that liberal ideas only could flourish in Indian soil to gain a political unity and effective administration. History never remained a record of past for him, but the basis of present and future action, not to revert back, but to advance further. His economic ideal developed along 'secular lines,' which was not 'non-religiousness,' rather moral and ethical, which aimed to create " a welfare-state" on modern and scientific lines.

He clearly understood that individuality could not be wiped away, and society could develop if individual was free with gentle guards and checks. If the 'self-motive' of the individual was granted and proper incentives were given, then only natural growth could take place. It was like granting freedom to a child in a house with certain measures of limitations with an aim of his welfare. This is why he chose to be a REPUBLICAN and a socialist and favoured virtues of the Capitalism and virtues of the Socialism.

He saw Socialism as a control of capital in the national interest rather than as an imposition of authority on private enterprise. He was an enemy of privilege of every kind and a believer in social control rather than dictation. That is why is ideal postulated a society, Indian in sentiment, and social habit, secular in its outlook and democratic in its working. Authoritarianism offended his sense of individual freedom, and he proposed for a scientific and practical Socialism. Not absolute Socialism of idealistic and theoretical type, which he aimed to achieve by granting due liberty and discipline both. This 'MIXTURE' was significant in the context of "synthetic" character of India. So he offered "Mixed Economy" with a supplementary role of public and private sectors to arouse awareness and the responsibility of the state and the citizens. The social responsibility of the private sector becomes inevitable and the process of socialization becomes natural and automatic in due course of time if "production" is optimum (Dr. Purnima P. Kapoor, 1985).

Production', he said, "is wealth" and this wealth can be abundant with vast labour potential, if "dignity of labour" is realized in every hand, and each and every work with proper and adequate conscience. There is no want of work, there is lack of 'intention' and 'interest'; a kind of dependence is deeply rooted in the Constitution of Indians, and he laid maximum stress on the spread of education for good technical training and development of human factor and improves the learning curve of industrial expansion. So political freedom was essential for stepping in the right direction that "without social freedom and socialistic structure of society and the state, neither the country nor the individual could develop much".

To inculcate his ideal he moved with the masses, organized state people's organization against the autocracy of the Indian Princess who controlled one third area of India. He took keen interest in the labour movement and held Presidential chair at different sessions. As a democratic Socialist he presented a minute of dissent to the Report on the future constitutional set-up of India and advocated for the establishment of a Socialist Republic for India.

Thus he rushed in where angles feared to tread. Like a seer of the past he pierced the veil of the future to show where all the social, economic and political forces could lead to. His magnanimous attitude, constant association of Gandhi and other leaders opened avenues for his analytical thinking. This evolved his scientific, modern and logical approach to economic problems. He learnt Economics through circumstances. It is the action that theorizes an idea. Economics is the study of man's actions in the ordinary business of life, and 'norms' form the nucleus of this study, which makes a person humanist before economist. Jawaharlal was the greatest humanist of his time. His approach to life was humane and he was an exemplary democrat. This democratic attitude helped him to be flexible in the formation of his ideology that he was ready to retrospect and improve in the area he had realization. Some people indulged in futile exercise of pitting him against Gandhi.

Needless to emphasize that the areas of agreement or disagreement between the two in the larger framework of Gandhism are very narrow. Only small men wanted to create a cleavage to serve their own interests. He was not a blind follower and made dispassionate analysis of ideas. He urged the masses through his vibrating eloquence and moving thoughts constantly at different levels of associations and opportunities, that by consistent iteration he got India committed to the objective of 'Socialism'. In this venture he remained a lone fighter and a lone visionary. Oppositions cautioned him and made him more logical and firm. He never turned back or lost faith in his ideal. His Western education proved a boon in disguise for his open mindedness, as he could raise the masses above superstitions and instill modern and scientific ideas into their minds. Education started spreading and awakened the sleeping spirit of the people. He planned for village uplift on modern lines. MODERNISATION stood violent criticism for additional cost and investment, but the main objective was not grasped, as this was to fructify plans of better standard of living good sanitation and progressive life which meant economizing in the longer-run with basic civic amenities and Social Welfare.

He believed that education was the greatest means to realize the social responsibility and individual awareness, so it has to be the incorruptible living wealth of a nation, which has to be self-evolved and authentic expression of the national spirit. It is essential for masses to understand the policy and decisions or nation divides into parts. Thus education aimed to prepare the desired consciousness to modernize people in the course of effective development that people will limit their families, realize responsibilities and process automatic development towards the economy of abundance to socialize eventually.

So education was to develop the collective instinct in man to feel that his individual good depends on the good of the society as a whole. He advocated compulsory education nation wide and played a vital role in planning quantitative and qualitative expansion of education. Transition of a traditional society to modernism traverses a tortuous path and sometimes in reverse direction. His talks and speeches developed a social-consciousness of the need of learning and scientific living. This helped to change the outlook of the Agrarian society and resulted in Green Revolution and scientific farming, which accelerated the growth of capital formation and the Gross National Product (Dr. Purnima P. Kapoor, 1985).

He was extremely logical in his hypothesis that only solid Industrial potential could strengthen the infrastructure and industrialize the country. It was not an easy task to raise the mind and heart of the people who were clinging to the age old ideas. He laid the foundation of basic and heavy industries in consonance with his avowed principle to uplift agriculture, which depends upon modern, scientific and improved inputs. He aimed to facilitate Production to create wealth, opportunity and capital. Only if there is capital, can it be distributed among people?

For this industrialization, he created a Mixed-Economy of Public and Private sectors to assume various dimensions of 'Production'. He knew that a country cannot flourish in a vacuum and it has to depend on other nations for its own benefit and benevolence. His socialism carried wider perspectives at different stages of learning; and gave wider implications. An independent India aspired through him to flourish economically in the global environment and he propounded a principle of co-existence to socialize resources among nations. He postulated the basic principles of FOREIGN-POLICY which was basically an economic policy for the furtherance of his ideal, and to open wider horizons of development. This policy aimed to maintain "individual-sovereignty" of the nation as a Trust and Socialization of capital and potential to uplift the under-developed nations. His foreign policy received international applause and proved extremely effective. He proved that he was a Republican in the true sense of the term and a great Socialist as he did not confine his ideal to the shores of his country. To him "nationalism" seemed a "narrow and insufficient creed "and he invited nations to develop in a co-operative spirit and benevolent way. This was unique Trusteeship in favour of social interest and international development.

There was unity given to the nation and the motto of 'service above self' spread a message of peace to other nations. The voice of poor nations was given a patient hearing. India stepped on the path of "Humanitarian-Socialism" This was a novel and practical philosophy. The country started humming with activities as factories, mills, laborties and machines of various types. A systematized economic development was processed with broad social objectives of achieving full employment, reducing inequality of income maximizing production and providing social justice.

Normative aspect of Material Welfare is the basis of economic science. When the country has developed materially then only can the Society take a Socialistic pattern. He channelized his economic philosophy and initiated Socialism— a rare philosophy developed in the mind of Jawaharlal as a pioneer to guide other nations through challenges and forces of time. His philosophy allowed A CHANGE ACCORDING TO NEED AND TIME and resented an "ism" or a 'dogma' to stick to it, because his foresight was tremendous and he envisioned before time. He called his experiences and "experiment", an innovation, which suited Indian myth and Economics, and raise a tremendous spirit of Renaissance.

Independence was not a victory for him; it was a relentless battle to fight poverty. Socialism in Democracy of innocents and illiterates appeared like the distant mountains which seemed easy access and climbing but as he approached. Difficulties surmounted higher he reached more laborious became his journey, and the Summit receded into clouds. "Yet the climbing was worth the effort and had its own joy and satisfaction".

It was not a smooth operation to drag a huge, unwieldy and amorphous body like Congress along the path, if not plainly of Socialism, but of 'progress' and modernization. He brought to the service of his country A LIFE FORCE that was deep down, truly tempestuous and gave God's plenty. The future before us is no more veiled in the glamour of a dream, but is lit with solemn glory of revelation and Truth.

NEHRU'S CONCERN FOR WORLD POVERTY

Nehru was always unambiguous as far as his role as a 'Head' of the largest parliamentary democracy like India. In his absence, we have lost a true democrat, an honest man and above all, a faithful leader who could guide the destiny of the nation selflessly. Not only that, he had a profound vision for the development of the world political and economic order through Socialism. He showed much concern for the establishment of the democratic system in the newly developing nations of the world. For them, he echoed concern in the United Nations. In this world body, he always pleaded for the freedom of the nations. His ideas and philosophy were readily accepted by the other emerging leaders all over the world, for example, Nassar, Sukarno, Kenneth Kaunda and Julius Nyerere. This concern of Nehru for all human beings sprang owing to his firm belief in individuality and liberty. Further, Panditji had a broad vision imbued with the kind of humanistic values which, in the wake of the unbridled conservatism of the world society cannot be minimized. He initiated new ideas and aspirations of the intelligentsia against the stubborn passions of vested interests and inculcated in the world community the passion for true democratic system and social justice. Striking the balance between the conflicting ideas and pressures put on him by other leaders of the nations in those times, to move forward to bring about social and economic transformation, was by no means an insignificant achievement. It was, indeed a very difficult task, particularly when the developed industrial nations were putting conditions on international trade and aid releases. Nehruji's appeal was for the cause of removal of world poverty by narrowing the gap between rich and poor nations. Since he championed the cause of world poverty, all people the world over endeared him (Dr. Ashok Vasanth Bhuleshkar, 1988).

DIFFERENCES IN APPROACH WITH GANDHIJI

For the abolition of poverty in India, Nehru convinced forcefully and effectively to his other colleagues in the Congress party and converted most of them to the faith of 'Democratic Socialism'. However, the only difference between Gandhiji and him was that he spoke the language of modern socialism which, by and large, appealed to the Indian intelligentsia. Gandhiji favoured indigenous technology and his ideas of economic development were based on intermediate technology suited to the local conditions in rural as well as in urban areas. Nehru was fascinated by advanced technology adopted in the western world since he wanted quicker progress and development. It may be mentioned that in view of the differences in approach to economic development, between him and Gandhiji, the common people were not amused by Nehru's socialist jargon; however, they were impressed by his transparent honesty, sincerity and by his abiding faith to uplift the downtrodden from the morasses of poverty and deprivation. Nehru thus dominated the Indian political scene particularly from 1928 and 1964, and the policies evolved during this period bear his imprint.

CREATION OF SOCIALIST PATTERN OF SOCIETY

It may be emphasized here that it was 'Nehru' who persuaded the then intelligentsia to adopt social planning since equality between man to man was innermost in his mind. He felt that economic opportunity can be provided to the common man if the key industries are nationalized, powers of the landlord class are curbed, monopoly of the vested interests is checked and controlled, free education to the society at large is provided and encouraged, and above all, social welfare measures such as health, sanitation and housing are initiated to create a healthy society. Ever since the goal of 'Socialist Pattern of Society', proposed for our country by Panditji, it is now clear that democratic society and socialist society has become a part and parcel of Indian way of life. Thus, the socialist society demands the creation of conditions of equality of opportunities for the large mass of people so that they may have the maximum scope for their self-expression and development. However, the objectives set before us by Panditji, one would like to ask a question—whether are we practicing it? From the point of view of the ends propounded by him under democratic socialism, if we examine on doctrinaire grounds, it can be remarked that we are far from achieving these objectives. We should now make constant efforts to carry forward the goals and ideals set before us by Panditji. His dream to set-up the Socialist Pattern of Society in India can only be achieved if we make sincere efforts. We have seen that during the Eighth five year plan, the goals of socialism have been reemphasized by our Prime Minister Shri Rajiv Gandhi, and therefore, we can rededicate ourselves to the cause of democratic socialism, to achieve the dream of Panditji.

NEHRU'S PHILOSOPHY OF INTERNATIONAL CO-OPERATION

Having said about the ideas of Panditji, in regard to Indian situation, we may like to look at briefly, his philosophy of international economic co-operation and its implications on Indian economic development. The fact remains that Nehru's philosophy of international co-existence and peace sprang up because he wanted peaceful economic transformation, uninterrupted by any upheavals of war. His foundation of peaceful co-existence was laid down through 'panchsheel'. The basic objectives and guiding principles of Nehru's international economic co-operation are implemented through co-operation with Asian countries, and India's immediate neighbours. He wanted to have regional harmony in Asia primarily to benefit from each other's resources. And this he started doing it even prior to attaining the Independence. After achieving our Independence, Panditji organized a loose confederation with the immediate neighbours under the Colombo plan. In 1955, he tried to extend the co-operation with the African countries by convening 'Afro-Asian Conference, at Bandung.' For Nehru, international co-existence and co-operation with the developing countries, was the basic principle on which he wanted to base the philosophy of economic co-operation, for the economic development of the developing countries. According to him economic co-operation between the different countries who have more or less, similar economic conditions, will provide an opportunity for creativity in the field of economics, which will in turn, revolutionalise the methods of production, for enhancing the levels of production. Thus, in short, Nehru's strong commitment to the cause of world poverty through international economic co-operation and peaceful co-existence made a deep impression on the international community. When the idea of United Nations was properly mooted, Nehru's heart was filled with Joy, because the concept and objective behind the formation of this world body closely fitted into his own ideals and therefore, he played a prominent role in the development of the United Nations, in his lifetime.

APPROACH TO WORLD PEACE AND ECONOMIC DEVELOPMENT

For Nehru the United Nations was of particular significance. It is through this body that he hoped to alleviate poverty and improve economic conditions of the masses the world over. It is worthwhile to point out here that 'the commonwealth' also provided him an equally important forum to vent his ideas on international political as well as economic matters, particularly international political as well as economic matters, particularly the philosophy of 'co-operative commonwealth'. His voice commanded increasing respect in these International bodies in view of his genuine concern for the unprivileged. Similarly, Panditji played an import ant role to propagate his philosophy of non-alignment and non-violence through these bodies. This helped him bring about peace and amity amongst the nations in those days of strong divided world, and lessen the cold war conflict between the big powers. It can be argued that to keep India out of cold war, Nehru strived hard as India's economic development was uppermost in his mind. He felt the country's economic planning would be jeopardized if war breaks out. He wanted to spend more money on dams, highways, steel plants and modern technologically oriented projects, to enhance the economic capabilities of the country than to divert the country's resources for building-up arms and ammunitions. Thus, it would not be wrong to say that the achievement of economic co-operation in various fields, and India's present amity between different nations, can be attributed to Nehru's legacy. The only snag which has aborted this concept, to a certain extent, is due to shortsighted policy of developed nations who, in order to protect their self-interest have ignored the real implications of his policy, for world economic development.

REGIONAL ECONOMIC CO-OPERATION

Nonetheless, during the late 1970's efforts at North/ South co-operation have resulted into better world under New International economic order. However, during the 1980's the intransigent policies adopted by the developed nations hampered the progress in achieving effectively the North/South economic co-operation between the developed and the developing nations. In view of such developments on the international scene, the developing nations among themselves thought it appropriate during 1980's, to have greater regional co-operation, resulting into emergence of South/ South economic co-operation. The establishment of 'South/ South Commission for Co-operation', will help India, to play a key role in economic development of the other Third world nations. Had Nehru been alive today his heart would have been filled with joy, to see the implications of his policy bearing a fruit in the practical sense. The basic concept of co-operation among the developing nations is the 'Complementarity' and 'reciprocity' of resource transfers, and 'mutual interests', and 'benefits', on equal terms, so that the regional/ sub-regional development is expeditiously attained, between the nations. Nehru's perspective of economic development embodied the inter-dependence of the nations in the world. He felt that the problem of economic development can be resolved globally since there is a mutuality of interest.

Today's efforts by the world leaders to evolve New International Economic Order can be greatly ascribed to the vision and wisdom of Panditji. He evolved strategies, from time to time, to convince the North, and kept on continuous dialogue with them, for the promotion of well-being of the world community at large. This shows his concern for the welfare of the entire human race. However, it is sad to observe that his dream is not yet accomplished, as it may be remarked that the developed nations have not as yet recognized the fact that the progress of both-the rich and the poor is mutually co-existensive and complementary. Therefore, the present efforts as referred to earlier, of contemplated South/ South dialogue, could help to bring about in a greater measure, the close ties between the developing nations, for furthering the cause of economic development. This may help to bring about social as well as economic justice for the mankind living in the southern region. Further, the regional economic co-operation, as visualized by Nehru, may help to tread the path of inter-regional economic co-operation, inter-dependent growth and development for the nations who will be involved in the formulation of economic policy in the southern region.

However, it would, at the same time, be prudent to pursue the goal of international economic co-operation between the developed and the developing countries, as propounded by Nehru, though, to bear the fruit, it may take more time, due to diversity of interests and the protectionist policies pursued by the developed nations. Countries in Asia, if they succeed in revitalizing their economies, the signs of progress may set an example to the other developing nations in the world. And this could be a glowing tribute to Jawaharlal Nehru, who strived hard in his life time to achieve togetherness of the world communities. However, in the initial stages, to harness, a new consensus for the management of the Asian economy can be considered an effort in the right direction. The wider implications of such a harmony may help to reduce the area of conflicts, between the nations in the Asian region. The present steps through arrangements such as South Asian Association for Regional Co-operation, (SAARC) and ASEAN, and the Gulf Co-operation Council, may be considered a step to forge closer relationships between the nations in the Afro-Asian regions, of reinforcing the process of mutual economic co-operation and strengthening the bond of bilateral as well as multi-lateral economic ties, helping to have regional and sub-regional arrangements and the global schemes of North/ South economic co-operation in the near future. Thus, finally it may be remarked, that with the clear message from Pandit Jawaharlal Nehru, the founding father of modern India, who strived hard for the world economic co-operation, it would not be far off, if we pursue the policy of togetherness which will help us to achieve the goal of universal brotherhood, peace, prosperity through the management of the world economies, for better future of the mankind in the emerging world of tomorrow.

NEHRU'S INTERNATIONAL APPROACHES

This confidence in bringing people together on a common platform for the defence of the rights of humanity were shaped into the world peace movement. The cultural backdrop of the statesmanship was by now completely prepared to organize all aspects to promote the ethos of peace movement. Another aspects of the international affairs, however, remained a kind of new challenge in the changing map of the world. The world was divided into developed and underdeveloped regions. All countries under the underdeveloped economies had freed themselves from the colonial bondages. In this infant stage after the freedom of colonial imperial power, they needed an environment of confidence. Panchsheel as the principles of international living were defined by Pandit Nehru for the collective security, prosperity and the friendship of the Asian countries. It should be remembered that Pandit Nehru had deep affection for the Chinese civilization. He had close contacts with democratic leadership of China. Students of Chinese economy can read the introduction by Pandit Nehru to a book, 'China Builds for Democracy'. The introduction is an essay that gives graphic philosophic interpretation of the emerging trends in the Chinese economy, politics and culture. It was, therefore, consistent for him to promote interactions with China's culture. Nehru's broadcast in 1946 as the Prime Minister, included one paragraph on China which is the evidence of what has been underlined above. Moreover, there had been ancient contacts. China's extension on Tibet was greatly debated in this context. How far the historic decision of India was strategically good or bad in respect of Tibet was and is still a point of reference from the humanistic point of view. Pandit Nehru, however, proved his merit. India does not have expansionist regional outlook. This was obviously declared in case of Tibet to the statesmen of the world. Perhaps this convinced the Soviet Union that Nehru can never promote warfare to claim the military superiority of India over its neighbouring countries. It was, therefore, easy to convince the leaders in China, Indonesia and the other neighbouring countries to accept the Panchsheel principles for international living.

References

1. Economic Thought of Jawaharlal Nehru, Dr. Purnima P. Kapoor, 1985, Deep & Deep Publications, New Delhi.
2. Indian Economy in the World Setting, Dr. Ashok Vasant Bhuleshkar, 1988, Himalaya Publishing House, New Delhi.
3. Indian Economic Thought and Development: Ashok V. Bhuleshkar, Popular Prakashan, Bombay, 1969.
4. Jawaharlal Nehru, The Discovery of India.
5. Jawaharlal Nehru, A Biography, Vol. 2, 1947-56.
6. Jawaharlal Nehru a study in Ideology and Social Change, R.P. Dube, Mittal Publications, New Delhi.
7. Jawaharlal Nehru Memorial, Volume II, Dr. V. Bhuleshkar, Popular Prakashan, Bombay, 1972.
8. Jawaharlal Nehru: Prime Minister, Amiya Rao, Sterling Publishers Pvt. Ltd, New Delhi, 1974.
9. Life and works of India's First Prime Minister—Jawaharlal Nehru, S. Balasubramaniam, 2007, Vijay Goel Publications.
10. Nehru: A Political Biography, Michael Breacher, 1969, Oxford University Press, London.

27

Economic Philosophy of Jawaharlal Nehru: Pregnant with Socialistic Content

BIRENDRA KUMAR JHA

> "Socialism is thus for me not merely an economic doctrine which I favour, it is vital creed which I hold with all my head and heart."
>
> —*Nehru*

Pandit Jawaharlal Nehru who strode like a colossus on the Indian sub-continent, fighter, statesman, historian and literateur but as a propounder of an economic ideology he was no less prominent than he was in his other various capacities. Pandit Nehru was not an original economic thinker. He was not associated with any school or ism but he, after picking up some ideas from here and there, wove them into a wreath. He borrowed the economic ideas freely from different schools of Economics and in this sense he was great economic eclectic. Like Adam Smith, Malthus, Marshall and Keynes his merit lies in successfully integrating different scattered ideas and reconciling antagonistic sets of thinking.

About his eclecticism Michael Brechor's observation is worth noting. In the realm of thought Nehru has always been a lonely traveler seeking answers that seem to elude his grasp. Almost all the ideological currents of the past half century appealed to his keen and receptive mind; first in time was classical liberalism with its emphasis on individual rights, then, at Cambridge, he was drawn to Fabian socialism, thereafter, he was influenced by the Gandhian stress on the purity of means and the message of non-violence; and in the late twenties and thirties by Marxist theory and the gospel of a classless society. He was also attracted to the ethical norms of western humanism, and later, during his long war-time imprisonment, to the precepts of the vedanta..... None of these dominated his outlook; all of them influenced his thought. Indeed, the key to his thinking is scepticism about all claims to absolute truth and virtue .... Nehru is an eclectic in intellectual matters. (Michael Brechor, 1959). His economic philosophy is dynamic, pragmatic, practical and scientific. None of his economic ideas is Utopian and speculative; all of them can be easily put to practice. Thus his philosophy was a living philosophy, social not individual, secular not-religious, practical not speculative, dynamic not static; disciplined not laissez faire; pragmatic not purely idealistic; and ethical not expediential. In his opinion only a living philosophy is competent for prescribing solutions to the cropped up problems. He remained always dynamic in his socio-economic thinking. His clear-cut concept on the desirability of change and flexibility can be expressed in his own words, "Even those basic principles which are said to be unchanging lose their freshness and reality when they are taken for granted and the search for them ceases (Nehru, 1946) He was a many-sided personality and our economic policy bears his indelible stamp.

Pandit Nehru's economic Philosophy was the result of so many influences both of ideas and persons but a seeker after truth like him can hardly be expected to lend himself to a single influence in a constantly shifting conditions of a dynamic world. In shaping and conditioning the corps of his economic philosophy some of the most important influences were his family atmosphere, British rule in India, impact of personalities like Gandhi, Tagore, Vinoba Bhave, Garbald, his personal contact with poor peasants and factory workers, his first visit to the U.S.S.R in 1927 and other foreign tours, jail imprisonments and his own deep and wide reading. His economic philosophy was a fusion of western and eastern economic doctrines. He himself accepted the fact that "A study of Marx and Lenin produced a powerful effect on my mind and helped me to see history and current affairs in a new light" (Nehru, 1946). Of course, he had borrowed from Marxism a scientific outlook, a zeal for making the country a better place to live in, an anxiety and enthusiasm for improving the lot of the poor through social ownership and control of means of production and a sense of understanding history but the Gandhian influence, as well as a streak of individualism and non-conformism, prevented him from embracing the creed completely. He was critical of Marxism for achieving the goal through violence and class struggle but "Communism has definitely allied itself to the approach of violence. Even if it does not indulge normally in physical violence, its language is of violence, its thought is violent and it does not seek to change by persuasion or peaceful democratic processes but by coercion and indeed by destruction and extermination. This is completely opposed to the peaceful approach which Gandhiji taught us.... speaking for myself I find this approach wholly unreasonable and uncivilized, whether it is applied in the realm of religion or economic theory or anything else" (Nehru, 1958). He accepted much in the Gandhian outlook but he never identified himself wholeheartedly with a rigid body of doctrine whether it was Gandhism or Marxism. As he never fully supported either Marxism or Gandhism he was looked with doubt and suspicion in both the campus (O.P. Mishra, 1978). According to Frank Moraes, "In Gandhi's life time Nehru had been accused of scaring Gandhites by his socialism and shocking socialists by his Gandhism. Neither intellectually nor morally did he feel at home in either camp, for in his reckoning the right road lay between. India must adopt a distinctive way of life suited to her own conditions which accepted neither the doctrinaire theories of Marxism or Socialism on the one hand nor Gandhi's belief in wealth as a trusteeship on the other"

(Frank Moraes, 1956). In this scenario it is but natural as Michael Brecher raised the question," where then shall we place him ? He is a liberal and democrat, a socialist and an individualist. Above all, he is a humanist in the best tradition of East and West. His creed is best defined as democratic socialism and refined and human materialism" (Michael Brecher, 1959). Thus, Nehru was not only a fighter of freedom, statesman, consolidator and maker of modern India but also a guide, friend and philosopher of the India's teeming millions in chief, and humanity in general. He was always in favour of seeking way out to maintain a balance between materialism and idealism. His failure to subscribe fully to the basic tenets of either Marxism or Gandhism was due to their lack of dynamic spirit and capability to solve the problems which make their ugly shape from time to time (O.P. Mishra, 1978).

Perhaps no other individual has so far shaped the course of development in India as did Pandit Nehru. He declared at the 1956 session of the Economic Commission for Asia and the Far East, "We are not going to spend the next hundred years in arriving gradually, step by step, at that stage of development which the developed countries have reached today. Our pace and tempo of progress has to be much faster." The course of development that Nehru envisaged for India was clearly egalitarian and this goal was prominent in all the Five year plans. The brief history of India's development experience can be viewed in terms of three visions viz Nehruvian socialistic vision, the LPG (Liberalization, Privatization and Globalization) vision and the HDM (Holistic Development and Management) vision. After the LPG experience, the need for HDM is being felt strongly. These three visions also represent the past, present and future of India's development vision (Subhash Sharma, 2003). Thus, departure from Nehruvian socialistic vision to the LPG vision proved failure in eradicating chronic economic problems like unemployment poverty and inequality. Those who have ultimate faith in market, believe that market is solution for all problems. For them market is God and God is market. But the reality lies in this fact that market is both a solution and a problem. As solution, it efficiently allocates resources, however, it fails to deliver equity. Thus, this God like other Gods, has also failed to deliver equality and justice. This God shows his own favouritism, justifying it in the name of the survival of the fittest.

PANDIT NEHRU: A TRUE DEMOCRATIC SOCIALIST

"The only key to the solution of World's problems and India's problems lies in socialism" This was Pandit Nehru's opinion expressed at the Lucknow Congress, 1936 in his presidential Address. Born to aristocratic parents; living in a superbly luxurious family atmosphere he developed a bourgeois outlook as he himself painfully admitted in these words. "I am typical bourgeois, brought up in bourgeois surroundings with all the early prejudice that his training has given me" (Nehru, 1936) but by the close of twenties he become a firm believer of socialism. He boldly accepted the fact as early as in 1929." I must frankly confess that I am a socialist and a republican, and am not believer in kings and princes, or in the order which produces the modern kings of industry, who have greater power over the lives and fortunes of men than even the Kings of old "Although he never believed in transplanting a foreign system in India, however promising, he was much more impressed by the achievements of Russian government. He enthusiastically spoke of its impact" So I turned inevitably with goodwill towards communism, for whatever its faults; it was at least not hypocritical and not imperialistic. These attracted me as also the tremendous changes taking place in Russia" (Nehru, 1936). His inclination towards socialism partly owes its origin to his contact with India's poor peasantry. Their sorrows and sufferings influenced his mental outlook profoundly. He expressed his feelings in these words. "Looking at them and their misery and overflowing gratitude, I was filled with shame and sorrow-shame at my own easygoing and comfortable life and our petty politics of the city which ignored this vast multitude of semi-naked sons and daughter of India. Sorrow at the degradation and overwhelming poverty of India. A new picture of India seemed to rise before me" (Nehru, 1936). Besides these, his visits to socialists countries time to time accelerated the speed of his thinking in regard to rejuvenating the Indian economy through increased public sector and state intervention. He being a friend of the poor and downtrodden people went on advocating and adopting socialism for India through democratic means for alleviation of their sufferings and bettering their life from 1929 till his death. Market mechanism was deemed to be a major cause of India's economic ills suffered during the British rule. The survival of the fittest is the market requirement while the survival of the weakest is a society requirement and so Nehruvian vision which was based on dominant role of the state was rooted in the Russian model and the socialistic vision of the World.

With the advent of the political freedom Pandit Nehru who took over as the first Prime Minister of free India and served the country in that capacity until his death on 27 May, 1964, found ample opportunity to give a concrete shape to his socialist ideas. On Nehru's initiative Directive Principles of State Policy contains socialistic element. Regarding this Dr. B.R. Ambedkar rightly remarked, "If the Directive Principles of State Policy are not socialistic in their direction and content, I fail to understand what more socialism can be". Pt. Nehru moved a Resolution on Aims and Objects in the Constituent Assembly on Dec. 13, 1946 which also contained socialistic element. It was largely on his initiative that the Indian National Congress in Jan, 1955 met at Avadi in Madras very clearly took decision in favour of establishment of a socialistic pattern of society in these words. "In order to realize the objective of the congress as laid down in Article 1 of the congress constitution and further the objectives stated in the Preamble and Directive Principles of the constitution of India, planning should take place with a view to the establishment of a socialistic pattern of society in which the principal means of production are under social ownership or control, production is progressively speeded up and there is equitable distribution of the national wealth". On the confusion raised regarding the meaning of socialistic pattern Pt. Nehru himself clarified this confusion in these words, "A socialistic pattern of society is socialism. Some people seem to make fine distinctions among socialistic pattern, socialist pattern and socialism. They are all exactly the same thing without the slightest difference" (Nehru, 1956). He feared that if a programme for socialism was not evolved and implemented immediately, "ten or fifteen years hence our people may lose faith in peaceful means and the problem may get more complicated" (quoted by Hiren Mukherjee, 1964).

But Nehru was also aware that socialism is devoid of democratic values and for the proper development of human personality and we growing of just society democratic values are indispensable. Therefore he combined the socialistic philosophy with the democratic socialism. The 68th Annual session of the Indian National Congress held on Jan, 9 and 10, 1964 and Bhubaneshwar decided to accept democratic socialism as its economic objective and adopted Resolution in Nehru's initiative like this. "The Congress is working for a revolution in the economic and social relationship in Indian society. The revolution is to be brought about through radical changes in the attitude and outlook of the people as well as the institutions through which they have to function.... The congress ideology may thus be summed up as democratic socialism based on democracy, dignity of the human individual and social justice". Thus, Pandit Nehru was a really democratic socialist. Hiren Mukherjee gave his remark that " More than any one man, he laboured to bring congress round to the recognization of a socialist society as India's goal. More than any one man, he plumped for active friendship and cooperation with the socialist third of the World" (Hiren Mukherjee, 1964) Pt. Nehru from the very beginning was of the opinion that "The famous 19th century saying about 'Government of the people by the people and for the people' failed to materialize in practice because under the capitalist system the Government was neither by the people nor of the people. It was a Government by the possessing classes for their own benefit. A real government can only be established under socialism." (Nehru,) India is perhaps the only country in the world which has launched the experiment of bringing about a socialist society through comprehensive economic planning under a democratic structure. In the western democracies like the U.S.A. and the

U.K. there has been what we may call piecemeal planning in the form of the 'New Deal' sponsored by President Roosevelt or the plan of social security enunciated by Lord Beveridge (Shriman Narayan, 1964). Due credit has to be given to his unique contribution in the form of democratic socialism which is based from the beginning on his deeply humanistic outlook. In the society based on the principle of democratic socialism, socialism and democracy are the means for the creation of a society in which exploitation of one class by another is abolished so as to raise level of living of its people and in which the individual possesses an unfettered right to self expression. He was very much sensitive towards injustice, inequality and suffering of any sort done to a human being and for him there is no justification for great disparities of income as have existed in India to continue. He had championed the case of democratic socialism for removal of these ills and he was of the opinion that democracy and socialism are compatible, complementary and inseparable. He believed that no democracy can exist for long in the midst of want and poverty and inequality and at the same time to him socialism through undemocratic means was a negation of individual liberty. Unlike the Russian Socialism Nehru's democratic socialism attached due importance to the individual and his dignity. While inaugurating the study circle of congressmen on Oct. 21, 1963 he said that the conditions in our country are different, and we cannot escape it. The communists proceed with their eyes closed ...... We have never to forget that while we must learn from everywhere, from outside, we have to follow our own path, our own methods. Undoubtedly, Nehru was a democratic socialist and his socialism was democratic socialism that was found most suitable in the Indian scenario for India.

PANDIT NEHRU'S ECONOMIC PHILOSOPHY: PREGNANT WITH SOCIALISTIC CONTENT

Pandit Nehru was a socialist by inclination and so his economic philosophy was pregnant with socialistic content. He tried his best to put the economy on a sound path of development through the mechanism of Planning. In his opinion for establishing a socialist society there should be first of all plenty of goods and services to provide a national minimum of food, shelter, clothing, education, medicine etc and for which we must, as Nehru stated, increase our production. We must increase our national wealth and the national dividend and only then can we really raise the standard of living of our people." If you do not produce more wealth, all your schemes of distribution fail because there is nothing much to distribute (Nehru, 1955). Nehru, the chief architect of development planning in India highlighted the importance and desirability of planning in India and put the very logical approach in this concern. Whatever it may be in other countries, in underdeveloped countries like ours, which have to develop fairly, equally and rapidly, the time element is important and the question is how to use our own our resources to the best advantage. If our resources are abundant it will not matter how they are used. They will go into a common pool of development. But, once resources are limited one has to see that they are directed to the right purpose so as to help build up whatever one is aiming at. Moreover he visualized planning essentially as "a process whereby we stop cumulative forces at work which make the poor poorer, and start a new series of cumulative which make them get over that difficulty. We have to support the cumulative forces which enable the poor to get over the barrier of poverty." (Nehru, 1957-63). He pleaded for controlling the cumulative forces which make the rich richer. Thus, the was in favour of adoption of planning at both ends. He had clear-cut concept in this regard as he pointed out that scientific planning enables us to increase our production, and socialism comes in when we plan to distribute production evenly. It is needless to say that his wider democratic perspective a scientific appreciation of planning concentrated on the problem of underprivileged and downtrodden to whom opportunities had been denied. He recognised that people are not equal in ability, in strength and in the capacity to work, but he strongly believed that everyone should be given equal opportunity to work and to prosper. He wanted to establish a welfare state with no major disparity in income. Jawaharlal's interest in and even passion for planning developed after his visit to the Soviet Union in 1927 and until his death in May 1964 his faith in planning as a powerful instrument of economic advance and social transformation not only remained undiminished but acquired increasing depth, insight and understanding from his experience of the formulation and implementation of the three plans in the country. This faith was part of his growing faith in socialism as a way to the future for the world as a whole and more particularly for India (Gyanchand, 1991) He was for basing the economic programme on 'human outlook and not on sacrifice of men to money as we find in the LPG version in the present era. The picture of India rose before him-naked, starving, crushed and utterly miserable'—remained a part of his intellectual outfit and was his constant inspiration in planning as in his whole life work. He worked to make this nightmare a matter of the past and poverty and exploitation of the masses remained for him a call of the future and planning the chief instrument for ending this misery.

Though Nehru was impressed by the experiment of Russian Revolution, when it came to the selection of suitable option for development of independent India, he preferred mixed economy model. This was not just political convenience but a thoughtful answer to the mode of economic organization suitable for Indian economy. One thing is very clear that at no stage of his life he adopted a free market philosophy but he knew vividly what heavy cost had to be paid in the Soviet Union and the other communist countries for social revolution and was very keen that the way of violence be avoided by our people, and a substitute for their dynamism—a democratic and peaceful substitute for force by which regimes in communist countries established socialist societies, had and has to be provided (Gyan Chand, 1991) Nehru dispensing with two extremes of capitalism and socialism devised a via media system between the two and that is known as mixed economy which is, thus, the outcome of the compromise between the two schools of thought in which both public and private sectors are allotted their respective roles in promoting the economic welfare of all sections of the community. Thus, mixed economy is said to have emerged out of the disenchantment with laissez-faire capitalism especially the shock in capitalist countries of the Great Depression of 1929-33 on the one hand and disenchantment with communism which was tried in the USSR during Stalinst regime with its most authoritarian planning administrative control and ruthless-suppression of individual freedom in the economic sphere reducing individual to the status of just a cog in the huge state's economic administrative machinery. Nehru's mixed economy system has forbidden several less developed countries from falling prey to militancy and communistic outlook. Nehru believed that the basic attraction of Marxism for millions of people was not its attempt at scientific theory but its passion for social justice. Yet, he believed that reduction in income disparities can be achieved only through state intervention. Left-to the blind forces of the market place he believed that disparities would grow. He wanted India to cross the barrier of poverty and to reach the stage of take off into sustained economic growth where growth becomes spontaneous (Eduardo Faleiro, 1989). With the intention to combine the best of both socialism and capitalism he preferred to have mixed economy but his inclination towards socialism appeared vividly. He was rightly hailed as the builder of the public sector in India. The ratio of public investment (Rs. 6300 crores) to the private investment (Rs 4100 crores) in the Third plan was approximately 60:40 while total investment in the First plan was Rs. 3360 crores (Rs. 1560 crores in the public sector and Rs. 1800 crores in the private sector) recording 47:53 ratio of public to private investment. In the Second Plan the total investment was to the order of Rs. 6750 crores (Rs. 3650 and Rs. 3100 crores respectively in the public and private sector) recording 54:46 ratio of public to private investment. Thus, the expansion of the public sector during his regime was intentional and the intention was to build up a socialist society in place of an acquisitive society. Of course, he gave the public sector the core position for equitable development of the economy but he was not averse to the private sector.

Pandit Nehru's vision and writings on land reform revealed his inclination towards socialism from very beginning when the country embarked on an era of planned development with Pandit Nehru as the leading light, it was felt that land reforms had a dual purposes to play: to ensure increased productivity and elimination of exploitation. In the meeting of the National Development Council held at New Delhi on 8 November 1963 Nehru said," Agriculture is more important than anything else, not excluding big plants, because agricultural production sets the tone to all economic progress. It is agriculture, that gives the wherewithal for progress. If we fail in agriculture, then we fail inevitably in industry too. I am laying stress on this because in spite of the emphasis on this, it appears to me that agriculture is often considered a routine job, not deserving to be taken charge of by the brightest of the Ministers". His strategy of development was essentially modernization of agriculture and the training of rural masses in making use of new tools and new methods of agricultural production. But he was aware of hidden exploitation in Indian agricultural system. He being a socialistic outlook felt unbearable pain to see the existing exploitation in Indian agriculture. The First plan endorsed the recommendations of the Congress Agrarian Reforms Committee (1949) in its report of land policy. The Agrarian Reforms Committee in its report held that" in the agrarian economy of India there is no place for intermediaries and land must belong to the tiller—in future subletting of land will be prohibited except in the case of widows, minors and other disabled persons.... The tenant should have the right to purchase the holding at a reasonable price..." The principal measures recommended in the First plan and reiterated in subsequent plans were abolition of intermediary tenures, reform of the tenancy system including security of tenure, fixation of fair rent and conferment of ownership right on the tenant, ceiling on land holdings and reorganization of the small farm economy through co-operative activity and prevention of fragmentation. It is but true that steps were taken soon after Independence. Almost all the states adopted legislations to end intermediary tenures. As a result of it more than 20 millions of tenants came into direct contact with the state. Waste lands also came under government control and about 4.5 million hectares of such land have since been redistributed to landless peasants. Legislation was passed in a number of states for converting tenants and sub-tenants into owners. More than 3 million tenants and share croppers acquired ownership of more than 3½ million hectares of land. In rent fixation, what was envisaged was that rent should not exceed 1/5th or 1/4th of the gross produce. Land ceiling legislation was enacted in all the states though the level varied. The programme of consolidation of holdings was also undertaken in a number of states (O.P. Mishra, 1978). Pt. Nehru had on unflinching faith in co-operation because in his view it helped in building up a human being and might play an active role in the adoption of democratic socialism in more effective way. In 1948 when he was appointed the chairman of the Congress Economic Programme Committee by AICC he made recommendations that cooperative societies should be established in as much number as possible. The First plan laid down "As an instrument of democratic planning, combining initiative, mutual benefit and social purpose, cooperation must be an essential feature of the programme of the implementation of the Five year plan. As it is the purpose of the plan to change the economy of the country from an individualistic to a socially regulated and cooperative basis, its success should be judged, among other things by the extent to which it is implemented through co-operative organizations". Then plan purposed to organize co-operation in the field of agriculture marketing, processing and cottage industries. The First plan also recorded" community development is the method and rural extension the agency through which the Five year plan seeks. It is to initiate a process of transforming the social and economic life of the village. No doubt land reform adopted by Pt. Nehru during his tenure have yet to show the results we expected, at least we have not had much violence in the rural areas, excepting some sporadic instances here and there. This is a great achievement and shows that Nehru's policy of land reform has worked well and his policy was essentially a reflection of his socialistic inclination. He deemed co-operation a forceful instrument for bringing about equality in the distribution of income and wealth, socio-economic justice materializing socialistic ideas into practice and ultimately building India a new.

Pandit Nehru, great visionary and planner he was, had as well realized that without rapid industrialization it was not possible for the country to come out of its poverty and raise the standard of living of her country men. But his attachment to industrialization does not mean that he was oblivious of the vital role of agriculture in the Indian economy. Initiating a discussion on the Third plan in the Lok Sabha on 22 August, 1960 he brought out succinctly the close nexus between agriculture and industry and the fact that these sectors cannot be viewed as watertight compartment in the context of growth and development. He said, "Having laid great stress on industrialization, we have to look in the direction of agriculture. We shall find that this industrial progress cannot be made without agricultural advance and progress. The fact is that the two cannot be separated. They are intimately connected because agricultural progress is not possible without tools without the new methods and techniques. There is no question of not giving priority to agriculture. Everyone knows that unless we are self-sufficient in agriculture we cannot have the wherewithal to advance in industries". As early as December 21, 1938 Pt. Nehru his first note to the National Planning Committee said, "There can be no planning if such planning does not include big industries. But in making our plans we have to remember the basic Congress policy of encouraging cottage industries". Undoubtedly, to him the rapid development of large scale machine industry was an urgent need of the country. But he never deviated from his basic outlook for socialism. In a talk broadcast from New Delhi on Aug., 15, 1947 he said, "And we have also to promote industrialization on a large and balanced scale, so as to add to the wealth of the country and thus to the national dividend which can be equitably distributed.". He said in a speech made at the meeting of the standing committee of the National Development Council, New Delhi on Jan, 18, 1963," In fact, you know that the big and powerful countries of the world are the countries which have industrialized themselves and thereby gained strength, whether for war or for peaceful purpose". In spite of the fact that basic industries and their development attracted his attention most he was enthusiastic to maintain an equilibrium between basic, heavy and machine industry and light industry. In a speech to All India Congress Committee, Indore, January 4, 1957 he said," we believe generally that the industrial progress of India will depend and must depend on the growth of heavy industry. There will be no industrial progress unless machines are made here, unless iron and steel are manufactured here. At the same time we have always to remember that unless we balance heavy industry with the growth of village industry, we shall produce an unbalanced structure which may crack up and fall to pieces. Therefore, the importance of village industry, household industry, cottage industry and small industry is very great". Thus, such sort of his view on industrial development is enough to reveal the fact that how far balanced he was in his approach in this concern. No doubt he had a great personal commitment and intense desire to see that Indian industry, particularly in the public sector, attains greater and commanding heights and contributes substantially to the economic growth and development but for him the emergence of public sector in India needed to play an important role side by side with the private sector. His intention was that large scale, basic and defense industries should be in the public sector and other types of industries should be organized either or private on co-operative lines. Thus, he stood for mixed economy. "That brings us to a transitional stage of economy.... It brings us to do things in such a way as continually to add to the wealth of the country, as well as to lead to a more equitable distribution of that wealth in the country..." It was his intension expressed in his words. While he had strong faith in private capital and also was impressed by the role of foreign capital in transforming the shape of an economy, but socialist that he was he wanted both Indian as well as foreign industrialists to work on terms and conditions that were within the socialist norms of the economy. And also special benefits and protections have been provided for the growth of medium and small industries which may prove on important source of employment, creative instincts and decentralized economic power.

Pandit Nehru had a scientific outlook and a great faith

in the ability of science and technology to transform society. For him," In modern life, science and the progency of science, techniques, technology, etc. are of the highest importance. They govern our lives and the conditions of living today. Therefore, we should understand and profit by them. What is happening today. Therefore, we should understand and profit by them. What is happening today behind the Five year plans and other economic programmes in India is the change-over from traditional society into a modern society." As early as in 1937, he wrote in a letter to Acharya P.C. Ray after visiting the All India Institute of Medical Research which read, "Personally I am greatly interested in and attracted to scientific research and I hope that when India is free, the state will encourage this in every possible way". He, as a student of science, understood and welcomed the revolutionary impact of science and technology and so when he became the Prime Minister of India he worked whole heartedly for the promotion and progress of science and its progeny-technology. He in 1958 announcing the new famous scientific policy resolution in Parliament, said "The Government of India have decided that the aim of their scientific policy will be to foster, promote and sustain, by all appropriate means the cultivation of science and scientific research in all its aspects, pure, applied and educational". Consequent upon the implementation of this resolution India made much headway in field of science and technology and he laid stress upon the cultivation of scientific temper and installing up of research laboratories and institutes. Before his death in 1964 there were about 30 laboratories and institutes scattered all over India from Kashmir in the north to Kerala in the south and from Bhavnagar in the West Jorhat in the east. His enthusiasm for these laboratories knew no bounds and he said," Even though we have completed a chain of national laboratories, we must not be content with this achievement. In fact, this is only the first step in the difficult ladder of progress which we have to climb". One contradiction of which he was keenly aware was the contradiction between large-scale organized industries with modern technique and village and small industries. He was all for the use of the latest science and technique in industry and knew that in basic industries there is no escape from the fullest possible use of modern technology and it was necessary and desirable to make use of it to the utmost degree. Thus, without his vision, imagination and stress on science and technology Indian could not occupy a place of pride on the industrial, scientific and technological map of the world. Really, Pandit Nehru was such a socialistic democrat who wanted to have more to distribute and he took steps towards scientific and technological advancement which could prove to be instrumental in bringing prosperity for the countrymen.

RESUME

Each and every action creates its own reaction. So is the economic philosophy of Pandit Nehru. A good number of economists appreciated his economic philosophy whereas economists like B.R. Shenoy, V.K. Vakil, Brahmananda and some others were critic of his economic philosophy. B.R. Shenoy emphatically stated, "The ambivalence of the Indian planners between democracy and communism cannot continue indefinitely. Either we take the road of economic liberalism which will ensure maximum economic development and a free society, or we get lured or forced into communism toiling along the soulless and fruitless path of regimentation." While most of the Indian economists followed Nehruvian mixed economic philosophy, Shenoy boldly prescribed Gandhian minimum state intervention principle for the development of India's economy. Shenoy's economic model is of laissez faire type as experienced by U.S.A., U.K., Israel and so on. He opined that since the pattern of production cannot change overnight, in the early stages of development, capital should be provided first for the expansion and modernization of agriculture and the lighter industries. Heavy industries must take their due turn thereafter. Whether in England or any other industrialized country of the World, the general pattern of development seems to have been to lay greater emphasis on consumer good industry. It is only after considerable development of consumer goods, and consumer durable industry, that a country usually developed a sufficiently large market for capital goods and then in the second stage, we see the development of capital goods industry as a natural consequence. In England, about seven to eight decades had to lapse between the Industrial Revolution of the textile industry and the emergence of engineering industry as a major component of the capital goods industrial structure. Pandit Nehru decided to launch upon major effort to develop basic and capital goods industries on top priority which has paid rich dividends. Indian industry is thus capable of making wide range of industrial products, both in the capital goods sector and the consumer goods sector, in short form soaps to satellites. This is, indeed, not an inconsiderable achievement for which the credit goes to Pandit Nehru's vision. Pandit Nehru was one of the few who understood the linkages amongst the various sectors and sub-sectors of the economy. He viewed planning as an exercise in balancing." Planning consists essentially in balancing: the balancing between heavy industry and light industry, the balancing between cottage industries and other industries. If one of them goes wrong, then the whole economy is upset. If you concentrate too much on industry, leaving agriculture to look after itself, the country gets into difficulties." He was aware of the fact that the enormous idle manpower in the country could not be used in modern industries and so long unemployment prevailed in the economy eradication of poverty seemed to be impossible. As early as in 1929 he realised the fact that "If we are to eradicate poverty, we must first to do away with this widespread unemployment". Decentralised rural industries were rightly for him as inescapable as organized modern industries for solving the most fundamental problems of Indian economy. He stated, "However rapid our industralization may be, it cannot be possibly absorbed more than a small part of the population of this country in the next ten, twenty or even thirty years. Hundreds of millions will remain who have to be employed chiefly in agriculture. These people must, in addition, be given employment in smaller industries like cottage industries and so on. Hence, the importance of village and cottage industries I think the argument one often hears about big industries versus cottage and village industry is misconceived. I have no doubt that we cannot raise the people's level of existence without the development of major industries in this country. We have to develop the village and cottage industry in a big way, at the same time making sure that in trying to develop industry, big and small, we do not forget the human factor. We are not merely out to get more money and more production. We ultimately want better human beings." His farsightedness is easily visible when he expressed his belief in these words;" The real change comes, of course from within the village and is not imposed from outside. It is a process of self development and self reliance. The outsider can only help a little, give some guidance and a push here and there. That little help, may, of course be of the greatest importance or it can light a flame which shed its light over very much areas. But the test of success is, how far the people of a village shoulder their own burdens and have developed a spirit of self-reliance and mutual co-operation." Pandit Nehru was very conscious and knew the fact as he stated, "To bring about socialism the planning is essential" He took steps in this direction boldly and he was eager to see India progressing much faster so that the socio-economic problems could be eliminated in time but he could not reap a bumper crop of planning as he desired. Of course," The economic course he set for the country and tried to implemented was on balance well conceived though not implemented well". (P.S. Lokanathan, 1965) Further he writes" If only he had been a little more firm and taken a stronger grip over the administration, the results of planning in Indian would have been very much different and the country would have advanced much further" (P.S. Lokanathan, 1965). The corruption and inefficiency of administration hampered the growth rate of the Indian economy as the resources were diverted towards non-developmental activities and merry-making but one should not forget the fact that India which had awaken from long slumber of slavery was economically backward and it was Pandit Nehru's farsightedness and vision which laid a strong foundation of the shattered economy of India. M. Brecher was right enough in his observation." Having said all this, it remains to be emphasized that India's progress is most impressive measured both against its on previous conditions and against the record of any other underdeveloped country which has chosen the democratic route to social and economic change. No less vital is the point, which cannot be overstressed, that whatever progress has been achieved is primarily due to the efforts of the Pt. Nehru. Indeed, he is the heart and soil and mind of India's heroic struggle to raise the living standards. There can be no doubt that he has been the Prime mover in India's massive planning effort". (M. Brecher, 1959). It may be borne in mind that Pandit Nehru provided us scientific methods of planning and necessary tools for achieving the goal of democratic socialism but if the tools could not be successful, the fault was in its execution and not with Pandit Nehru's economic philosophy; pregnant with socialistic content.

References

Nehru (1946), Discovery of India, Signet Press, Calcutta.

Michael Brecher (1959), Nehru—A Political Biography, Oxford Press.

Nehru (1958), The Basic Approach in the Economic Review, Aug, 15.

Frank Moraas (1956), Jawaharlal Nehru—A Biography, Macmillan, New York.

O.P. Mishra (1978), The Economic Philosophy of Pt. Jawaharlal Nehru, Chugh Pub., Allahabad.

Subhash Sharma (2003), Markets, State and Society in the New Age: Towards Holistic Development and Management, in *Southern Economist*, Vol. 41, No. 17, Jan. 1.

Nehru (1936), Autobiography, Bodley Head, London.

Nehru (1956), Address at Conference of the All Indian Manufacturers' Organization, New Delhi, April 14.

Hiren Mukherjee (1969), The Gentle Colossus, Manisha Granthalaya, Calcutta.

Sriman Narayan (1964), Socialism in Indian Planning, Asia Publishing House.

Nehru (1955), Towards a Socialistic Order, New Delhi.

Nehru (1959-63), Collection of Speeches, Vol. IV, Publication Division, Delhi.

Gyan Chand (1991), Nehru and Planning in *Khadi Gramodyog*, Vol. XXXVIII, No. 2, November.

Eduardo Faleiro (1989), Nehru and Balanced Economic Growth in *Khadi Gramodyog*, Vol. XXV, No. 12, Sept.

P.S. Lokanathan (1965), The Quality of His Greatness in the *Eastern Economists*, Annual No., Dec.

Science Reporter Nehru Commemoration, Vol. 1, Nos. 7-8, July-Aug. 1964, *Kurukshetra*, Vol. XLI, No. 2, Nov. 1992.

Different *Yojanas*.

28

Nehru's Achievements and Failures in National Perspectives

R.P.L. Jain

INTRODUCTION

The achievements of Pandit Nehru in almost every field of national life (viz., economic, social, political and cultural) show that he was known as an outstanding political leader, great social thinker, freedom fighter, peasant leader and later on as a policy-maker during the country's independent era. He was a cultured person, humane in his approach to the problems whether it was political, economic, administrative or personal. He was a towering personality of India, the Great, and did not allow anybody to underestimate him in any field.

An attempt is made here to assess the achievements of Pandit Nehru in diverse areas of national life considering country's aspirations, plans and potential and the actual results during his stewardship which gives a complex picture and leads to even endless debate on this issue. Evaluation can be a mixture of objectivity and subjectivity and of quantity and quality of the performance. Some achievements and some miserable performances have been observed. However, there are ways of reviewing the achievements/failures of Pandit Nehru during the country's independent era. One way is to go by the Prime Ministerial regime and the other way is to consider the country's performance among various fields. However, it should be kept in mind that the two ways of observing the country's progress and problems are not really alternatives. Both approaches have to be adopted because they are very much interconnected.

OBJECTIVES

The prime objective of the study is to assess the contributions of Pandit Nehru in various fields of the country as a whole. More elaborately, it aims at:

1. To analyse the achievements of Pandit Nehru in various fields viz., (i) Democratic system of parliamentary pattern, (ii) Planning, (iii) Land reforms, (iv) Mixed economy, (v) Industrialisation, (vi) Science and Technology, and (vii) International relation, etc. of the country as a whole;
2. To examine failures of Pandit Nehru with respect to country's performance; and
3. To conclude main observations of the study and to make best possible use of all the best that Pandit Nehru gave to the nation during his lifetime.

ECONOMIC PHILOSOPHY OF PANDIT NEHRU

The economic philosophy of Pandit Nehru is expressed here regarding various important aspects of the economy as under:

(i) Democratic System of Parliamentary Pattern

During his Prime Ministership, the functioning of the cabinet was unparallel on account of a substantial measure of collective responsibility. It was not because that there were other stalwarts like Sardar Patel, Rajaji, Govind Vallabh Pant, Maulana Azad, John Mathai and C.D. Deshmukh but also because of confidence in the cabinet principle of consultation and collaboration with one person to another. The entire collective team functioned in a very fairly relaxed manner without fears and tensions irrespective of portfolio allotment.

(ii) Planning

Nehru's focus was also attached to economic planning. He took the concrete steps for its implementation and was inspired not too much by the Soviet experiment as its conviction that without economic planning, the country could not achieve rapid progress in the process of transformation from agricultural economy to a modern economy with a balanced sectoral pattern, capable in eradication of poverty and employment creation. He also created an adequate planning organisation.

(iii) Land Reforms

Nehru was of the opinion that Indian farmers could become the agent for modernization of agriculture if they were enabled to do so. The first enabling act was land reforms that gave them entitlement to land. Nehru followed by undertaking large investment in irrigation, power, rural roads, market expansion, communications, scientific research and technology. Nehru introduced Community Development Programme in the mid 1950 with a view to raising the awareness and uplifting of the villages through an appropriate network of Community Development Programmes and extension services.

(iv) Mixed Economy

Nehru was not a doctrinaire socialist. He was a realist and pragmatist. He deliberately chose the concept of mixed economy in which private initiative was to be quite crucial in certain areas. Although, he gave the core position to the public sector for the equitable development of the economy. He also did not underestimate the initiative and enterprise of the private sector. However, he was of the view that public sector was to play a central role in development of rural infrastructure, basic research and extension and social infrastructures like education, health and public services with a view to building an equitable society.

(v) Industrialisation

Nehru favoured the policy of developing heavy industries during his stewardship. It was essential not only from the point of view of diversifying the economy rapidly but also for modernizing agriculture so that inputs like tractors, fertilizers, pesticides and power can only obtain from manufacturing sector. Attention was also given to substantial expansion of irrigation facilities, though initially the preference was for mega projects. During his period, the country achieved the reasonable economic growth with substantial price stability. The fiscal position was rather good with surpluses on revenue account.

(vi) Science and Technology

Nehru was a very good statesman by following the traditional and tried to establish relationship with the modern approach especially in the sphere of science and technology. He was successful in establishing big industrial units in engineering, steel and oil refineries. Nehru was also instrumental in establishing many national scientific laboratories, institutes of technology and institutes of management during his stewardship.

(vii) International Relation

Nehru also made valuable contribution in raising India's status at international level. It was the Nehru's personality that India stood as a free country establishing her status in international affairs. He also played not a little role in the emancipation of Asian countries from colonialism, the outstanding example being that of Indonesia.

FAILURES

In recent years, especially after the implementation of economic reforms measure in 1992, it had become almost a fashion to blame Pandit Nehru for slow growth of the Indian economy and his planning model for having restricted private initiative. It is usually said that no man is perfect and Nehru was not an exception to it. Nehru contributed much towards promoting national integration but could not succeed in reorganising various states due to their pressures on linguistic basis. He also did not set good example in grooming a successor until the retirement from Prime Ministership in the age of seventy. It was humiliating one when our country suffered at the hands of China, for whose cause Nehru campaigned in many forums, was a sad episode during his distinguished career as Prime Minister. The dismissal of Kerala State Government dominated by Communist Party with Namboodripad as the Chief Minister was also a lapse on his part.

CONCLUDING OBSERVATIONS

On the whole, Nehru helped to strengthen national independence, set-up industrial base, strong public sector, introduce planning on a nation-wide scale and gradually abolish the old feudal system of landownership. Thus, the Nehru era was the best in the country's performance from the view point of Indian democracy based on a federal pattern.

Keeping in view, the contributions of Pandit Nehru in the context of the national economy, it is observed that nation should make best possible use of all the best that Nehru gave during his stewardship. There is no doubt that Pandit Nehru was the founder of present India.

REFERENCES

Nehru, Jawaharlal (1962), An Autobiography, Allied Publishers, New Delhi.

Nehru, Jawaharlal (1961), The Discovery of India, Asia Publishing House.

Martyshin, Qrest (1989), Jawaharlal Nehru and his Political Views, Progress Publishers, Moscow.

Simha, S.L.N. (2007), 'Independent India, 1947-97 and Beyond: Some Reflections', Southern Economist, Vol. 46, No. 13, Nov. 1, ed.

29

Nehru's Vision of Science and Technology

Hari Narayan Prasad Singh

INTRODUCTION

Jawaharlal Nehru was born in Allahabad on 14th November, 1889. He was the only son of Pandit Motilal Nehru, an imperious and successful lawyer of Allahabad. Nehru's Childhood some what "Sheltered and uneventful one." He spent his early time mostly in listening to grown up talks of the elder member of his family, taking interest in Arabian Nights and tales narrated to him by Munshi Mubarak Ali. The stories from old Hindu methodology and from the epics—Ramayana and Mahabharat, also touched his heart which he used to listen from his mother an anent.

At home he was being educated by a series of English teacher's and governess, one of his prominent tutors was an European by the name of Ferdinand, T. Brooks, who was an ardent theosophist and an amiable teacher.

After Independence of the country in August 1947, Jawaharlal Nehru became the first Prime Minister of

Independent India and continued uninterruptedly in that position from August 1947 to his death on 27th May 1964 an uninterrupted stretch of 17 years as Prime Minister.

VISION OF SCIENCE AND TECHNOLOGY

Jawaharlal Nehru was a great freedom fighter, statesman, historian, and literateur. His Contribution to the vision of Economic Planning, Industrialisation, Socialism, Agriculture, Modern Science and technology. The Economic Vision did not grow in a vacuum. The Economic Vision of Pandit Nehru were firmly rooted in pragmatic idealism, dynamism, scientific temper, etc. and they strike a means between Gandhism and Marxism.

The First Prime Minister of Free India, Nehru was a new direction and role of science and technology in India. Pandit Nehru was a great admire of modern science and scientific attitude and modern technology. Thus he wrote: "I am....a great admirer of the achievements of modern civilization, of the growth and application of science and technological growth. Humanity has every reason to be proud of them." He continued: " Technical achievements of science are obvious enough, its capacity to transform an economy of scarcity into one of abundance is evident."

Nehru had an abiding faith in modern science and was convinced that the solution to the basic problems of massive poverty and economic backwardness was through science and technology. He declared: "I am a great believer in science– and the scientific approach has changed the world completely. I think that if the world is to solve its problems, it will inevitably have to be through the means of science and not by discarding science."

Dr. Rajendra Prasad, wrote about Nehru: " Jawaharlal Nehru is essentially a man of science and technology, with undoubted faith in their progress and achievements. All the same at the back of it all, there is in him a spiritual strain which is marked. While placing full reliance on the development of science and harnessing scientific knowledge for the eradication of misery and poverty, he is conscious of the limitations of such material progress without submission to some kind of spiritual principal."

He declared that the three fundamental requirements of India are heavy engineering and machine building Industry scientific research institutions and electric power. He was a man of ideal with great determination. When he once set his heart on a particular objective he would work for it for all he was worth and would not count any sacrifice too great for it. Keeping in view the trend in the advanced nations he saw to it that immediately after Independence scientific research in India was organised by the Govt. A National research laboratories with provisions of research in pure and applied science was established. Nehru had the foresight to the importance of nuclear power and set-up the Atomic Energy Commission in 1948.

Nehru's deep interest in science and passed 1958 Science Policy Resolution of Govt. of India. The objective of Science Policy Resolution are:

(a) To secure for the people of India the benefits from the acquisition of Scientific Knowledge and its application.
(b) To foster and cultivate science and scientific research in all aspects, namely, basic applied and educational.
(c) To encourage individual initiative for acquisition and dissemination of knowledge.
(d) To train scientific and technical personal to fulfil the needs in various fields like agriculture, Industry, defence, etc. and to have an adequate supply of scientists.

He was found of "Scientific Temper" and wanted it to be included as part of education in India right from the school days. He went so far as to apply science to religion and advocated essential on scientific attitudes even in religions matter. He had started to believe quite stoutly that the whole method of science the approach of science is essential for the survival of humanity. He linked science and planning and developed planing science in action.

A conference of industries, it was accepted then that the problem of poverty and unemployment, of National defence and economic regeneration could not be solved without rapid industrilisation. A National Planning Committee under the Chairmanship of Pandit Jawaharlal Nehru was appointed to draw up a comprehensive scheme of National Planning. It was thus a first attempt of its kind on the part of the people of India to draw up a co-ordinated plan for national economic regeneration. The National Planning Commission was setup in March 1950. Five years plan periods were adopted.

Jawaharlal Nehru was aware that planning necessarily implied priorities and in fixing those priorities he was guided by the hard realities of life though his faith in basic Industries was never shaken. The First Plan for example emphasized agricultural development. The first plan accorded the highest priority to agriculture. It recorded that it would be impossible to sustain a higher tempo of Industrial development." The high priority given to agriculture in public sector programmes was at the cost of a low priority given to Industries, Agricultural Production targets however mere not only reached but even exceeded..

The Second Plan was conceived in an atmosphere of economic stability. Agriculture was assigned a lower priority and the plan aimed at rapid industrialisation with particular emphasis on the development of basic and heavy industries. The development of such Industries which manufacture machines need economic progress. He believed that only large scale industrialisation would be in a position to provide increasing employment opportunities to the country's population and would help produce wealth in increasing quantities and thus help removed mass poverty. Nehru believed that "poverty in India cannot be removed without rapid industrialisation. It may be rightly said that it was Pandit Nehru who laid the foundation of industrialisation of the country." Thus high priority was given for the iron and steel, fertilizer, coal, cement, heavy engineering and heavy electrical. The three steel plants at Durgapur, Bhilai and Rourkela were set-up. Since then another plant at Bokaro has started production and the Salem Plant is Producing cold-rolled steel. Now India is a net exporter of steel. Today India's heavy engineering and machine tools industries command respect in the world.

Pandit Nehru emphasised the human factor in the whole planning process. He observed that "Planning in not merely a question of drawing up a list of projects and finding resources to execute them. The financial aspect is important but is far less important the human aspect." When he inaugurated the Indian industries fair in New Delhi on October 29, 1955, he observed that we should utilise modern technology with understanding, humanism, tolerance and compassion in order to achieve a proper balance between man and machine. In his inaugural speech of 44th Session of the Indian Science Congress in Culcutta on January 14, 1957, he said, "If science divorced it self completely from the realm of morality and ethics, then the power is possessed might be used for evil." Later, on the other occasion, he further opened that "the more we advance in science, the less we seem to progress in the field of civilisation."

Pandit Nehru emphasised the importance of modern science and technology. He wrote. "I arrived again at science, when I realised that science is not only a pleasant diversion and abstraction, but was of the every texture of life, without which our modern world vanish away. Politics led me to economic and this led me inevitably to science and the scientific approach to all our problems and to life itself. It was science alone that could solve these problems of hunger and poverty of insanitation and illiteracy, of superstitions and deadening customs and traditions, of vast resources running to waste, of a rich country inhabited by starving people." And therefore, he held the view that "a country survive to day if it has enough of scientific and technical personnel."

If modern science and Technology have done a great amount of good to mankind. Nehru was also aware of the tremendous harm which they can do to mankind. But then he said that that was not the fault of modern science and technology but people who put it to bad use.

Thus we can say that Nehru was a practical economist. He firmly believed that, if one's going to build the house of India's future, strong, secure and beautiful than he has to dig deep for the foundation. When house was to be rebuilt with different orientation. He realised the harmfulness of define the scheme of house in rigid terms. But he did not define these objective of his economic vision like an academician, yet he had planned process of action and interaction. He was trying to co-ordinate ideals and actions in a scientific way.

To conclude, we see that the visions of Pandit Jawaharlal Nehru on science and technology are important guidelines to our development programmes even today. While appropriate technology would be adopted whenever possible, the human aspect should be kept in mind. Science and technology can help to solve the basic problems of poverty,. unemployment and economic backwardness. Science and technology can usher in a better society, a better civilization.

REFERENCES

S. Radhakrishnan (1965) on Nehru, Publication Division, New Delhi, p. 59.

R.R. Mehrotra, A.K. Agarwal, S. Ganguly, Nehru, Man Among Men. Mittal Publication, New Delhi.

S.S.M. Desai, Development of Indian Economic Though, Publication Himalaya Publishing House, Bombay, p. 248.

Jawaharlal Nehru (1946), The Discovery of India, Signet Press, Culcutta, p. 10.

5. Speech (1949-53), pp. 146, 361, 396.
6. The Unity of India, p. 26.
7. A Bunch of Old Letter, p. 30.
8. Glimpses of World History, Vol. II, p. 694.

30

Structural Changes in Indian Economy from 1947 to 2000 A.D.: From Nehru to Manmohan Singh

KISHORE KUMAR ROY CHOUDHURY

HISTORICAL BACKGROUND

The principal pre-occupation of free India's government has been economic planning. At that time India has 14.6 percent of the entire human population, but it has only 2.4 per cent of the world's land area. The per capita income was nearly the lowest in the world. Floods and droughts frequently brought about acute food shortage amounting to famine Food, clothing and housing were problems confronting the planners. In the first phase of 1950, India was in a weak position in respect of food production. At that time the position of commercial crops like cotton and jute was more satisfactory. It can be said that India's industrial position was not greatly affected by the partition except that a large number of Muslim mechanics migrated to Pakistan. At that time the policy of the Government was to encourage private enterprise and to welcome foreign capital. The

Government of India took a realistic view and openly stated the policy of the state was to encourage the development of industry in the private sector. Then it was a popular debate on the issue of private and public sector. But Nehru wanted to encourage private enterprise. According to Nehru's opinion, private sector was desirable to encourage nation's growth and production.[1] Though three was another view. According same policy-makers, trade in essential commodities could be done better by the states than by private agencies and that middlemen were parasites who should be eliminated. At that time state Trading Corporation was given a monopoly of imported cement, caustic soda, raw silk and of export of iron ore. The Second Five Year Plan shows an all round increase over the First Five Year Plan. The index of industrial production shows an increase of 94 percent, production of steel ingots rose one and a half times. The area of irrigation, food grain production and transportation were very impressive.

It can be the said that during the first plan period both agricultural and industrial production recorded substantial increase. But during the second plan, the rise of national income amounted to only 20 percent as against the target of 25 percent. But from the second plan period India was able to produce increasing quantities of machine tools and machinery for use in agriculture and transport and for such industries as chemicals and pharmaceuticals, textiles, jute, cement, tea, sugar, etc. Sect oral and structural changes were started from the Second Five Year Plan in India.

Sectoral Changes: From 1950 to 2000 the sectoral contribution of national income depicts a clear picture about the composition or distribution of national income by industrial origin. Table 1 shows that the contribution of primary sector has gradually declined from 58.3 percent of NDP in 1950-51 to 35.2 percent in 1989-90. The secondary sector has increased its share of NDP from 15.1 percent in 1950-51 to 25.5 percent in 1989-90. The share of tertiary sector has gradually increased from 26.6 percent in 1950-51 to 39.3 percent in 1990. Among the major components or tertiary sector the share of transport, communication and trade has also increased from 10.7 percent in 1950-51 to 17.7 percent in 1987.[2]

TABLE 1

Distribution of Net Domestic at Factor Cost Percentage Distribution

(At 1980-81 Prices)

Sector	*1950-51*	*1970-71*	*1980-81*	*1989-90*
A. Primary Sector	58.3	47.8	41.2	35.2
1. Agriculture	50.1	41.8	36.4	31.5
2. Forestry	6.4	4.3	2.8	2.4
3. Fishing	0.7	0.7	0.9	
4. Mining and Quarrying	1.1	1.3	1.3	1.3
B. Secondary Sector	15.1	21.2	23.0	25.5
5. Manufacturing	11.4	15.3	17.0	20.0
6. Construction	3.4	5.2	5.2	4.3
7. Electricity, Gas and Water Supply	0.3	0.7	0.8	1.2
C. Tertiary Sector	26.6	31.0	35.8	39.3
8. Trade, Transport etc	10.7	13.8	16.4	
9. Finance and Real Estate	7.3	7.3	8.4	
10. Community and Personal Service	8.6	9.9	11.0	
Total: Net Domestic Product (A+B+C)	100.00	100.00	100.00	100.00

Source: Compiled from National Accounts Statistics, 1990 and New Series on National Accounts Statistics (1990-81 to 1985-86) Feb. 1998 and C.S.O. Quick Estimates (1991).

Collected from: Dhar, P.K., Indian Economy, *op. cit.*, p. 39.

Table 2 reveals a board trends in changing composition of the domestic production. This table shows the share of the primary sector has gone down from 55.3 percent in GDP in 1950-51 to 26.4 percent in 1997-98. It also shows that the share of secondary sector as shown a steady increase from 16.1 percent of G.D.P in 1950-51 to 27.0 percent in 1997-98. The share of manufacturing in GDP increased from 11.4 percent in 1950-51 to 17.6 percent in 1997-98. The share of tertiary sector improved from 28.5 percent in 1950-51 to 46.6 percent in 1950-51 46.6 percent in 1997-98.[3]

TABLE 2

Share of Gross Domestic Product by Industry of Origin (at 1980-81 prices)

	Percentage Distribution			
	1950-51	*1970-71*	*1980-81*	*1997-98**
(I) Agriculture, etc.	55.2	44.5	39.1	26.4
1. Agriculture	48.6	39.7	34.7	24.2
2. Forestry	5.0	4.0	2.7	1.1
3. Fishing	0.7	0.8	0.8	1.1
(II) Mining Manufacturing, etc.	16.1	23.6	25.9	27.0
1. Mining and Quarrying	1.1	1.3	1.5	2.3
2. Manufacturing	11.4	16.1	17.7	17.6
(a) Registered	5.4	9.4	10.0	12.0
(b) Unregistered	6.0	6.7	7.6	5.6
3. Electricity, gas and Water supply	0.3	1.2	1.7	2.4
4. Construction	3.3	5.0	5.0	4.7
(III) Transport, Communication and Trade, etc.	11.0	14.2	16.7	23.3
(IV) Finance and Real Estate	9.0	8.0	8.8	11.4
(V) Community and Personal Service	8.5	9.6	10.5	11.9
A. Commodity Sector (I+II)	71.5	68.1	64.0	53.4
B. Service Sector (III+IV+V)	28.5	31.9	36.0	46.6
Total	100.00	100.00	100.00	100.00

*At 1993-94 pieces and R. Dutta and K.P.M. Sudharam: Indian Economy, *op. cit.*, p. 39.

Source: Complied and computed from CMIF Basic Statistics Relating to the Indian Economy, Vol. I, All India, August 1994 and CSO National Accounts Statistics, 1999.

It shows a structural change in the composition of national income by industrial origin from 1951-52 to the end of the 20th Century. The growth of NDP at factor cost started from 1960-61 to 1970-71. The Table 3 shows that annual average rate of growth of agricultural output which was 3.0 percent during 1950-51 to 1960-61 gradually declined to 1.8 percent only. But the annual average rate of growth of

TABLE 3

Growth of NDP at Factor Cost (at 1970-71 Prices)

Heads	*Annual Rate of Growth of NDP*		
	1950-51 to 1960-61	*1960-61 to 1970-71*	*1970-71 to 1984-85*
A. Primary Sector	3.0	1.6	1.8
1. Agriculture	2.5	1.5	2.9
2. Forestry	2.3	4.6	4.0
3. Fishing	5.5	3.3	5.7
4. Mining and Quarrying	5.8	4.8	1.8
B. Secondary Sector	5.4	5.0	4.2
5. Manufacturing	5.7	4.8	4.5
6. Construction	4.3	4.5	2.2
7. Electricity, Gas and Water Supply	1.0.9	10.1	7.6
C. Tertiary Sector	5.9	4.6	5.8
8. Transport, Communication and Trade	5.4	4.9	5.1
9. Banking Insurance and Real Estate	4.6	5.6	5.8
10. Public Administration and Defence	4.9	7.2	9.2
11. Other service	5.9		
Total: Net Domestic Product	3.8	3.2	3.7

Source: Complied from National Account Statistics (1970-71 to 1976-77) January 1979, CSO's White paper and RBI, Report on Currency and Finance 1985-86, and Dhar P.K India Economy, *op. cit.*, p. 41.

manufacturing sector during 1970-70 to 1984-85 was over of 4.5 percent.

Table 4 shows that a growing industrialization took place in that phase. Indian economy was gradually being transformed from an agricultural one to an industrial one. These growth rates has resulted structural change in the composition of national income of the economy. The rate of growth of agriculture showed a decline from 3 percent during 1950-51 to 3.6 percent during 1980-81 and 1990-91. Those entire figure shows a slow but steady structural change in the

TABLE 4

Rates of Growth of GDP by Industrial Origin (At 1980-81 prices)

	Compound Annual Growth rate Between					
	1950-51 and 1960-61	*1960-61 and 1970-71*	*1970-71 and 1980-81*	*1980-81 and 1990-91*	*1950-51 to 1990-91*	*1990-91 to 1996-97*
I. Agriculture, etc.	3.0	2.3	1.5	3.6	2.6	2.8
1. Agriculture	3.3	2.2	1.7	3.9	2.8	2.9
2. Forestry	0.3	3.0	-0.9	-1.0	0.3	*1.0
3. Fishing	5.5	3.5	2.8	5.7	4.4	6.5
II. Mining and manufacturing	6.2	5.4	4.0	6.7	5.6	6.6
4. Mining and Quarrying	5.6	39	4.9	6.7	5.3	3.4
5. Manufacturing	6.0	5.2	4.0	7.2	5.6	6.9
6. Construction	6.3	5.5	3.0	3.6	4.6	4.6
7. Electricity, gas and Water supply	10.3	11.1	6.8	9.0	9.3	7.6
III. Service Sector	4.1	4.6	4.3	6.6	4.9	7.4
8. Transport Communications and Trade	5.3	5.0	4.7	6.4	5.4	8.0
9. Banking Insurance and Real Estate	3.0	3.4	4.0	7.2	4.4	8.8
10. Public Administration and Defence	3.1	3.9	3.0	5.5	3.9	4.0
11. Other service	3.1	3.9	3.0	5.5	3.9	5.5
Gross Domestic Product	3.9	3.7	3.1	5.6	4.1	5.8

Source: CMIF, Basic Statistics Relating to the India Economy, Vol. I, August 1992 and CSO, Ntional Accounts Statistics (1998) and R. Dutta and K.P.M. Sudharam, *op. cit.*, p. 19.

post reform period. But after the reform period (1990-91 to 1996-97) the period shows, agriculture growth rate declined on an average to 2.8 per cent but mining and manufacturing improved to 6.6 percent and the service sector to 7.4 per cent.

Thus with the growing industrialization in the country, Indian economy is gradually being transformed from an agriculture one to an industrial one. This type of

TABLE 5

Agriculture Growth Rate (1980-1996)

Country	*Growth Rate in %*
China	5.86
Pakistan	4.00
USA	3.86
Thailand	3.70
Malaysia	3.89
Indonesia	3.23
India	3.10

Source: *Yojona*, Vol 47, Nov. 2003, p. 20 (Publication Division).

TABLE 6

Sectoral Real Growth Rates in GDP

S. No.	*Item*	*1995-96*	*1996-97*	*1997-98*	*1998-99*	*1999-00 (P)*	*2000-01 (Q)*	*2001-02 (A)*	*2002-03*	*Average Growth Rate*
I.	Agriculture and allied activities	-0.9	9.6	-2.4	6.2	0.3	-0.4	5.7	-3.1	1.87
II.	Industry	11.6	7.1	4.3	3.7	4.8	6.6	3.3	6.1	5.93
III.	Service	10.5	7.2	9.8	8.4	10.1	5.6	6.8	7.1	8.18
IV.	Total GDP	7.3	7.8	4.8	6.5	6.1	4.4	5.6	4.4	5.86

A: Advance Estimates; Q: Quick Estimates; P: Provisional.
Source: Economic Survey, 2002-03, p. 11.

transformation resulted structural change in the composition of the national income. At that phase there was a special need for enhancement of growth process both agriculture and industry. But there has been a little positive impact of economic reforms, on agriculture sector in India. But there were some cases where it had been showing negative trend.[4] Comparing at the international standards Indian agriculture has been witnessing slow average annual growth rate even in the economic reforms period. Table 5 shows the clean picture that during the period of economic reforms Indian agriculture sector suffered in comparison with china, Pakistan, U.S.A. Thailand, Malaysia and Indonesia. At this phase, India economy was in need of agriculture led growth for effective rural development.

From the different statistical support it is seen that agriculture is still the dominant sector in Indian Economy. A number of measures have been taken places which have directly benefitted this sector. As a result agriculture and agro-processed exports have boomed in the first half of 1990's.[5] But more in flow of investable resources in the agriculture sector is needed. This will impart a new dynamism to the rural poor.

Recent Situation: Result of the structural change in India economy may be revealed with the help of

NSSO data published in July 2005-June 2006. Some of the important findings of the survey are as follows.[6]

1. About 74 Percent of the Households belongs to the rural India and accounted for nearly 76 percent of the total population.
2. Literacy rate for population of all ages was about 66 percent for male and 47 percent for female in rural areas.
3. About 50 percent of persons in all age group (5-29 Years) were currently attending education institutions.
4. About 56 person of rural males and 31 percent of rural females belonged to the labor force.
5. More than half of the employed in rural areas were self employed out of that 57 parent among males and nearly 62 person among female.
6. The percentage of regular salaried/wage employees was relatively lower among females as compared to male in both rural and urban India

These besides among the persons of age 15 years and above in rural area, only 5 percent got Public Works.[7] It is observed that the Contribution of Primary sector in NDP was

58.3 percent, secondary sector was 15.1 and Tertiary sector was 26.6 percent. All these figures are arranged at 1980-81 Price. After crossing tenth five years of plan these figures are 20.5 percent 24.4 percent and 55.1 percent (at 1999-2000 Prices). In the year 1999-2000 the per capita income of most of states in India is quite satisfactory. Though poverty has been prevailing (26.1 percent).[8]

Thus we can say from Fisher and Clark's idea that India is now experiencing gradual expansion. After analyzing Lewis concept Indian industrial sector is attracting workers from rural areas. Poverty has been Prevailing (26.1 Percent).[9] But Table 6 reveals that there is marginal increase of 1.87 percent P.A. in agriculture sector as compared to industry, service and GDP at factor cost in the period of economic reforms. This table shows that from 1995-96 to 2002-03 the agriculture growth rate in India remained negative or insignificant. It is seen from the Table 5 that these is clearly indication of uneven and erratic growth rate. The reasons for these uneven growths are as follows:

1. Wide inter-crop differences in growth performance.
2. In the relative contribution of area and yield changes to output growth.
3. Poor communication capacity in rural area.
4. Weak research extension linkage.

We can analyze different phases of economic growth from Jawaharlal Nehru as a Prime Minister to the last half of the 20th Century. Nehru says "We want greater wealth, higher standards of living and greater production" we have to achieve these objectives not nearly mechanically but also in a social sense which is very important".[10] At that time the Planning Commission emphasized on the process of a change in occupational structure through. Immediately after independence, with her vast and growing population and low per capita income with poor agricultural productivity, India defined her development priorities based on self refinance, distributive social justice individual freedom.[11] After crossing different phase India reaches a better position. The structural change is taking place. But it is seen that the inter-state pattern of human development in India is at present full of contrasts. The states with faster economic growth would see a trend of slowing down.[12] And there are same states that have lopsided pattern of development.

Analyzing the social structure from 1959 to 2000 one important thing is remarkable. The impact of urbanization and industrialization is slowly undermining the rigorous of the caste system. The growth of communication has brought about an economic tradition in India. The traditional village industries declined, and people have been forced by economic necessity to move out to the new development areas.

CONCLUSION

After fifty-eight years of planning India still is experiencing a higher population growth. India also suffers from dualistic feature. One segment of the economy is the subsistence type and suffers from backward elements. At present the major problem of India is food security Sustained growth of agriculture sector is very vital at this stage.

I would like to mention here that the socio-economic thinking of Nehru is still relevant in this present phase. Nehru drew up the first Five Years plan in 1951 which started the government investments in Industries and agriculture. He also pioneered a series of community developments programs aimed at spreading diverse cottage industries and increasing efficiency into rural India. He also launched India's program to harness nuclear energy.

According to some social scientist, Nehru Mahalanobis model growth had neglected agriculture and the small sector. But it is wrong idea. There is no conflict between the heavy industry and the agriculture sector. Another group of social scientists argued that Rao-Manmohon Model has followed the IMF world Bank prescription of stabilization and structural adjustment.[13] But this idea is debatable. It is possible to describe these concepts in these selected lines. I would like to say that Nehru had an optimum Economic philosophy depending on Indian reality. We have received this philosophy when India was facing a vast and steady growing population very low per capita consumption and low real per capita income. Also there was poor agricultural productivity and industrial structure was very poor. In conclusion, let us note that certain specifics of India economic development during the last fifty years. One of them is some contradictions become extremely acute both in the sphere of society and politics second food security problem has emerged as the top issue in these years. And third what has been happening to poverty? To unemployment? And to high price rise? We are thinking about a path agriculture sustainability means development not in only terms of output but also in terms of socio-economic and ecological parameters.

India in recent years has actively participated in international campaigns related to atmospheric research. India consistently reiterated its commitment to the unity, sovereignty and integrity with Asian countries and African countries. Recently the Foreign Ministers of the non-alignment movement (NAM) met in Cartagena Colombia. The meeting assumed special significance of Terrorism.

In the 21st century one of the important achievement is the advancement in information technology. This sector has a profound impact in countries economy and the quality of human life. But unfortunately at present the world's vital problem is terrorism. Local terrorism and international terrorism are the basic problems among the social scientists.[14]

To discuss the different phases of structural changes in Indian economy one important aspect should be mentioned here. That is the risks emanating from climate change, resulting from anthropogenic green house gas emissions. The need for cooperative global action to meet the challenge of climate change. At present different actions are taken by the different Government. Nehru pursued land redistribution and launched program to build irrigation canals, dams and spread the use of fertilizers. He introduced Community Development Program in the mid 1950 with a view to raising the awareness. In this sphere I can say that Nehru's system was directly applicable to different problem of structural developments in India, Obviously, Nehru was a good prophet and he was right in predicting the need for optimum rural developments. Nehru cherished the dreams National amity, peace, harmony and rural- urban linkage. In spite of all these developments are Nehru's dreams translated in realty.

Notes and References

1. Nilkanta Sastri and Srinivasachari: Advanced History of India: Allied Published: New Delhi, Reprint 1971, p. 773.
2. Dhar P.K: Indian Economy—Its Growing Dimensions: Kalyani Publishers: New Delhi, p. 40.
3. Ruddar datt and K.P.M Sundharam: India Economy: S. Chand and company: New Delhi Print 2002, pp. 39-40.
4. Article by Dr. P.K Singh: Reforms in the Agriculture Sector, *Yojana*, Vol. 47, Nov. 2003.
5. Article by Montek Singh Ahluwalia: Ensuring a Prosperous Future, *Yojana*, Independence Day, 1994 (Special Issue).
6. Article Dr. Jitendra Ahirrao: Employment and Unemployment Situation in India, 2005-06, *Kurukshetra*, March 2008, p. 27.
7. Ibid. and Report No 522 based on the date of 62nd round Survey of NSSO in the Ministry of Statistics and Programme Implementation, Government of India.
8. Article: Dhirendranath Konar and Subhabrate Chakrabarty: The North-Eastern States of India: A Demographic Profile, Developmental Issues of North-East India, D.N. Konar Subhabrata Chakraborty, Akansha Publishing House, New Delhi, pp. 24-25 (edited).
9. Article Dr. P.K Singh *op. cit.*, p. 20 and Article O.P. Mishra, Utpal Barman, Kamini Bisht, Pushpa Kumari and Neelam Yadav: New Initiative in Agriculture and Rural Development, *Kurukshetra*, March 2008.
10. N.N. Chatterjee: Nehru's Thought on National Topics, Publications Divisions, Government of India, 2002, p. 38.
11. I.C. Dhingra: The Indian Economy: Resource Planning Development and Problem, Sultan Chand & Sons, New Delhi, 1994, p. 1.
12. Dhirendranath Konar: The Scenario of Population Growth in India, Akansha Publishing House, New Delhi, p. 179.
13. R. Datt and K.P.M Sundharam: *op, cit.*, p. 163.
14. India: 2002: Publication Division, Government of India, edited by Research, Reference and Training Division, pp. 160 and 675.

References

M. Chalapathi Raw: Building of Modern India: Jawaharlal Nehru, Publication Division Ministry of Information and Broadcasting, Government of India.

P.D. Tandon: The Unforgettable Nehru: National Book Truest, India.

Social Stratification: ed. By Dipankar Gupta, Oxford in India, Readings in Sociology and Social Anthropology, Oxford University Press, Modern Print, 1992.

50 Years of Indian Republic: Editor M.K. Santhanam, Publication Division, Government of India.

31

Re-visiting Nehru's Mixed Economy Model

A.P. Tiwari

This paper re-visits Nehru's mixed economy model of planned development. It starts with the basic premise that neither 'extreme left' nor 'extreme right' but the 'middle path' has been the central paradigm of Nehru's 'mixed economy' model. Nehru believed that rapid growth was not an end in itself. Growth was required to be made compatible with independence and democracy. Economic independence was imperative for a strong base of heavy and defence industries. Nehru's cohesive economic design was based on modernity characterised by economic development and democracy. His mixed economy model relied upon bureaucracy to implement economic plans.

Nehru's mixed economy model was primarily aimed at making all- round simultaneous changes in a balanced manner so as to hasten the process of structural transformation. Significantly, Nehru's mixed economy model was aimed at concurrent realisation of three ends incorporating state-directed industrialisation, constitutional democracy and socio-economic redistribution. Nehru contemplated that the strengthening of heavy capital goods industries would enable the nation to generate a higher rate of investible surplus and thereby promote more rapid industrialisation and growth concomitant with self-reliance.

Nehru's 'mixed economy' model was well enjoined upon in the tripartite categorisation of industries in the IPR, 1956. The ultimate aim of his mixed economy model was to make the country economically strong with special focus on establishing an egalitarian society. Nehru was committed to democratic social transformation. Indeed, this commitment was supposed to be an integral part of his development strategy. Nehru envisioned mixed economy development strategy as a 'third way' which took the best from the then existing systems and sought to create a system most suited to the Indian history and philosophy. Thus, his mixed economy model was seemingly rooted in the great Indian tradition of 'madhya marg' signifying 'middle path' of development. Nehru's model could succeed in ensuring moderate growth, democratic legitimacy and economic stability. Finally, the paper laments that Nehru's mixed economy model gave paramountcy to public sector with its dominant role in national economic development. But this focus has shifted in favour of private sector under the neo-liberal policy regime. However, in view of the post-reform widening disparities, socio-economic exclusion and financial volatility, Nehru's economic ideology of a strong public sector needs to be re-vitalised.

32

Nehruji's Vision on Industrialisation and its Contemporary Relevance

Srinivasan Ramachandran

I. INTRODUCTION

Nehruji was basically a law graduate from Cambridge University. Though he was not a direct student of the social studies, during his student days in London, Nehruji was influenced by the first thoughts of Fabianism and Socialism, by the works of Lowes Dickinson, and by Meredith Townsend's 'Europe and Asia',[1] Nehruji's study of all the works by the founders of the scientific socialism has a profound impact on the formation of his social outlook. It strengthened his interest in the sociologist ideals which he maintained throughout his entire life.[2] With these thoughts, he imagined that the growth of public sector was not by itself the growth of socialism, but it would help to lay the foundation of socialism by enabling the material basis for a socialist management of the economy.[3]

Nehruji laid much emphasis on the detrimental effect on the Indian economy of the British policy of discouraging the growth of Indian industry.[4] So Nehruji believed that the application of modern science and technology were the remedy to eradicate unemployment and poverty of India.[5] Therefore he did not share Gandhiji's faith in village self sufficiency and emphasis on cottage and small scale industry as against heavy industry. Nehruji believed that industrialisation was essential for the modernisation of India and emphasized in particular, heavy and basic industries, river valley schemes atomic research and exploration of the farther frontiers of scientific knowledge.[6] From this, one can understand that Nehruji was the builder of modern India on a socialist's line.

Through the concept of democratic socialism within the parliamentary form of Government, Nehruji enabled India to build the public sector as a prime mover for industrialisation and also he gave freedom for private enterprises and individuals talents and desires.[7] Then he felt that the private sector helping in increasing the national wealth even while the public sector gradually expanded, it would overlaped finally overwhelmed the private sector. Meantime India would be modernised, would be producing moré than enough for her requirements and would become self reliant; and there would be enough for all.[8] From this one can concluded that Nehruji was the father of the public sector in India. Hence, it is decided to evaluate Nehruji's efforts to develop public sector industries during his period and their relevance after him.

2. IMPACT OF NEHRUJI'S VIEWS ON INDUSTRILISATION IN INDIA

Independent India under Nehruji did not adopt the Gandhian model of economic development as he fully supported industrialisation as the decisive prerequisite for independence and progress: It can hardly be challenged that, in the context of the modern world, no country can be politically and economically independent, even within the framework of international interdependence, unless it is highly industrialised and has developed its power resources to the utmost. Nor can it achieve or maintain high standards of living and liquidate poverty without the aid of modern technology in almost every sphere of life. An industrially backward country will continually upset the world equilibrium and encourage the aggressive tendencies of more developed countries. Even if it retains its political independence, this will be nominal only and economic control will tend to pass to others. This control will inevitably upset its own small-scale economy which it has sought to preserve in pursuit of its own view of life. Thus an attempt to build up a country's economy largely on the basis of cottage and small scale industries is doomed to failure. It will not solve the basic problems of the country or maintain freedom, nor will it fit the world framework, except as a colonial appendage".[9]

Further, Nehruji firmly believed that the Indian economy could be developed on sound lines only by the adoption of a process of intelligent, imaginative and integrated planning and democratic principles. Therefore, India entered into the era of planned economic development, within the framework of a democratic constitution. It was certainly the vision and wisdom of Nehru that had been responsible for firmly laying the foundation of modern planned economic development of the country.[10] The main objective of planning has been to eliminate poverty and transform the stagnant levels of life into a dynamic phase of economic activities, which will assure self-accelerated and regular growth. In this scheme of planning the first and critical operation objective is rapid industrialization without which living standards of the masses could not be improved. Therefore, the strategy of planning aimed at building-up of an industrial base through heavy industries to be followed up subsequently by a spread of ancillary consumer goods industries.[11] The emergence of the public sector is main contribution of Nehruji to the Modernisation of the economy and the attainment of the goals of socialism. Of course it has been one of the Gandhian ideologies on industries. He believed that in view of the vastness of the country and the magnitude of the tasks confronting it rapid progress would be possible only by creating, expanding and strengthening Public sector.[12] But at the same time, Nehruji was realistic enough to accord equally important role to the private sector in developing the economy. He therefore felt that the country needed a mixed economy, in which both the public and private sectors closely co-operate each other in speeding up the country's economic progress. Accordingly the government decided to reserve the strategic industries and those require huge financial and technical resource for the public sector, while the others be left open to the private sector.[13]

In the year 1956 Jawaharlal Nehru launched the Second Five Year Plan based on the Mahalanobis Model,[14] Which developed the growth parameters in two distinct sectors viz., investment goods and consumption goods. Starting from the initial two-sector model covering labour and capital inputs, the Mahalanobis model provided the basic strategy for the plan.[15] The objectives of the Second Plan are to substantially increase industrialisation, employment and national income and reduce inequality of income and wealth and it laid heavy emphasis on public investment and rapid industrialisation. Not only, was the basic pattern of investment thus shifted from agronomy to industry, but within the industrial sector itself the focus was on spectacular capital intensive heavy industries highlighted by an emphasis on steel. The plan thus envisaged a setting-up of three steel plants in the public sector, expansion of two private sector plants; a seventy percent rise in production of coal; trebling cement production and extensive development of the capacity and infrastructure of the Indian railways.

Though there has been a significant growth in the industrial sector in the Second Plan period it could not achieve its targets.[16] It was mainly due to the continuous absorption of a substantial percentage of working force in the agriculture and allied sectors. This would mean that our planned effort has not been able to make a significant impression in shifting the population to secondary and tertiary sectors rapidly enough to make an impact on the primary sector. Nor primary sector has thrown up surplus to create conditions favourable for expansion elsewhere. With the addition to work force on the normal rate of increase in population, the backlog of unemployment continues to remain at over ten million. This is a very important factor in considering the nature of industrial revolution, which we want to bring about in our economy from the depth of poverty and low income.[17] During the seventeen years of Nehruji's premiership, Indian economy achieved spectacular progress towards self-reliance in many crucial areas. Although Nehru did not achieve much success in making the administration development-oriented, he certainly rendered splendid service to the country's economic progress by giving it a modem progressive outlook and by inspiring the people with high ideals.[18]

3. INDIRA GANDHI AND THE RICH TRADITION OF NEHRUVIAN PHILOSOPHY

Indira Gandhi's contribution to India's economic development has been even more substantial than that of her father. She continued most of the major policies initiated by Nehru; but what is more significant, she also displayed considerable originality introducing new ideas to accelerate the growth of the economy. Indira Gandhi nationalised the coal industry and the commercial banks enlarged, the public sector gave many incentives to the private sector so that it might play a more active role, facilitated a large inflow of foreign capital and technology and brought about closer economic relations between India and the rest of world.

Indira Gandhi was keen on alleviating poverty in the country. She took many bold steps in this direction, the most remarkable one amongst them was the nationalisation of fourteen Commercial Banks on July 19, 1969. In 1980, six more Commercial Banks were nationalised and banking was brought into the fold of the public sector. This has given a new turn to the working of the banking system in the country. Gradually, the public sector banks (i.e., 20 nationalised banks and the State Bank of India group) transformed the concept of banking from "class" banking to "mass" banking. The banks now developed a social perspective in the business approach and functioning. Their credit policy has been moulded in favour of the priority sector advances.

The country launched upon the Sixth Five Year Plan for the period 1980-85 which coincided with the beginning of a new decade. The major goal of the Sixth Plan has been spelt out in the plan document as 'the realisation of economic and social order based on the principles of socialism and self-reliance'. In general, the Sixth Plan successfully restored economic stability and put the economy on a sound track of rapid growth and development, giving a new hope for the country's future. It has been rightly felt that the sound base of infrastructure established over the last forty years should enable the Indian economy to face the challenges that may emerge in the years to come. Like Nehru, Indira Gandhi did not achieve much success in the economic development as Indira Gandhi's tenure as Prime Minister showed the weaknesses in the implementation of the various programmes. For example, the number of large sick units with outstanding bank credit up to rupees one crores or more had increased to 513 at the end of June 1984 from 435 these units went up to Rs. 2,112 crores at the end of June 1984 from Rs. 1,729 crores at the end of June 1982.[19]

4. MARCH TOWARDS PRIVATISATION

Rajiv Gandhi also had firm faith in socialism,[20] Rajiv Gandhi expressed his views thus "our aim is higher productivity, rapid advancement of social justice and continuous modernisation".[21] From this one can reasonably conclude that Nehru Played a pioneering role laying a strong foundation for the public sector as a catalyst of planned economic development. Indira Gandhi gave necessary stimulus to nurture and strengthen it. With the liberalisation of industrial policy, Rajiv Gandhi has added a new dimension to the public sector with a view to improving its efficiency. Arjun Sengupta Committee which was set-up in September 1984, to evaluate the performance of the public sector, to identify the constraints, and to suggest measures to improve their working felt that on the whole the public sector had failed to achieve its objectives for which it has been set-up.

During 1980, improving the efficiency of the public sector is a problem, which has been exercising the minds of governments in many developed and developing countries. Some of them have tried to tackle it by adopting the policy of privatisation. It was the British government headed by Margaret Thatcher that first initiated in 1979 a bold programme for reducing the role of the state in the economic activity. Some companies have been privatised. The British experiment in privatisation has created enormous interest in many countries and attracted several foreign delegations to make and in depth study of its techniques. The US Government has also introduced a programme of privatisation as an important element in its strategy for accelerating economic growth. Some of the privatisation proposals were carried out in 1987 and in the subsequent years. Similar programmes have been implemented in Canada, France, West Germany, Turkey, Pakistan and Bangladesh. It is not surprising therefore, that in India also some economists and industrialists have urged the government to initiate privatisation.[22]

As it is, privatization has become a global phenomenon in the 1980s. Gorbachov's policy reforms-Perestroika (restructuring) and Glasnost (openness) have aroused world-wide interest in the issue of privatisation and liberalisation.

This is evident from the fact that during the Seventh Plan the share of private sector has increased to 48 per cent from 43 per cent from the Sixth Plan. The move towards privatisation has been made because corruption, nepotism, inefficiency have been devilled the management of public sector undertakings. If corruption and delays are eliminated, and state enterprises are managed more efficiently and made more productive, the tendency to privatisation may well curtailed if not reversed. Socialism demands this for and unchecked growth of private sector often generates distortions in the economy.

5. INDUSTRIALISATION IN THE ERA OF GLOBALISATION

In the midst of 1991, when the Narashimha Rao's government took over power, Indian economy was facing a serious crisis. The new government announced a series of measures, one after the other, to restore balance in economy. All these measures have been grouped under 'New Economic

Policy' and broadly they have been classified into stabilisation measures, and structural adjustment or economic reforms. As part of the marketisation of the economy the new policies also aimed at the globalisation of the Indian economy. Globalisation is considered as an important element in the reform structure and several interrelated sets of measures have been taken to achieve this object such as (1) doing away with the licensing of major part of import and export; (2) private sector is also being expanded by permitting the foreign companies to set-up their establishments within the country independently or in collaboration with the Indian company, and so on. This issue is of great importance in the post WTO scenario undoubtedly global markets offer opportunities for all, but opportunities do not guarantee the desired.[23]

The process of global integration and the effects of the WTO agreement were expected to cause increases in India's export of agricultural goods, textiles and garments, leather and gems and jewelry. However, all of these categories have actually declined in share of exports. Instead, chemicals and engineering goods showed substantial increase in export shares.[24] It is observed from this the labour categories' share in exports has been declining.

New economic reforms have bypassed the agriculture which is the mainstay of any programme of economic stabilisation has shown a very low rate of growth. Even the large manufacturing sector, growth rate during the last three years has been very sluggish. The capital goods sector has suffered a sharp decline and thus weakened the fundamentals of the economy. Besides this, the entire process of new economic reforms has initiated a process of jobless growth. The silent implementation of exit policy has led to voluntary retirement on a massive scale. It has led to casualisation of labour that enjoyed better security earlier. The capital-intensive path of development whether with the help of Indian private sector or foreign direct investment through multinationals, is responsible for the phenomenon of jobless growth.[25] Therefore, a genuine fear is being expressed everywhere that the new moves will adversely affect our economic self sufficiency, generate unemployment and will make the country to dependent upon the multinationals.

6. CONCLUSION

From the above discussion one can conclude that the recent trend in our economy has been completely deviated from the path shown by Nehruji. Foreign Direct Investments may help in the process diversification of production structure, modernisation of the economy, but their overall developmental impact is not of a catalytic nature and is 'generally felt much more within the urban sector. Nehruji's views on industrialisation and full employment, did not materialise much in practice due to the fact the policies of various governments took a deviant route. It may be stated here that under new economic reforms regime the public sector has become neglected the growth rates of employment in the orgnised sector. (both public and private) witnessed a declining trend from 1.44 per cent in 1991 to 0.04 per cent in 1999). The decline was more sharp in the public sector (from 1.52 per cent 1991 to 0.19 percent in 1996 and zero growth in 1999 than the private sector from 2.21 per cent in 1992 to 0.11 per cent in 1993)[26] Therefore Nehruji's vision on industrialisation, should receive due attention of policy-makers leading to appropriate policy changes in the positive direction.

Notes and References

1. Lord Butler "Jawaharlal Nehru—The Struggle for Independence", in John Grigg, (ed.), *Nehru Memorial Lectures 1966-1991*, (Delhi: Oxford University Press, 1992), p. 4.
2. Erik Komarov, "Nehru's Views on History Society and Politics," in The Institute of Oriental Studies USSR Academy of Sciences, (ed.), *Jawaharlal Nehru Reminiscences*, (New Delhi: Sterling Publishers Private Limited, 1989), p. 49.
3. Sarvepalli Gopal, *Jawaharlal Nehru A Biography Volume Three 1956-64*, (Delhi: Oxford University Press, 1984), pp. 289-90.
4. This policy he tells us was in some degree maintained even as late as the Constitution Act of 1935. So successful were these British policies during the nineteenth century that India became increasingly ruralized. In almost every progressive country there has been, during the last century, a shift of population from agriculture to industry and from village to town. With this shift went generally increased wealth. In India this process was reserved, due in part to the deliberate action of the British Government. In the middle of the

nineteenth century about 55 per cent of the population is said to have been dependent on agriculture; by the second decade of the twentieth century the ratio was about 75 per cent. In Nehru's view the appalling poverty of the Indian people is of rather recent origin and was due in part to the opposition of Britain to the industrialisation of India. See, Lord Blackett, "Aspects of India's Development", in John Grigg, (ed.), *Nehru Memorial Lectures 1966-1991,* (Delhi: Oxford University Press, 1992), pp. 59-60.

5. Lord Blackett, *op. cit.*, p. 61.
6. T.N. Kaul, Nehru the Idealist and Revolutionary", in John Grigg, (ed.), *Nehru Memorial Lectures 1966-1991*, (Delhi: Oxford University Press, 1992), p. 159.
7. Shankar Dayal Sharma, Nehru's Internal Impact on India as Prime Minister", in John Grigg, (ed.), *Nehru Memorial Lectures 1966-91*, (Delhi:Oxford University Press, 1992), p. 226.
8. Sarvepalli Gopal, *op. cit.*, pp. 290-91.
9. Jawaharlal Nehru, *The Discovery of India,* (New Delhi: Oxford University Press, 2003), p. 301.
10. R.J. Venkateswaran, D.M. Mithani, *Rajiv Gandhi: Economic Perspective Towards 21st Century,* (Bombay: Himalaya Publishing House, 1989), p. 2.
11. Oleg Malyarov, *Nehru on India's Social and Economic Development*, Institute of Oriental Studies, USSR Academy of Sciences (ed.), (New Delhi: Sterling Publishers Private Limited, 1989), p. 100.
12. R.J. Venkateswaran, D.M. Mithani, *op. cit.*, p. 3.
13. Nehru was aware of the fact that Indian industrialists had, during the British Period, achieved considerable success in promoting the growth of the economy by starting such major industries as ship building, steel, cement, cotton textiles, jute and chemicals, as a result of which exports had been stepped up to some extent and imports had been correspondingly reduced. They had also acquired extensive experience and expertise in various other fields of industry, commerce and finance. He, therefore, felt that what the country needed was a mixed economy in which both the public sector and the private sector would not merely co-exist but closely and sincerely co-operate with each other in speeding up the country's economic progress. See, R.J. Venkateswaran, D.N. Mithani, *op cit.*, p. 3; R.C. Dutt, *Socilalism of Jawaharlal Nehru,* (New Delhi: Abhinav Publications, 1981), pp. 200-1.
14. Prof. Mahalanobis has probably been the most profound influence on Nehru's economic thinking since the autumn of 1954, He became a member of the British Royal Society in 1923 and later held the post of Honorary Statistical Adviser to the Government of India. Prof. Mahalanobis had been greatly influenced and impressed by the planning procedures adopted in Russia. He wanted a similar approach to be made in India. He played a major role in shaping the Second Five Year Plan with its emphasis on heavy industry and expansion of the public sector. See, R.J. Venkateswaran, D.M. Mithani, *op. cit.*, p. 175.

15. Prof. Mohalanobis prepared his well known Plan-Frame, the object of which was to activate the Indian economy by providing for sophisticated machine building plants, as well as high technology industrial products, while reserving the less sophisticated consumer goods for the decentralised sector. Agriculture and irrigation were not neglected., and while the allocations for these two items fell in percentage terms both in the Plan Frame as well as in the final draft of the Second Plan, compared to the allocations made in the First Plan in absolute terms the funds allotted rose from Rs. 785 crores to 950 crores in the Plan Frame and to Rs. 1054 crores in the final draft of the Second Plan. It was for Industry and Mining, however, that the Plan Frame made a strong bid, and sought an allocation of Rs. 1100 crores constituting 25.6 per cent at the total plan outlay against Rs. 173 crores or 8.4 percent of the outlay in the First Plan, and it was here that the private industrialists sensed danger. They succeeded in reducing the allocation to Rs. 890 crores or 18.5 per cent of the total outlay in the final draft of the Second Plan. On the other hand, the private industrialists were in favour of higher allocation to Transport and Communication which benefited them and succeeded in raising it from Rs. 950 crores to 1,385 crores See, R.C. Dutt, *op. cit.*, p. 217.
16. R.C. Dutt, *op. cit.*, p. 22; Babubhai M. Chinai, India's March Towards Democratic Socialism, (Bombay: Shri Brihad Bharatiya Samaj, 1972), pp. 138-40.
17. See, R.C. Dutt, *op. cit.*, p. 239.
18. P. Thirayan, *India the Critical Decade After Nehru,* (New Delhi: Sterling Publishers Pvt., Ltd., I 974), pp. 95-97.
19. R.J. Venkateswaran, D.M. Mithani, *op. cit.*, p. 20.
20. R.J. Venkateswaran, D.M. Mithani, *op. cit.*, p. 54.
21. R.J. Venkateswaran, D.M. Mithani, *op. cit.*, pp. 55-61.
22. R.J. Venkateswaran, D.M. Mithani, *op. cit.*, pp. 14-20.
23. Nirmal Bindra, "Impact of Economic Reforms on Indian Economy," in J.L. Singh, K.D. Gaur, eds., *Human Resources and Economic Development*, (Delhi: Sunrise Publications, 2004), pp. 443-44.
24. Jayati Gosh, "The export growth Story", *Deecan Chronicle,* 1: 327, Chennai: (20 Feb., 2006), p. 6.
25. Ashu Pasricha, *WTO, Self-Reliance and Globalisation,* (New Delhi: Deep & Deep Publications Pvt. Ltd., 2005), p. 183.
26. Government of India, *Economic Survey,* New Delhi: Ministry of Finance, Economic Division, (2000-01), p. 139.

Index